Critical Essays on
JOHN DONNE

CRITICAL ESSAYS
ON
BRITISH LITERATURE

Zack Bowen, General Editor
University of Miami

Critical Essays on

JOHN DONNE

edited by

ARTHUR F. MAROTTI

G. K. Hall & Co. / New York
Maxwell Macmillan Canada / Toronto
Maxwell Macmillan International / New York Oxford Singapore Sydney

G. K. Hall & Co.
Macmillan Publishing Company
866 Third Avenue
New York, New York 10022

Maxwell Macmillan Canada, Inc.
1200 Eglinton Avenue East
Suite 200
Don Mills, Ontario M3C 3N1

Library of Congress Cataloging-in-Publication Data

Critical essays on John Donne / edited by Arthur F. Marotti.
     p.   cm.—(Critical essays on British literature)
    Includes bibliographical references and index.
    ISBN 0-8161-8769-X
    1. Donne, John, 1572–1631—Criticism and interpretation.
I. Marotti, Arthur F., 1940– . II. Series.
PR2248.C75   1994
821'.3—dc20   94-14588
                                                CIP

The paper used in this publication meets the minimum requirements of American National Standard for Information Sciences—Permanence of Paper for Printed Library Materials. ANSI Z3948-1984. ⊖™

10   9   8   7   6   5   4   3   2   1

Printed in the United States of America

Contents

◆

General Editor's Note

◆

The Critical Essays on British Literature series provides a variety of approaches to both classical and contemporary writers of Britain and Ireland. The formats of the volumes in the series vary with the thematic designs of individual editors, and with the amount and nature of existing reviews and criticism, augmented, where appropriate, by original essays by recognized authorities. It is hoped that each volume will be unique in developing a new overall perspective on its particular subject.

Marotti's introduction briefly summarizes the history of Donne's inauguration into the modernist canon following Grierson's 1921 edition of *Metaphysical Lyrics and Poems of the Seventeenth Century*. Donne's works, with their complex intellectual self-referentiality, endeared him to formalists and New Criticism, and, more recently, new historicism, cultural materialism, feminism, and deconstruction. Marotti outlines the historical and biographical aspects that attracted critics, and notes Donne's tendency to write for a small coterie, implying the intimacy of communication shared with a highly select group. His witty and intellectually complicated verse, which destroyed "rational discrimination and control for the sake of emotional and intuitive apprehension of complex or mysterious subject matter," lends his work to a variety of constantly shifting post-modernist interpretations. The seven selected essays, all published since 1977, include a new treatment written especially for this volume by Ronald Corthell. Together the essays explore a variety of contemporary critical stances to Donne's work.

ZACK BOWEN
University of Miami

Publisher's Note

◆

Producing a volume that contains both newly commissioned and reprinted material presents the publisher with the challenge of balancing the desire to achieve stylistic consistency with the need to preserve the integrity of works first published elsewhere. In the Critical Essays series, essays commissioned especially for a particular volume are edited to be consistent with G. K. Hall's house style; reprinted essays appear in the style in which they were first published, with only typographical errors corrected. Consequently, shifts in style from one essay to another are the result of our efforts to be faithful to each text as it was originally published.

Introduction

◆

ARTHUR F. MAROTTI

By now the history of Donne criticism in the twentieth century is an old story.[1] Interest in Donne was energized by late nineteenth-century biographies by Augustus Jessopp and Edmund Gosse, the second of which included most of Donne's letters. Their work, together with that of more recent biographers and biographical critics, has given the life story of this self-referential author a very prominent place in discussions of his poetry and prose. Sir Herbert Grierson's magisterial Oxford edition of the verse elevated Donne's status as a canonical author after some two centuries of relative neglect, providing scholars, students, anthologists, and general readers with easier access to his poetical work.[2] This edition, along with the same editor's later anthology of metaphysical poetry, brought Donne to the attention of T. S. Eliot and a generation of modernist poets and critics,[3] who "kidnapped" him, making him over in their own image.[4] The New Critics of the 1920s, 1930s, and 1940s found the poetry, especially the lyrics, to be a perfect test case for their own techniques of formalist analysis, discovering in Donne's complex verse the wit, ironies, paradoxes, and ambiguities of which they were so fond.[5] Scholars wishing to counter the modernist appropriation of Donne with an approach that emphasized his historical otherness, turned to literary and intellectual history to explicate his works, finding in Donne's intellectuality and concetticism a path to Renaissance learning, ideas, and conventions.[6] More recently, new historicist, cultural materialist, feminist, and deconstructive critics have redefined the texts of this early-modern author in terms of new notions of textuality, culture, literary production and reception, and gendered writing and reading. From the time of Eliot's (re)discovery of Donne and the metaphysicals to the present, large issues of our own cultural and political history have framed the discussion. It is no wonder then that any one critic's version of Donne should stimulate debate or provoke controversy.

    R. C. Bald's extraordinarily useful biography of Donne, *John Donne: A Life*,[7] has become the starting point for contemporary scholarship on Donne.

Claiming that Donne is "the earliest major poet in English of whom an adequate biography is possible,"[8] Bald not only interprets the rich data of Donne's life, but also recreates the social and political environments in which Donne functioned over the course of his secular and ecclesiastical careers. This biography has a wealth of information about the political and social worlds of Elizabethan and early Stuart England, and about the individuals with whom Donne had contact—material that scholars have been able to reconstruct for a variety of interpretive purposes. Bald's portrait of Donne goes against the grain of the hagiographical scheme established by Sir Isaac Walton's *Life and Death of Dr. Donne*,[9] pointing out some of this writer's less-than-noble motives and behavior, especially in the five or six years before he entered the ministry,[10] but Bald's tact and historical meticulousness have made his study accessible and useful to scholars and critics with different argumentative aims.[11]

In directing scholars toward the historical contexts of Donne's life and writings, Bald's biography has encouraged the newer historical approaches to Renaissance texts identified with those politically charged forms of criticism labelled "new historicist" and "cultural materialist"—both of which schools include feminist scholars. These scholarly and critical movements have resulted in a general, though by no means wholesale, shift from the explication of individual works—especially lyrics from the *Songs and Sonnets*—to more wide-ranging considerations of groups of texts and of Donne's work as a whole in their sociocultural matrix.[12] The scholarly discussion of Donne has also expanded from its traditional literary-historical and intellectual-historical frameworks to include social, economic, and political contexts. Thus, thanks partly to Bald, the authorially focused approach to texts has been able to incorporate more broadly based historical analyses.

Donne was a poet who confined his work largely to manuscript circulation, allowing only few of his poems to be published during his lifetime. Since the posthumous 1633 edition of his poetry cannot serve as a secure basis for a modern critical edition, textual scholars from Herbert Grierson through Helen Gardner, Wesley Milgate, and John Shawcross have had to turn to the various lines of manuscript transmission of Donne's verse.[13] These have helped them to establish the texts hypothesized by traditional "idealistic" textual scholarship, those that represent the author's "final intentions." But since an authorial holograph survives for only two of Donne's poems, the Latin epigraph on his wife and "A Letter to the Lady Carey, and Mrs Essex Riche,"[14] the situation is far from stable and many textual disputes have arisen.

In the past few years two changes have altered the textual situation for Donne in important ways. First, the process of discovering manuscripts containing Donne poems has continued beyond the documents known by his Oxford editors, producing a list of some 250 manuscripts, a richer documentary legacy than for any other English Renaissance poet.[15] Second, revisionist textual scholars like Jerome McGann have attacked the idealism of traditional textual scholarship and argued for a cultural materialist and sociocentric approach to texts—one that respects textual changes and variations as interesting in their own right, instead of dismissing them as "corruptions" of hypothetically "pure" originals.[16] The presentation of texts and the textual apparatus of the in-progress *Donne Variorum* should reflect these changes.[17] Scholars have begun to acknowledge the social history of Donne's writings, particularly the poetry, and the inevitable textual malleability built into the manuscript system of transmission in which he functioned.

It was partly in response to the manuscript situation of Donne's poems that I formulated my own approach to Donne in my book, *John Donne, Coterie Poet*.[18] In it I argue that Donne thought of almost all of his verse and much of his prose as coterie literature, designing his work for manuscript circulation in a succession of social environments in which he functioned. He wrote for an audience of friends, acquaintances, patrons, patronesses, and the woman he married, treating poetry as an avocation, part of a life and career whose main goals, even for some time after his ordination, were social status and advancement. Since Donne's poems were rooted in their biographical and social contexts, it makes sense to discuss them first in relation to their original audiences, paying particular attention to the rhetorical enactment of the author's relationships to peers and superiors through the conflicting styles of egalitarian assertion, social iconoclasm, and deferential politeness. It is also useful to relate the poetry to the contemporary prose Donne wrote either for private circulation or for publication, dealing with his choice of different literary forms in terms of his changing sociopolitical circumstances.

Influenced by A. Alvarez's account of privately circulated poetry, and by J. W. Saunders's articles on manuscript transmission and the "stigma of print,"[19] I examined some of the actual documents in which Donne's verse is preserved and became convinced that the authorial conception of Donne that has survived in literary-historical accounts written through the perspective of print culture distorts the original conditions of his poetry's production and reception. My book developed as an attempt to understand the socioliterary dynamics of the poetry as coterie verse composed within a succession of different social contexts over a number of years, as work whose generic and rhetorical coordinates were originally adjusted to particular readers who knew the poet and were known to him. Whatever their subsequent historical vicissitudes in the media of manuscript and print, the poems' initial conditions of production and reception explain much about the workings of these texts.[20]

Donne's poetry needs to be viewed in the context of the system of manuscript transmission of literature to which the poetry of most courtly and satellite-courtly authors belonged. Most poems written by gentlemen-amateurs like Donne were occasional in nature, rooted in their biographical and social contexts. Self-advertising coterie writing like Donne's was the social performance of a poet who could play the sometimes bland generalities of poetic conventions against perceived particularities of his personality and social circumstances. Donne engaged in self-reflexively autobiographical discourse, calling his coterie audience's attention to his implication in both the text and contexts of his writing, as he fashioned distinctive utterances from literarily and culturally familiar material. Virtually all of the basic features of Donne's poetic art are related to its coterie character: his creation of a sense of familiarity and intimacy, his fondness for dialectic, intellectual complexity, paradox and irony, the appeals to shared attitudes and group interests (if not, also, to private knowledge), the explicit gestures of biographical self-referentiality, the styles he adopted or invented all relate to the coterie circumstances of his verse. Donne was obviously most comfortable when he knew his readers personally and they knew him. Ideally, the social relationship with a known audience made possible the kinds of communicative transactions Donne found congenial.

Donne expected certain intellectual, aesthetic, and social knowledge or sophistication of his readers—the capacity to understand the nuances of his witty manipulation of literary conventions, genres, cultural codes, and specific social and rhetorical circumstances. "I will have no such Readers as I can teach," he proclaimed in the preface to *Metempsychosis*, expressing a wish for what Ben Jonson called an audience of "understanders,"[21] the admission to which was not simply a matter of moral and intellectual qualifications, as it was for Jonson. It was probably the coterie character of Donne's audience that led Jonson to postulate that "Done himself for not being understood would perish,"[22] a statement that has proved accurate enough in predicting some of the historical vicissitudes of Donne's verse.

In his letters, Donne set forth a model of communication with his coterie reader that I believe he sought in most of his poetry and much of his prose. In one missive, he told his close friend Sir Henry Goodyer that he conceived of letters as "conveyances and deliverers of me to you":[23] the interpersonal relationship, then, not the circumstantial content, was what mattered. He wished for or fantasized a perfect mutual understanding with his correspondent-friend: "Angels have not, nor affect not other knowledge of one another, then they list to reveal to one another. It is then in this onely, that friends are Angels, that they are capable and fit for such revelations when they are offered" (*Letters*, 109-10). In another letter, Donne emphasized the metacommunicative aspect of epistolary communications, telling Goodyer, "I have placed my love wisely where I need communicate nothing" (*Letters*, 115)—by which he meant that the letters' information content was much less important than the friendship they mediated. Defending the absence of "news" from his prose epistles, Donne said that "their principall office . . . [is] to be seals and testimonies of mutuall affection, but the materialls and fuell of them should be a confident and mutuall communicating of those things which we know." He regarded the content of his letters as "nothing" (*Letters*, 121), but such "nothing" was the rhetorical space in which the interpersonal transaction with his reader could take place. This negation or absence of discursive meaning is that condition towards which all Donne's writing moves—not only his poems, but also his prose, especially his *Sermons*. Critics like Joan Webber and Donald Friedman recognize that in both his *Sermons* and in some of his best poetry Donne enacts a process of discovery that necessitates the witty destruction of rational discrimination and control for the sake of emotional and intuitive apprehension of complex or mysterious subject matter.[24] Given this situation, it is no surprise that more recent critics have found that Donne's writing invites deconstructive readings.[25]

Problems arose for Donne's contemporary readers, no doubt, when the complexities of his writing exceeded the limits of their capacities and they found themselves unable to maintain social and intellectual contact through the medium of a relentlessly perplexing text. Donne's elegists point to the combination of competence and incapacity in those who read this poet's work. Carew, who proclaimed Donne "a King, that rul'd as hee thought fit / The Universal Monarchy of wit,"[26] acknowledged Donne's intellectual advantage over his readers. Jasper Mayne, himself one generation younger than Donne's original audience, called *The First Anniversarie* "so farre above its Reader . . . that wee are thought wits, when 'tis Understood." "What was thy recreation turnes our braine," Mayne wrote, "Our rack and paleness, is thy weakest strain."[27] Though Mayne's confusion may have exceeded that of Donne's primary readers, I think that what he says points to some of the difficulties they probably encountered. Donne's metacommunicative affirmation of the bonds of feeling, of understanding, and of social intimacy with his readers may have been designed partly to counteract some of the effects of the deliberate difficulties of his work. Donne thus seems to have created a kind of double relationship with his readers, at once adversarial and intimate, occasionally insulting and complimenting them at the same time. Perhaps it was necessary for him to feel both distance and immediacy in the coterie circumstances in which he wrote.

To read Donne's verse as coterie poetry, one must not only interpret it in terms of its immediate biographical and social matrices, but also locate it more generally in the Elizabethan and early Stuart sociocultural contexts that encoded the literary genres, modes, conventions, and languages that Donne used. In recent years, scholars have paid increasing attention to the historical circumstances of English Renaissance literature and to the ideological assumptions of both the texts themselves and of the critics interpreting them. As the essays in this collection demonstrate, Donne has benefitted from this new wave of historical criticism, including work with specifically feminist emphases.

This anthology of Donne criticism is one of a series of collections that have appeared since Theodore Spencer's *A Garland for John Donne, 1631–1931*, which commemorated the three-hundreth anniversary of Donne's death.[28] I avoid repeating selections that are reproduced in earlier anthologies and concentrate on newer work, substantial essays that range widely through Donne's writings or that have broad implications for Donne criticism. I have tried to include selections that examine groups of poems or combinations of prose works and verse within the context of large cultural, historical or methodological issues. In one way or another, all the pieces in this book are exercises in historical analysis, but they approach the historical embeddedness of literary texts and their interpretation in markedly different ways. Thus, the feminist pieces foreground certain issues not strongly emphasized in the other essays, but expand our historical understanding of Donne, the culture of which he was a part, and the historical vicissitudes of reading and interpretation. Given the space limitations of this volume, I have decided not to present extended treatments of single poems or prose works: therefore, I (reluctantly) have not included some very fine essays—for example, Richard Strier's and Joshua Scodel's discussions of Satire 3 or Elizabeth Harvey's analysis of "Sapho to Philaenis."[29] I have also passed over other pieces that seem directed to a more specialist scholarly audience—for example, Alison R. Rieke's treatment of Donne's relation to a tradition of poetic riddles, Elaine Scarry's discussion of Donne and Renaissance conceptions of the human body, and Heather Dubrow's treatment of Donne's wedding poems in her book on the Stuart epithalamion.[30]

The collection opens with Achsah Guibbory's essay, " 'Oh, let mee not serve so': The Politics of Love in Donne's *Elegies*." In it Guibbory argues, first, that love and sex are political in Donne's elegies, and that the poet's misogyny is a reaction to threats posed to patriarchal masculine "superiority" by (among other things) the existence of a female monarch: "the attack on female rule in amatory relations spills over into an attack on female rule in the public world." She demonstrates the ways in which the *Elegies* show a recurring tension between the male mastery asserted and an implicit female resistance to mastery which undermines the restoration of male sovereignty." These poems have a subversive political potential in suggesting that, just as a mistress's power depends on the submission of a lover, who can withdraw allegiance, so too a (male or female) monarch relies on the consent of subjects as the basis of power. This sociopolitical observation is analogous to the one made by David Aers and Gunther Kress in their essay on the verse letters. Guibbory offers a feminist analysis of Donne's masculinist frame of reference without either distorting his at times antifeminist expressions and assumptions or dismissing his sexual politics as odious. Like other recent feminist scholars, she has taken a fresh look at Donne's work, pointing to the inescapable impact of gender on writing, reading, and interpretation.[31]

Janel Mueller's discussion of Donne is excerpted from her essay, "Women among the Metaphysicals: A Case, Mostly, of Being Donne for." Having argued elsewhere that Donne's lesbian love elegy "Sapho to Philaenis" imagines full reciprocity and equality in love,[32] Mueller examines the way in which Donne, as the "last English poet of the metaphysics of heterosexual love," creates very different roles for women in his love poetry, religious verse, and verse letters. Women are "indispensable to the poetry and to the identities of the discoursing males who are its mouthpieces." Mueller contends that the love poems sometimes imagine equality of the sexes, yet "inscribe at key points the asymmetry of outlook and sexual role that casts the male as the persuader and possessor, the female as the persuaded and possessed." On the other hand, she believes that in devotional poems and verse epistles Donne was forced "to discourse differently of love." Mueller characterizes the verse letters to noblewomen and the *Anniversaries* as "preparatory exercises and masterworks on the symbolic power of femininity." The verse letters present patronesses as "authority figures who, through their attentions to him, set the worth of his person and the direction of his life." Although Aers and Kress's essay takes a somewhat different approach to the relationship between poet and patroness in the verse letters, Mueller's essay overlaps with it in her analysis of the power relationships figured in the poems.

Richard Halpern's innovative essay on Donne's *Songs and Sonnets* utilizes the concept of "autopoiesis" to reconceptualize the notion of "lyric autonomy," which has been attacked in recent years by Marxist, new-historicist, and poststructuralist critics. Originating in the biological sciences, the theory of "autopoiesis" has been taken up by other fields to refer to "informationally closed systems" that "do not receive or process input from their environments, nor . . . produce output of any kind." In Niklas Luhmann's "grim narrative of modernity," for example, the sociologist uses the term to characterize "the specialized social systems which constitute modern industrialized societies." They are "self-referring communicative networks . . . cognitively open to one another but normatively closed." The theory of "autopoiesis" is one that treats language as "consensual, not informational—connotative, not denotative." (Information theorists might add "analogue, rather than digital.") Halpern uses Donne's *Songs and Sonnets* as a test case for the "theory of social autopoiesis," one that can "resituate the terms of the relation between history and lyric autonomy." He locates these poems "within a history of sexuality which at once respects the formal boundaries of the lyric and questions some of the assumptions behind a Foucauldian understanding of sexuality." He argues that "in declaring the birth of a literary space distinct from other social spaces,"[33] a poem such as Donne's "The Canonization" "attests indirectly to a more general if incipient process of social differentiation which . . . characterizes modernity in its broadest sense." "The autonomy of lyric is thus itself a form of historical and social testimony . . . ," he argues. Halpern accepts Luhmann's argument that "Love . . . is [historically] a compensatory mechanism which surmounts mutual indifference among persons. . . . a generalized symbolic medium of communication" that establishes "a personal sphere of mutual receptivity in contrast with a public world which to the individual appears increasingly indifferent and incomprehensible." Thus Donne's emphasis on passion as antagonistic to the social contract is an instance of "a seemingly autonomous eros which resists institutionalization," but, on the other hand, "the code of love is just one more autopoietic system added to the others."

Donne's love lyrics are a prime example, then, of the detachment of sexuality "from its instrumental role in a social matrix." And Donne's shift from metonymic to metaphoric connection between love and the public world is a vivid illustration of this fact. Emphasizing Donne's creation of *"difficult* poems, full of cybernetic noise," Halpern characterizes Donne's *Songs and Sonnets* as "voyeuristically open but informationally closed," reinforcing other critics' observations about Donne's communicative strategies. His final remarks on the question of lyric autonomy in relation to Marxist theory are both thoughtful and provocative.

Halpern's essay is followed by an excerpt from my book, *John Donne, Coterie Poet*, in which I discuss the devotional poetry and prose that Donne wrote before he entered the ministry in their Jacobean sociopolitical context. I acknowledge, but do not heavily emphasize the relevance of this work to Donne's own spirituality (though I do foreground his agonizing over whether to pursue a secular or ecclesiastical career).[34] Since Walton, there has been a false separation of Donne's spiritual and political interests. Therefore, I have highlighted the relevance of the sacred poems (and *Essays in Divinity*) to Donne's secular ambitions and to the political world in which he functioned.[35] Thus, for example, I see the relationship of the speaker(s) and God in the religious poems as shaped by a model of Jacobean royal patronage with which the poet was preoccupied in the period between his loss of government employment and his ordination. Private, spiritual struggles found expression in a familiar public, political language.

I discuss *La Corona*, the *Holy Sonnets*, "A Litanie," and "Goodfriday, 1613. Riding Westward" as coterie texts rooted in Donne's sociopolitical circumstances and social relations. I call attention to the way the realignment of favored literary genres in an era in which England was governed by a king who had himself written religious verse made it possible in *La Corona* for Donne to accept the identity of poet—a role which he had earlier consistently rejected. In the *Holy Sonnets* I see the enactment of a conflict between autonomy and dependence, or of assertion and submission, appropriate to Donne's situation as an ambitious but frustrated seeker of preferment—a conflict the poet also dramatized in his encomiastic verse letters to patronesses.[36] Specifically, this is manifested in "the portrayal of male authority, the rhetorical elaboration of the struggle of spiritual pride and humility, the subversive indecorum of particular works, and the general transformation of a (religiously expressed) passive aggression into an aesthetically sadomasochistic relationship with his readers." I consider one devotional prose work from this period, the *Essays in Divinity*, which I read as "a text whose powerfully satiric force has not been properly acknowledged"—a work that not only signals "a crisis of motive, belief, and commitment" in a man who was uncertain about whether he should pursue secular or ecclesiastical advancement, but also contains strong (and pointed) political criticism.[37] I conclude with a discussion of "Goodfriday, 1613. Riding Westward" as a religious lyric in which Donne's attempt to reconcile secular and religious goals was performed, like his earlier amorous verse, for knowledgeable coterie readers.

David Aers and Gunther Kress's discussion of some of Donne's verse letters, " 'Darke texts need notes': Versions of Self in Donne's Verse Epistles," uses a stylistic approach to call attention to the poems' sociopolitical coordinates and to their roots in Donne's conflicted attitudes toward his social superiors. Aers and Kress are conscious of the need to find a "descriptive and theoretical framework within which the real interest of these poems can be perceived and analysed."[38] In Donne's verse epistles to patronesses they detect conflicting versions of the self: "one version . . . refers an autonomous self to inherent values which would doubtless be recognized in a platonic utopia or by stoic and platonic individuals who have detached themselves from existing societies . . . the other version of self sees it as socially constructed and dependent, either through equal relationships (as those between friends) or the social relations of the market based on rareness, use and contingency."

Treating Donne as a characteristic "alienated intellectual," Aers and Kress describe Donne's conflict between sociopolitical subversiveness and submission in terms of the contradictory (yet complementary) versions of selfhood found in the verse letters: "in his version of self the subtle sycophant was always accompanied by the critical 'troublemaker' who deployed the platonic model subversively against the values of the leading social groups into which he longed to be incorporated." In the epistles to patronesses, Donne suggests that the value of these women as objects of praise depends as much on the encomiastic poet as on their supposedly intrinsic merits. In the epistles to friends, Donne's stoic stance is undercut by the need for the kind of social interactions that the poems structure. In Aers and Kress's sensitive sociolinguistic analysis, these poems, which modern readers have either ignored as uninteresting or discussed in terms of the "topoi of praise" they embody,[39] seem on the contrary rich and dynamic.

Ronald Corthell's psychoanalytic essay on Donne's *Anniversaries* examines the poems' logic of desire as it works in their "construction of the subject of Donne"—by which he means at once the "speaking subject who produces (and is produced by) Elizabeth Drury as 'the Idea of a Woman,' " "the academic subject 'John Donne' produced by readings of the *Anniversaries*" and "the reading subject who produces (and is produced by) that 'John Donne' and whose thinking also instantiates a relationship between the Renaissance and the present." Using Lynda Boose's observation about the absence of the daughter from patriarchal narrative and Julia Kristeva's account of abjection, Corthell argues that "the signifying economy of loss and recuperation that produces the empowered reading subject of the *Anniversaries* is also a male economy of desire." For Corthell, Kristeva's analysis of the abject as the underside of the symbolic illuminates the connection between Donne's satiric anatomy of the dead world and the idealization of the poems' "shee." Corthell returns to Freud's remarks on narcissism, narcissistic loss, and melancholy to point out the ways in which the *Anniversaries* present a (male) "gendered symbolics of loss" through the "identification of the ego with the abandoned object." Corthell explores the psychodynamics of the poems' patronage context, dealing not only with the poet-client, but also with the patron-reader, suggesting that a father's narcissistic investment in his daughter might have made "the extravagance of the *Anniversaries* . . . resonate to the loss of Robert Drury," the "shee" of the poem thus serving poet, patron, and potential male readers as "the site of men's discourse on loss and recuperation." Corthell's reading makes sense of the poems' misogynistic elements as well as of their extraordinary acts of idealization, but it also contributes to the feminist discussion of the gendered acts of production and reception of Donne's writings.

One of the effects of the rehistoricizing of Donne that has taken place in the last 15 or 20 years is that scholars have been reexamining Donne's prose more carefully, often referring to it in discussions of the poetry. Although we still lack a modern critical edition of the letters, editions of the *Paradoxes and Problems, Essays in Divinity, Biathanatos, Pseudo-Martyr, Ignatius his Conclave, Devotions*, and *Sermons* have facilitated these scholarly efforts.[40] An earlier generation of scholars produced valuable books and articles on Donne's prose, particularly the Sermons.[41] But now that the boundary between "literary" and "non-literary" discourses has been blurred by historical approaches that resituate texts within the larger field of cultural production, it makes more sense to read the prose along with the poetry, as Annabel Patterson does in her rich discussion of the politics of Donne's writing.

Patterson's essay on Donne's politics explores the "self-division and self-contradiction" enacted in his work.[42] Arguing against the notion of Donne's opportunistic acceptance of royal absolutism and his status as "the king's man," she concentrates on the poetry and prose of "Donne's transitional period, from 1606 to 1615," but argues that all his work, from the Satires through the Sermons, demonstrates a complexity of attitude, belief, and feeling. She begins with a brief discussion of the Satires, particularly Satire 5, which she interprets as courageous political criticism of the Elizabethan system. The distinction drawn in the Satires, between the scholar in retreat from a corrupt world and the "motley humorist" immersed in it, is seen as characteristic of Donne's stance in the work to follow. In the Jacobean era, Patterson argues, even when Donne served James as a controversialist attacking the king's international Catholic enemies, he showed signs of sympathy for and connection with "the [domestic] opposition group in the troublesome Jacobean parliaments." Although Patterson chooses Elegy 14 ("A Tale of a Citizen and His Wife"), a poem of debatable authenticity, to illustrate Donne's willingness to criticize Jacobean government and the ideology of royal absolutism, her points are confirmed by other evidence of Donne's predilection for the "discourse of opposition" developing inside and outside of the parliaments in the first half of the Jacobean era.

Patterson focuses on the question of royal prerogative and on the "constitutional" struggle in which it was implicated. She notes that Donne's (manuscript-circulated) paradoxical defense of suicide, *Biathanatos*, was a politically dangerous text requiring, like all formal paradoxes, an intellectually agile and sophisticated reading in order to understand its subversive suggestions about royal prerogative and the traditional liberties of Englishmen. The printed *Pseudo-Martyr* similarly contains a perspective critical of the king's ideological position and the subsequent *Conclave Ignatii* is a "radically unstable text" "written in the alienated voice of satire . . . and . . . from the 'reconciling' perspective of the official propagandist," perhaps embodying the Jesuit technique of "equivocation," a quality Patterson attributes to the epithalamion Donne wrote (belatedly) for the scandalous Somerset-Howard marriage. Patterson discusses Donne's difficult position as a member of the 1614 ("Addled") Parliament, which was preoccupied with the rigging activities of those members who functioned as royal "undertakers."

In the lyric poetry, Patterson concentrates on terms like "favorite," "prerogative," and "liberty," that in light of her discussion of Donne's conflicted political position, are quite insistent and revealing. She concludes with a brief discussion of an early sermon preached at Paul's Cross, which she interprets as "a claim that integrity . . . can be reconciled with patronage," and in which, in the face of an audience of dignitaries and government figures, Donne "came out . . . swinging his political principles." For her, it is a gross caricature of Donne to regard him as simply a "kingsman" or cynical careerist. Her finely crafted argument should give future scholars pause before adopting such reductive versions of Donne.[43]

Patterson's work and that of the other contributors to this collection demonstrate the continuing vitality of Donne scholarship and criticism. Having first survived long periods of neglect, then modernist appropriation, John Donne has emerged as a writer and historical figure whose writings should continue to attract historical scholars, feminist critics, those interested in textual criticism (if not also historical bibliography), and a more general literary audience fascinated by their style, energy, and complexity. It is no accident that such a self-conscious, performative writer, whose works so often call attention to their own modes of operation and rhetorical dynamics, should appeal not only to literarily sophisticated readers prepared for the challenges and pleasures of difficult texts, but also to intellectually curious scholar-critics well versed in contemporary literary and cultural theory who find Donne's work, as have earlier generations, an irresistible object for their interpretative practices. Not too many years hence, another editor, assembling another selection of Donne criticism, should be able to find essays whose arguments and insights develop some of the ideas found in the pieces in this anthology, but whose shape and specificity most contemporary scholars are not quite ready to imagine.

Notes

1. See, for example, Deborah Aldrich Larson, *John Donne and Twentieth-Century Criticism* (Rutherford, NJ: Fairleigh Dickinson University Press; Toronto: Associated Universities Presses, 1989); and Leonard Unger, *Donne's Poetry and Modern Criticism* (Chicago: Henry Regnery, 1950). John Roberts's two annotated bibliographies of Donne criticism are valuable resources: *John Donne: An Annotated Bibliography of Modern Criticism, 1912–1967* (Columbia: University of Missouri Press, 1973) and *John Donne: An Annotated Bibliography of Modern Criticism, 1968–1978* (Columbia: University of Missouri Press, 1982), as is his essay, "John Donne's Poetry: An Assessment of Modern Criticism," *John Donne Journal* 1 (1982): 55–67. For a collection of critical commentary on Donne from his own time to 1889, see A. J. Smith, ed., *John Donne: The Critical Heritage* (London and Boston: Routledge & Kegan Paul, 1975).

2. *The Poems of John Donne*, edited with introductions and commentary by Herbert J. C. Grierson, 2 vols. (Oxford: Oxford University Press, 1912).

3. *Metaphysical Lyrics and Poems of the Seventeenth Century: Donne to Butler*, selected and edited, with an essay, by Herbert J. C. Grierson (Oxford: Clarendon Press, 1921). Eliot's review of this volume originally appeared in the *Times Literary Supplement*, 20 October 1921, 669–70.

4. See Merritt Y. Hughes, "Kidnapping Donne," *University of California Publications in English* 4 (1934): 61–89. See also Leonard Unger, *Donne's Poetry and Modern Criticism* (Chicago: Henry Regnery, 1950).

5. See Larson, Chapter 3 (90–112).

6. Larson claims: "Since the 1940s, Donne scholars have . . . tried to remove Donne from the influence of the New Critics. To do this, they have used . . . three main methods: a return to biographical studies, a reinterpretation of Donne's skepticism, and a study of his place in Renaissance poetic traditions" (106). See, for example, such works as C. M. Coffin, *John Donne and the New Philosophy* (1937; reprint, New York: The Humanities Press, 1958) and Donald Guss, *John Donne, Petrarchist* (Detroit, MI: Wayne State University Press, 1966).

7. R. C. Bald, *John Donne: A Life* (New York and Oxford: Oxford University Press, 1970).

8. Bald, 1.

9. This biography was first published in the 1640 edition of Donne's *LXXX Sermons*, then appeared separately in 1658 and was included in Walton's *Lives* (1670). See David Novarr, *The Making of Walton's Lives* (Ithaca, NY: Cornell University Press, 1958) for a study of Walton's biographical method.

10. For example, in reference to Donne's attempts to win patronage and preferment from Robert Carr, Earl of Somerset, in the period before his ordination, Bald states, "Donne's life during his last eighteen months as a layman does not present a particularly edifying spectacle" (300).

11. By contrast, John Carey's *John Donne: Life, Mind, and Art*, 2nd ed. (Oxford: Oxford University Press, 1990), which presents Donne as an ambitious, conflicted apostate with a bad conscience, de-idealizes him so thoroughly that many readers have responded negatively and underestimated the value of this intelligent and perceptive study.

12. Carey's book is a prime example of this phenomenon.

13. See the following editions of Donne's poems (in addition to Grierson's): *The Divine Poems of John Donne*, ed. Helen Gardner, 2nd ed. (Oxford: Clarendon Press, 1978); John Donne, *The Elegies and The Songs and Sonnets*, ed. Helen Gardner (Oxford: Clarendon Press, 1965); John Donne, *The Epithalamions, Anniversaries, and Epicedes*, ed. Wesley Milgate (Oxford: Clarendon Press, 1978); John Donne, *The Satires, Epigrams, and Verse Letters*, ed. Wesley Milgate (Oxford: Clarendon Press, 1967); *The Complete Poetry of John Donne*, ed. John T. Shawcross (Garden City, NY: Doubleday & Co., 1967).

14. For a discussion of the manuscript remains of Donne's works, see Peter Beal

(compiler), *Index of English Literary Manuscripts*, vol. 1, 1450–1645, part 1 (London and New York: Mansell Publishing Ltd., 1980), 243–61.

15. Ted-Larry Pebworth, "Manuscript Poems and Print Assumptions: Donne and His Modern Editors," *John Donne Journal* 3 (1984): 20, notes that 246 manuscripts containing transcriptions of Donne poems have been found.

16. See Jerome McGann, *A Critique of Modern Textual Criticism* (Chicago and London: University of Chicago Press, 1983) and *The Beauty of Inflections: Literary Investigations in Historical Method and Theory* (Oxford: Clarendon Press, 1985), part 2, "Textual Studies and Practical Criticism," 67–132. See D. C. Greetham's discussion of the issues at stake between a traditional author-centered approach to textual study and the "social" school of textual criticism in "Textual and Literary Theory: Redrawing the Matrix," *Studies in Bibliography* 42 (1989): 1–24. See also my own essay, "Manuscript, Print, and the English Renaissance Lyric," in *New Ways of Looking at Old Texts: Papers of the Renaissance English Text Society*, ed. W. Speed Hill (Binghamton, NY: Medieval & Renaissance Texts & Studies in conjunction with Renaissance English Text Society, 1993), 209–21.

17. This important project, under the general editorship of Gary Stringer, will be published by Indiana University Press. Whereas Gardner, for example, only regularly collated a few representative manuscripts in her editions, the *Variorum* editors are using computer collation to bring together all available manuscript and print evidence. See Gary Stringer, "The Donne Variorum Textual Collation Program," *Computers in the Humanities* 21 (1987): 83–89. The textual editors for this project are John Shawcross, Ted-Larry Pebworth and Ernest W. Sullivan, II. Sullivan has edited two related manuscripts containing Donne's poetry, *The First and Second Dalhousie Manuscripts: Poems and Prose by John Donne and Others, A Facsimile Edition* (Columbia: University of Missouri Press, 1988). See his discussion of these documents and of their textual significance (1–12; see also his article, "Replicar Editing of John Donne's Texts," *John Donne Journal* 2 (1983): 21–29. In addition, see John Shawcross, "Scholarly Editions: Composite Editorial Principles of Single Copy-Texts, Multiple Copy-Texts, Edited Copy-Texts," *TEXT* 4 (1988) 297–317.

18. Arthur F. Marotti, *John Donne, Coterie Poet* (Madison and London: University of Wisconsin Press, 1986). In this paragraph and the six paragraphs following, I use material from the Preface and Introduction to this study. I am grateful to the University of Wisconsin Press for permission to do so.

19. A. Alvarez, *The School of Donne* (1961; reprint, New York and Toronto: New American Library, 1967); J. W. Saunders, "The Stigma of Print: A Note on the Social Bases of Tudor Poetry," *Essays in Criticism* 1 (1951): 139–64; and "From Manuscript to Print: A Note on the Circulation of Poetic MSS. in the Sixteenth Century," *Proceedings of the Leeds Philosophical and Literary Society* 6:8 (1951): 507–28. I also found useful Alan MacColl's account of "The Circulation of Donne's Poems in Manuscript," in A. J. Smith, ed., *John Donne: Essays in Celebration* (London: Methuen, 1972), 28–46 and Margaret Crum, "Notes on the Physical Characteristics of Some Manuscripts of the Poems of Donne and of Henry King," *The Library*, 4th ser., 16 (1961): 121–32.

20. My forthcoming book, *Manuscript, Print, and the English Renaissance Lyric* (Ithaca and London: Cornell University Press, 1994) discusses manuscript transmission more fully. See also Mary Hobbs, *Early Seventeenth-Century Verse Miscellany Manuscripts* (Aldershot, England: Scolar Press, 1992); Harold Love, *Scribal Publication in Seventeenth-Century England* (Oxford: Clarendon Press, 1993); Ted-Larry Pebworth and Claude J. Summers, "'Thus Friends Absent Speake': the Exchange of Verse Letters Between John Donne and Henry Wotton," *Modern Philology* 81 (1984): 361–77; and Richard B. Wollman, "The 'Press and the Fire': Print and Manuscript Culture in Donne's Circle," *Studies in English Literature* 33 (1993): 85–97.

21. See the "Preface to the Reader" in *The Alchemist*, in *Ben Jonson*, ed. C. H. Herford, Percy and Evelyn Simpson, 11 vols. (Oxford: Clarendon Press, 1925–52), 5:291.

22. *Jonson*, 1:138.

23.   *Letters to Severall Persons of Honour (1651)*, a facsimile reproduction with an introduction by M. Thomas Hester (Delmar, NY: Scholars' Facsimiles & Reprints, 1977), 109—further citations will be noted in the text.

24.   See Joan Webber, *Contrary Music: The Prose Style of John Donne* (Madison: University of Wisconsin Press, 1963), 12; Donald Friedman, "Memory and the Art of Salvation in Donne's Good Friday Poem," *English Literary Renaissance* 3 (1973): 421. See also Rosalie Colie, *Paradoxia Epidemica: The Renaissance Tradition of Paradox* (Princeton: Princeton University Press, 1966), 501n.

25.   See, for example, Tilottama Rajan, " 'Nothing Sooner Broke': Donne's *Songs and Sonnets* as Self-Consuming Artifact," *ELH* 49 (1982): 805–28; Thomas Docherty, *John Donne, Undone* (London and New York: Methuen, 1986); and Judith Scherer Herz, " 'An Excellent Exercise of Wit that Speaks So Well of Ill': Donne and the Poetics of Concealment," in Claude J. Summers and Ted-Larry Pebworth, eds., *The Eagle and the Dove: Reassessing John Donne* (Columbia: University of Missouri Press, 1986), 80–91. Although some interesting deconstructive readings of Donne have appeared in recent years, I am convinced that the best historicist interpretations have incorporated deconstructive methods and insights and that deconstructive criticism in its less historically specific forms has been a dead end in Donne studies. See the discussion of Docherty's book in the Afterword to the second edition of John Carey's *John Donne: Life, Mind and Art*, 266–75, 280.

26.   Thomas Carew, "An Elegie upon the death of the Dean of Paul's, Dr. Iohn Donne," in Smith, ed., *John Donne: The Critical Heritage*, 95.

27.   Jasper Mayne, "On Dr. Donnes death," in Smith, ed., *John Donne: The Critical Heritage*, 97–98.

28.   Theodore Spencer, ed., *A Garland for John Donne, 1631–1931* (Cambridge, MA: Harvard University Press and London: Hutchinson, 1931). Other anthologies of criticism include: Helen Gardner, ed., *John Donne: A Collection of Critical Essays* (Englewood Cliffs, NJ: Prentice Hall, 1962); Peter Amadeus Fiore, ed., *Just So Much Honor: Essays Commemorating the Four-Hundreth Anniversary of the Birth of John Donne* (University Park and London: Penn State University Press, 1972); Smith, ed., *John Donne: Essays in Celebration*; John Roberts, ed., *Essential Articles for the Study of John Donne's Poetry* (Hamden, CT: Archon Books, 1975); Harold Bloom, ed., *John Donne and the Seventeenth-Century Metaphysical Poets* (New York: Chelsea House, 1986); and Summers and Pebworth, eds., *The Eagle and the Dove*. Robert's anthology, though limited to the poetry, contains the largest selection, some 39 essays.

29.   Joshua Scodel, "The Medium is the Message: Donne's 'Satire 3,' 'To Sir Henry Wotton' (Sir, more than kisses), and the Ideologies of the Mean," *Modern Philology* 90 (1993): 479–511; Richard Strier, "Radical Donne: Satire III," *ELH* 60 (1993): 283–322; Elizabeth Harvey, "Ventriloquizing Sappho: Ovid, Donne, and the Erotics of the Feminine Voice," *Criticism* 31 (1989): 115–38 (reprinted in *Ventriloquized Voices: Feminist Theory and English Renaissance Texts* [London and New York: Routledge, 1992], 116–39, 153–57).

30.   Alison R. Rieke, "Donne's Riddles," *JEGP* 83 (1984): 1–20; Elaine Scarry, "Donne: 'But Yet the Body in his Book,' " in *Literature and the Body: Essays on Populations and Persons* (Baltimore and London: Johns Hopkins University Press, 1988), 70–105; Heather Dubrow, *A Happier Eden: The Politics of Marriage in the Stuart Epithalamion* (Ithaca and London: Cornell University Press, 1990), 151–200.

31.   See also James Holstun, " 'Will You Rent our Ancient Love Asunder?': Lesbian Elegy in Donne, Marvell, and Milton," *ELH* 54 (1987): 835–67; Ilona Bell, "The Role of the Lady in Donne's *Songs and Sonnets*," *Studies in English Literature* 23 (1983): 113–29; and Janet Halley, "Textual Intercourse: Anne Donne, John Donne, and the Sexual Politics of Textual Exchange," in *Seeking the Woman in Late Medieval and Renaissance Writings: Essays in Feminist Contextual Criticism*, ed. Sheila Fisher and Janet F. Halley (Knoxville: University of Tennessee Press, 1989), 187–206. Bell and Halley take rather different views of Anne More Donne's reading abilities. Halley uses Eve Sedgwick's notion of male homosocial bonding to suggest

that Donne was less interested in writing for the woman he married than in "plac[ing] his image of his wife into circulation" (193) among a male coterie.

32. "Lesbian Erotics: the Utopian Trope of Donne's 'Sapho to Philaenis,'" *Journal of Homosexuality* 23:1–2 (1992): 103–34.

33. See Anthony Low, "Donne and the Reinvention of Love," *ELR* 20 (1990): 465–86.

34. The religious and spiritual thematics of Donne's devotional verse have been well discussed by Louis B. Martz, *The Poetry of Meditation: A Study of English Religious Literature of the Seventeenth Century*, rev. ed. (New Haven and London: Yale University Press, 1962); William Halewood, *The Poetry of Grace: Reformation Themes and Structures in English Seventeenth-Century Poetry* (New Haven and London: Yale University Press, 1970); and Barbara Kiefer Lewalski, *Protestant Poetics and the Seventeenth-Century Religious Lyric* (Princeton: Princeton University Press, 1979), esp. 253–82. See also William Kerrigan, "The Fearful Accommodations of John Donne," *English Literary Renaissance* 4 (1974): 337–63; John Stachniewski, "John Donne: The Despair of the 'Holy Sonnets,'" *ELH* 48 (1981): 677–705; and Richard Strier, "John Donne Awry and Squint: The 'Holy Sonnets,' 1608–1610," *Modern Philology* 86 (1989): 357–84.

35. See also my discussion of Donne's politics and his other early Jacobean prose in *John Donne, Coterie Poet*, 183–95.

36. See *John Donne, Coterie Poet*, 202–32, and the essay by Aers and Kress in this collection.

37. In discussing this work, Annabel Patterson's essay (reprinted in this collection) fleshes out the historical contexts to which I refer.

38. In recent years some other critics have usefully discussed the verse letters and, in particular, Donne's relationship with Lucy, Countess of Bedford: see, especially, Margaret Maurer's two essays, "John Donne's Verse Letters," *Modern Language Quarterly* 37 (1976): 234–59, and "The Real Presence of Lucy Russell, Countess of Bedford, and the Terms of John Donne's 'Honour is so sublime perfection,'" *ELH* 47 (1980): 205–34; and Barbara K. Lewalski's "Lucy, Countess of Bedford: Images of a Jacobean Courtier and Patroness," in *Politics of Discourse: The Literature and History of Seventeenth-Century England*, ed. Kevin Sharpe and Steven N. Zwicker (Berkeley, Los Angeles, London: University of California Press, 1987), 52–77.

39. See Barbara Kiefer Lewalski, *Donne's* Anniversaries *and the Poetry of Praise: The Creation of a Symbolic Mode* (Princeton: Princeton University Press, 1973), esp. 11–70.

40. See *Paradoxes and Problems*, ed. Helen Peters (Oxford: Clarendon Press, 1980); *Essays in Divinity*, ed. Evelyn M. Simpson (Oxford: Clarendon Press, 1952); *Biathanatos*, ed. Ernest W. Sullivan, II (Newark: University of Delaware Press and London: Associated University Presses, 1984); *Pseudo-Martyr*, ed. Anthony Raspa (Montreal: McGill / Queen's University Press, 1993); *Ignatius His Conclave*, ed. T. S. Healy, S. J. (Oxford: Clarendon Press, 1969); *Devotions upon Emergent Occasions*, ed. Anthony Raspa (Montreal: McGill / Queen's University Press, 1975); and *The Sermons of John Donne*, ed. George R. Potter and Evelyn Simpson, 10 vols. (Berkeley: University of California Press, 1953–62). Some of the letters from manuscript sources are printed in Evelyn Simpson's *A Study of the Prose Works of John Donne* (1924; second edition, Oxford: Clarendon Press, 1934). See also John Donne, *Selected Prose*, chosen by Evelyn Simpson, ed. Helen Gardner and Timothy Healy (Oxford: Clarendon Press, 1967).

41. See, especially, Simpson, *A Study of the Prose Works of John Donne*; William Mueller, *John Donne, Preacher* (Princeton: Princeton University Press, 1962); and Joan Webber's two groundbreaking studies, *Contrary Music: The Prose Style of John Donne* and *The Eloquent "I": Style and Self in Seventeenth-Century Prose* (Madison and London: University of Wisconsin Press, 1968).

42. There are some obvious similarities to the argument advanced by Aers and Kress and to my own approach to Donne's politics in *John Donne, Coterie Poet*.

43. See also Mary Ann Radzinowicz's "The Politics of John Donne's Silences," *John Donne Journal* 7 (1988): 1–19. Radzinowicz addresses four "silences" in Donne's work: "Donne's silence about England's colonization of America, about her pacification of Ireland, about the sociopolitical role of exceptional women, and in English about other poets" (2). She uses my

own work (on the conditions of coterie writing) and that of Patterson (on censorship), Aers and Kress (on class), and Richard Helgerson (on the literary system) as modes of entry into the four topics. For another ambitious discussion of Donne's politics, see David Norbrook, "The Monarchy of Wit and the Republic of Letters: Donne's Politics," in *Soliciting Interpretation: Literary Theory and Seventeenth-Century English Poetry*, ed. Elizabeth D. Harvey and Katharine Eisaman Maus (Chicago and London: University of Chicago Press, 1990), 3–36.

"Oh, let mee not serve so": The Politics of Love in Donne's *Elegies*

Achsah Guibbory*

For modern readers, accustomed to distinct separations between private and public, love and politics may seem strange bedfellows. But recent studies have made us aware of important connections between amatory poetry and patronage, between the discourse of (courtly) love and the seeking of advancement by aspiring men at Queen Elizabeth's court.[1] Arthur Marotti, especially, has analyzed the political circumstances and dimensions of Donne's amatory poetry, arguing that we should see it as "coterie" poetry written in an "encoded" language, embodying Donne's frustrated ambitions for socioeconomic, political power even when, *especially* when, he is writing about love.[2]

Marotti's discussion of the interrelations between politics and the languages of love is deservedly influential. But his argument (both in the book on Donne and in his important earlier article on Elizabethan sonnet sequences) fosters a certain distortion, for repeatedly Marotti's language implies that the *real* subject of this poetry is socioeconomic power and ambition. While he brilliantly shows the political dimensions of the languages of courtly love as used in Elizabethan poetry, the effect of his argument is to suggest not so much the *inter*relations between love and politics but the centrality of socioeconomic concerns. Love becomes merely the vehicle of the metaphor; the tenor is invariably political. In the interest of deciphering this political "meaning," amatory relations between men and women tend to all but disappear.

I want to build on Marotti's sense of the political dimension of Donne's witty love poetry, by arguing not that love is a metaphor for politics but that love itself is political—involves power transactions between men and women. By privileging neither Donne's ambitions for socioeconomic power nor his personal need for a fulfilling emotional relationship with a woman, I reevaluate the interrelationship between love and politics. I will focus on Donne's depictions of amatory relationships—his representation of the female body, sexual relations, and sexual difference—to show how he represents power relationships in love and how love repeatedly intersects public politics. In Donne's

*ELH 57 (1990) 811–833. Reprinted by permission of the Johns Hopkins University Press.

treatment of love in the *Elegies*, the public world of politics and the intimacies of the private world are often inseparable.[3]

The "direct, natural, and necessary relation of person to person is the *relation of man to woman*."[4] Though the words are Karl Marx's, the notion was well understood in the Renaissance. As Milton's portrayal of the "society" of Adam and Eve makes clear, the relationship between man and woman is thought to constitute the basic unit of society. Apparently natural but also culturally determined, that relationship offers a potential image of the organization and distribution of power in the larger society. Milton's treatment of Adam and Eve in *Paradise Lost* reveals his awareness of a political dimension to interpersonal, sexual relations. Donne, too, understood the political dimension of amatory relations, exploiting it in his *Elegies*. Donne repeatedly in these poems envisions relations between the sexes as a site of conflict, thereby mirroring a larger society in which there is considerable anxiety about the lines and boundaries of power.

Exploring male/female relations, Donne's *Elegies* focus insistently on the body, especially the female body. The human body commonly functions as what the anthropologist Mary Douglas has called a "natural symbol" of society—a "model" symbolically expressing the values and orders, powers and dangers, of the social body.[5] Thus it is not surprising that Donne's representations of the body, as well as of male/female sexual relations, have a sociopolitical significance.

In discussing the male/female relations in the *Elegies*, I will deal with the misogyny evident in many of these poems, but often repressed in critical readings of Donne.[6] There is in many of the *Elegies* a persistent misogyny, indeed a revulsion at the female body, which has provoked various responses. Some readers give these poems scant attention, preferring to focus on the more easily admired poems of the *Songs and Sonnets* like "The Good-morrow," "The Canonization," or "The Ecstasy," which celebrate a mutual love that attributes to the mistress special importance and value. Others see the misogyny as simply a matter of "literary convention" (which skirts the issue of why authors are attracted to some literary conventions and not to others), or as an example of Donne's desire to shock or his outrageous wit, or as one posture among many that Donne tries out in his poetry. But these critical responses effectively tame Donne's *Elegies*. Yes, Donne is being outrageously, shockingly witty, but why are women the subject of degradation in so much of the wit? Granted there is humor in these poems, but jokes often have a serious dimension and reveal much about the person. And though Donne adopts various personae and tries out a variety of postures, at some level he possesses an ability to identify (even if briefly) with these roles. It is unfair to Donne's poetry, and inconsistent, to treat the misogynous, cynical poems as rhetorical posturing or as exercises in witty manipulation of literary convention (hence, not "really" meant) while reading the celebrations of mutual love as indicative of Donne's "true" feelings. Though we may not like to admit the presence of misogyny in one of the greatest love poets in the English language, we need to come to terms with it, especially in the *Elegies* where it appears so strongly. What I will be arguing about the *Elegies* is not meant to be taken as the whole picture of Donne—obviously, the canon is extensive and various, and his attitudes are quite different in many of the *Songs and Sonnets*—but it is one part of Donne's works that needs to be understood and historicized rather than repressed if we are to have a fuller understanding of the poet and the canon.

Many if not most of Donne's *Elegies* were written in the 1590s, when England was ruled by a female monarch who demanded faithful service and devotion from aspiring men.[7] The mere presence of a female monarch is insufficient to account for the *Elegies*, but it does suggest an initial historical context for these poems. Elizabeth, the "woman on top" (to use Natalie Zemon Davis's phrase) was an anomaly in a strongly patriarchal, hierarchical culture in which women were considered subordinate to men.[8] It is difficult to ascertain the effect that rule by a female monarch had on the position of women. Though she may have provided an encouraging example for women, it is likely that, as the exception, she actually confirmed the rule of patriarchy in English society.[9] But for men there were tensions inherent in submission to the authority of a queen in what was otherwise a culture in which power and authority were invested in men. As Constance Jordan remarks, the prospect of a female ruler "could hardly have been regarded with anything but concern"; and the actual presence of a woman on the throne in England gave focus to a debate about the legitimacy of woman's rule.[10]

Tensions over submission to female rule are strikingly evident in Donne's representation of private love relationships in the *Elegies*. Many poems attack or reject female dominance in love and attempt to reassert male control. Though Marotti has well described fantasies of control in these poems, it has not been sufficiently appreciated how much the degradation and conquest of women is presented as essential to that control, nor how these efforts to control woman have a special sociopolitical meaning. "Private" relations between man and woman are closely connected to the pattern of relations in the larger social body—a point recognized by Milton in his divorce tracts, for example, when he set about to reform the institution of marriage. Though the private and public spheres became increasingly separated in England during the seventeenth century, in the world of Donne's *Elegies* they are still closely interrelated.[11] Repeatedly, the attack on female rule in amatory relations spills over into an attack on female rule in the public world. Private love and public politics become subtly intertwined as Donne's amatory elegies are inscribed in politically resonant language. Many of the poems are both explicitly amatory *and* covertly political. Hence they possess a politically subversive potential at the same time as they probe the dynamics of amatory relations.

The conventions of courtly love poetry, with its chaste, unattainable, superior woman, desired and sought by an admiring, subservient, faithful male suitor, were especially appropriate for articulating complex relationships between Queen Elizabeth and the ambitious courtiers seeking her favors.[12] That Donne rejects and mocks these conventions in his poetry has not gone unnoticed. As Marotti well puts it, Donne in his *Elegies* is rejecting "the dominant social and literary modes of the Court, substituting plainspeaking directness for polite compliment, sexual realism for amorous idealization, critical argumentativeness for sentimental mystification, and aggressive masculine self-assertion for politely self-effacing subservience" (*Coterie*, 45). But it has not been sufficiently appreciated that the rejection of courtly love and the assertion of self are achieved in large part through a ritualized verbal debasement of women. It is common to speak of Donne's Ovidian "realism," but in some elegies, "realism" seems too mild a term for the debasement Donne substitutes for idealization.

Repeatedly, Donne's *Elegies* represent women, not as idealized creatures, closed and inviolable in their chastity, but as low, impure, sometimes even disgusting creatures. Donne rejects "classical" representations of the female body (finished, elevated, pure), which characterized courtly and Petrarchan love poetry, in favor of the "grotesque" female body—not so much out of an attraction toward the vitality of the grotesque body as out of an impulse to demolish the idealized image of woman, thereby making her undesirable and hence, no longer an object of worship.[13]

Elegy 2: The Anagram wittily, systematically subverts the conventions of female beauty as the speaker tells how Flavia has "all things, whereby others beautious bee" (2), but in the wrong order, proportion, places, or forms. Her small and dim eyes, large mouth, jet teeth, and red hair make her grotesque and "foule" (32). Like Shakespeare's sonnet 130 ("My mistress' eyes are nothing like the sun"), this elegy playfully mocks conventional Petrarchan descriptions of female beauty (golden hair, small mouth, pearly white teeth), but Donne's details may also glance at the physical appearance of the aging Queen Elizabeth, who in her later years had visibly rotten teeth and wore a red wig.[14] The poem itself reenacts the descent from high to low not only in its announced subject (the ugly mistress) but also in its movement from describing her face to describing her genitals, which are guarded by a "durty foulenesse" (42) that will keep out all rivals and ensure her chastity for the man who dares marry her. "Though seaven yeares, she in the Stews had laid, / A Nunnery durst receive [her], and thinke a maid" (48–49). Even "Dildoes" would be "loath to touch" her (53–54). The language of the poem unpleasantly links her face and her genitals—both are "foule" (32, 42). Just as the foulness of the one reflects the foulness of the other (and Donne uncovers both), so the larger implication of the poem is that this low grotesque female body mirrors, even in its distortion, the traditionally beautiful female body. She has all of "beauties elements" (9) and is thus an "anagram" of beauty. As in his *Paradoxes and Problems*, Donne delights in being outrageous, in exercising his wit in defending the indefensible. The paradox here serves to undermine the idea of female beauty (and hence desirability) and to suggest that "beauty" (and the power of beautiful forms) is humanly constructed—Donne suggests that the man can rearrange Flavia's "parts" to make her beautiful just as we arrange "letters" different ways in order to produce a variety of pleasing "words" (15–18).

If *The Anagram* presumes a continuity (not merely a contrast) between the ugly and the beautiful female body, *Elegy 8: The Comparison* makes this connection explicit.[15] The poem begins by contrasting idealized descriptions of the female body with grotesque ones:

> As the sweet sweat of Roses in a Still,
> As that which from chaf'd muskats pores doth trill,
> As the Almighty Balme of th'early East,
> Such are the sweat drops of my Mistris breast,
> And on her necke her skin such lustre sets,
> They seem no sweat drops, but pearl carcanets.
> Ranke sweaty froth thy Mistresse brow defiles,
> Like spermatique issue of ripe menstrous boils.
>
> (1–8)

The focus on excretions, however, defiles the pure, classically beautiful body. Beneath the oppositions between high and low runs the sense of what these two supposedly different women share—an open, sweating, excreting, potentially diseased body. As in so much of his writing, Donne is obsessed with decay and death, here particularly associated with the female body. The nausea which surfaces elsewhere in Donne (for example in the *Satires* and *The Second Anniversary*) here is evoked by woman. Like *The Anagram, Elegy 8: The Comparison* tends to conflate face and genitals, the high and low parts of the body, metaphorically linking "menstrous boils" and "thy Mistresse brow" and moving from descriptions of the women's heads to descriptions of their breasts and finally to their genitals.

The idealized description of female beauty is progressively undermined by the grotesque one. In spite of the contrasts drawn, the differences come to seem more those of perception or description (that is, verbal and imaginative constructs) than of "objective" material reality. If the "ugly" woman is associated with death, so too is the beautiful one:

> Round as the world's her head, on every side,
> Like to the fatall Ball which fell on Ide,
> Or that whereof God had such jealousie,
> As, for the ravishing thereof we die.
>
> (15–18)

Beneath the appearance or illusion of beauty is foulness, dirt, disease, death. Though *his* mistress's breast seems "faire," the breasts of the rival's mistress are "like worme eaten trunkes, cloth'd in seals skin, / Or grave, that's durt without, and stinke within" (24–26).[16] And her breasts are an anticipation of things to come. Though *his* mistress's genitals are like a "Lymbecks warme wombe" (36),

> Thine's like the dread mouth of a fired gunne,
> Or like hot liquid metalls newly runne
> Into clay moulds, or like to that AEtna
> Where round about the grasse is burnt away.
> Are not your kisses then as filthy,'and more,
> As a worme sucking an invenom'd sore?
>
> (39–44)

Mere touch is contaminating, defiling. The disgusting descriptions of the female body as diseased, impure, and polluting, themselves contaminate the idealized representation of woman so that by the end of the poem, the speaker's denunciation seems to include not just "comparisons" and the "ugly" mistress but woman generally: "Leave her, and I will leave comparing thus, / She, and comparisons are odious" (53–54). Perhaps the two mistresses described in the poem are not different women but rather a single woman seen in two ways. The misogynist thrust of the poem, which betrays the male speaker's desire to keep uncontaminated, may explain the discomforting comparison used to represent the speaker's sexual relations with the beautiful mistress: "Such in searching wounds the Surgeon is / As wee, when wee embrace, or touch, or kisse" (51–52). The delicacy of mutual tenderness jars with the queasy sense of exploring tender (open? bleeding?) wounds.

The repulsion toward the female body evident in so much of the poem makes it difficult to worship or adore woman. By deidealizing woman, Donne reconstructs male/female relationships—as embodied in the sex act—to confirm a hierarchy in which the male remains superior:

> Then like the Chymicks masculine equall fire,
> Which in the Lymbecks warme wombe doth inspire
> Into th'earths worthlesse durt a soule of gold,
> Such cherishing heat her best lov'd part doth hold.
>
> (35–38)

This passage does more than describe the temperate heat of his mistress's genitals (which contrasts with the barrenness and excessive heat of the other woman's). By drawing on the Aristotelian association of the male with fire and spirit and of the woman with earth and lower forms of matter, it also reconfirms the traditional hierarchy in which men were seen as naturally superior. As Aristotle explains in *De generatione animalium*, "the female always provides the material, the male provides that which fashions the material into shape; this, in our view, is the specific characteristic of each of the sexes: that is what it means to be male or to be female. . . . the physical part, the body, comes from the female, and the Soul from the male."[17] In generation, which for Donne as for Aristotle confers a purpose or end on sexual intercourse, woman is like the warm limbeck, the necessary container—and at the same time the (in itself) worthless dirt, the earth—the material that needs to be informed by a masculine soul. Merging Aristotelian sex differentiation with Paracelsian alchemy, Donne represents man as contributing the heat, the "Chymicks masculine equall [in the sense of the original Latin *aequus*, 'even'] fire," as he "inspire[s]" the "durt" with a "soule of gold." Thus even the seemingly idealized description of woman at last reconfirms her inferiority and subordination to man.

Donne's emphasis on sex, on the body, and notably on female genitals in these poems has typically been seen as characteristic of the Ovidian influence, and of his "realism." But it is a peculiar realism that focuses so exclusively on one part of the body. The speaker in the witty, satirical *Elegy 18: Loves Progress* assumes a superior posture as he denies woman the qualities of "virtue," "wholesomeness," "ingenuity" (21, 13) and defines her essence as her genitals, the "Centrique part" that men love (36). Men should pay no attention to the face and those higher parts of the female body, which are dangerous distractions that threaten to waylay or even "shipwracke" (70) men on their journey to the harbor of love: her "hair" is "a forrest of ambushes, / Of springes, snares, fetters and manacles" (41–42), her lips give off "Syrens songs" (55), her tongue is a "Remora" (58); her "navell" (66) may be mistaken as the port; even her pubic hair is "another forrest set, / Where some doe shipwracke, and no farther gett" (69–70). Seduction becomes a journey of exploration and discovery, but also potential entrapment for the unwary male. The female body he traverses actively seeks to thwart him.

Satirizing Petrarchan idealizations of women, Donne implies that such refinements are new and monstrous perversions of nature: "Love's a bearewhelpe borne; if wee'overlicke / Our love, and force it new strange shapes to take / We erre, and of a lumpe a monster make" (4–6).

If worshipping woman from a distance and praising her virtue and beauty are modern, monstrous innovations, Donne implies he is restoring older, natural, and correct amorous relations. Mocking the platonic ladder of love (set forth first by Diotima in Plato's *Symposium* and later by Bembo in Castiglione's *The Courtier*) whereby the lover ascends from the beauty of a particular person to an admiration of beauty generally to a vision of ideal, transcendent beauty, Donne sets up a different pattern of love whereby men may "ascend" if they "set out below" and start from "the foote" (73–74).[18] The "progress" of love is thus a journey of progressive mastery, in which the goal or "right true end of love" (2) (the female genitals) is kept firmly in sight at all times. The refusal to idealize, indeed the impulse to debase that "end" of love shapes the poem's final lines, which first describe sexual intercourse as paying "tribute" to woman's "lower" "purse" and then compare the man who uses the wrong means to attain this end to a person who foolishly tries to feed the stomach by purging it with a "Clyster" (91–96).

What we have here, as in so many of the *Elegies*, are strategies for reasserting male control in love. To some extent these are reminiscent of Ovid. Alan Armstrong's description of Ovid's contribution to the development of the elegy suggests both his special appeal for Donne and also a parallel in these two poets' redistribution of power in love relationships. Much as Donne would subvert Petrarchan conventions, Ovid himself undercut Latin elegiac conventions such as the enslaved lover, asserting instead that love is an art with the lover in control rather than ruled by his passions and mistress. Ovid gave the "elegiac lover a degree of rationality and self-control reflected in his urbane wit and complete self-consciousness."[19] Such a description of Ovid, with its emphasis on mastery, is more valuable in explaining the appeal and usefulness of Ovid to Donne than the commonplace label of "Ovidian realism." Ovid's concern with control may have had a political dimension (though obviously not identical to Donne's), expressing a desire for independence in a society of limited freedoms, in which one could be exiled at the pleasure of the emperor. (One thinks of the premium Cicero and Horace in their own ways placed on rationality, self-control, and self-sufficiency as means of insulation from dangerous political vicissitudes.) Ovid's love elegies continue the stance of political non-conformity evident even earlier in Catullus and Propertius. But there are differences between Ovid's and Donne's elegies, for gender assumes a special importance in Donne's efforts at mastery. The misogyny that surfaces in Donne's poems, and becomes a strategy for defining the male speaker's superiority, recalls not Ovid's elegies so much as Juvenal's *Satires*.[20]

Since the conventions of courtly love were an integral part of the ideology of Queen Elizabeth's court, appropriated and encouraged by the queen as articulating and confirming her power, Donne's sharp rejection and subversions of these love conventions might be expected to have political implications. His choice of genre itself reflects not simply his literary taste but a political stance, for he is distancing himself from the preferred discourse of the Elizabethan court. He elects in the 1590s to write not sonnets of courtly love but satires and elegies—genres marked by misogyny and insistence on the male speaker's power and control. The anti-establishment implications of his choice of genres and of the misogyny in Donne's elegies accord well with our knowledge that in the mid 1590s Donne was associated with the Essex circle, having embarked on two expeditions against Spain under Essex in 1596 and 1597.[21]

Throughout the 1590s Essex was engaged in a prolonged struggle for power with the queen that set him against the court establishment and that ended only in 1601 with his trial and execution for treason. His conflicts were not only with Cecil and Ralegh, his rivals for political favor, but also with the queen herself—a point evident in J. E. Neale's conclusion that "had she let a man of Essex's nature pack the royal service and the Council with his nominees, she would probably in the end have found herself a puppet-Queen, in tutelage to him." Disdaining the subservience that characterized his stepfather Leicester's relation with the queen, Essex found it difficult to subject himself to Elizabeth's will, repeatedly betraying in his actions and letters a particular and growing dislike of serving a woman.[22] A letter of advice from Francis Bacon after the Cadiz expedition warned Essex that his all too evident resistance to Elizabeth's authority was dangerous: describing Essex as "a man of a nature not to be ruled," Bacon asked "whether there can be a more dangerous image than this represented to any monarch living, much more to a lady, and of her Majesty's apprehension?" (*Lives and Letters*, 1:395).

Essex was ambitious for glory and honor. But that matters of gender were also involved is startlingly evident in the violent public argument that took place between Essex and the queen in summer 1598 over the appointment of a governor for Ireland. Angry at the queen's rejection of his candidate, Essex turned his back on her in a "gesture of contempt," which prompted the queen to strike him on the ear. Essex put his hand on his sword, swearing that "he would not put up with so great an indignity nor have taken such an affront at the hands of Henry VIII himself" (*Lives and Letters*, 1:489–90). His anger at having to take this abuse from a woman is apparent in the letter he afterwards wrote Elizabeth, complaining of "the intollerable wrong you have done both me and yourself, not only broken all laws of affection, but done against the honor of your sex" (*Lives and Letters*, 1:493). Essex's feeling that there was something perverse in her exercise of authority, in his having to submit to a female ruler and accept her humiliations, was not limited to this occasion, and it was apparently shared by others. Young men surrounding Essex were privately saying that they would not submit to another woman ruler, thus reviving the issue of gender that Elizabeth had faced at the beginning of her reign.[23] In 1597 the French ambassador Sieur de Maisse observed that, though Elizabeth's government pleased the people, "it is but little pleasing to the great men and the nobles; and if by chance she should die, it is certain that the English would never again submit to the rule of a woman."[24]

Such sentiments find an echo in Donne's privately circulated *Elegies*. The *Elegies* embody attitudes toward female rule that were also being expressed by Essex and his circle. The whole pattern of Donne's anti-Petrarchanism and revisions of gender relations betrays a discomfort with (indeed, a rejection of) the political structure headed by a female monarch. Intimate private relations between man and woman and the power structure of the body politic mirror and reinforce each other. If the private and the public are so closely related, perhaps a change in relations in the private realm will generate a corresponding change in the world of politics.

The political dimension of Donne's love elegies is particularly evident in the sense of seduction as mastery that pervades *Elegy 19: To his Mistres Going to Bed*, in which Donne moves easily between the bedroom and the political realm of empires and monarchs. In this witty, exuberant poem we are far from the degradation and disgust of *The Anagram* or *Comparison*. For the speaker joy, enthusiasm, and delight reign.[25] But even here, as the speaker commands his mistress to undress, Donne transfers power from the woman, desired and praised, to the man who hopes to possess her. She is wittily idealized and commodified through a variety of stunning conceits that aim to conquer her (his "foe" [3]) through hyperbolic praise: she is a "farre fairer world," a "beauteous state," "flowery meades," an "Angel," "my America," the repository of "whole joys" (in Donne's wicked pun) (6, 13, 14, 20, 27, 35). But the other side of compliment, admiration, and reverence is the desire to possess and thus master the colonized woman. The speaker affirms his power not only through the accumulated verbal commands of the poem but also through a crucial shift in metaphor in lines 25–32:

> License my roving hands, and let them goe
> Before, behind, above, between, below.
> O my America, my new found lande,
> My kingdome, safeliest when with one man man'd,
> My myne of precious stones, my Empiree,
> How blest am I in this discovering thee.
> To enter in these bonds, is to be free,
> Then where my hand is set my seal shall be.

At the beginning of this passage the woman is the monarch, providing a license; but the moment she gives this license she loses her sovereignty. What was implicit from the first now is clear. The man becomes not only explorer but conquerer, and she becomes *his* land and kingdom. The repeated possessives reinforce the sense of his mastery, and by the end of this passage he has now become the monarch, setting his "seal." Self-aggrandizement, of course, characterizes much of Donne's poetry, even his divine poems, but the metaphors and images in these lines have a distinctive political resonance as they dethrone the woman and restore sovereignty to man.[26]

As soon as this politically subversive note has been sounded, Donne momentarily retreats from its implications, first praising "full nakedness" (33) then flattering the woman as both a "mystique book" and a divinity who imputes "grace" to the special few allowed to see her mysteries "reveal'd" (41–43). But once her confidence in female superiority has been reestablished, Donne gives a final twist to the argument that conclusively and wittily reasserts male supremacy by placing the man "on top": "To teach thee, I am naked first: Why than / What need'st thou have more covering than a man" (47–48). The act of sex confirms what is seen as the legitimate, rightful mastery of man—a mastery that conflicts both with the conventions of courtly love and with the political situation in England in the 1590s. Seduction fantasies, even as they represent woman as supremely desirable, complement Donne's strategy of debasement, for both aim at restoring male sovereignty.[27]

But, as readers have noticed, the mastery and control Donne's speakers strive for in the *Elegies* is often frustrated or incomplete.[28] The very metaphors describing women contain a disturbing potential for suggesting women's resistance to any individual man's control. The *Elegies* show a recurring tension between the male mastery asserted and an implicit female resistance to mastery which undermines the restoration of male sovereignty. The land, despite man's attempts to enclose and possess it, is always vulnerable to being "possessed" by other men, as the speaker of *Elegy* 7 ("Natures lay Ideot . . .") only too well has learned. His mistress's husband may have "sever'd" her "from the worlds Common" (21), enclosed her as private property, and her lover may have further "Refin'd" her into a "bliss-full paradise" (24), but these acts prove inadequate attempts to civilize her. For all the speaker's position of superiority (he claims to be her teacher, even her God-like creator who has "planted knowledge" and "graces" in her [24–25]), she has thrown off his authority and is leaving him for other lovers. The poem ends with angry, impotent outbursts, in which verbal degradation reveals both the desire to control the woman through what *Elegy 16: On his Mistris* calls "masculine persuasive force" (4) and the striking inability to do so:

> Must I alas
> Frame and enamell Plate, and drinke in Glasse?
> Chafe wax for others seales? breake a colts force
> And leave him then, beeing made a ready horse?
> (27–30)

The female body's "openness" subverts all attempts at permanent masculine control, and insures that dominance will always be unstable and precarious. As the speaker in *Elegy 3: Change* puts it, "Women are like the Arts, forc'd unto none, / Open to'all searchers" (5–6). The conventional representations of woman as land/earth and as water convey a sense of her openness, her essential resistance to boundaries or limits, which Donne wittily exploits:

> Who hath a plow-land, casts all his seed corne there,
> And yet allowes his ground more corne should beare;
> Though Danuby into the sea must flow,
> The sea receives the Rhene, Volga, and Po.
> (17–20)

Embodying the Aristotelian identification of woman with the supposedly lower elements of earth and water, such representations both suggest the difficulty of mastering woman and reinforce the notion of her necessary inferiority to man, making male sovereignty seem natural and imperative. Though the receptiveness of their bodies shows women were not made to be faithful to one man, the speaker argues that women are made for men in much the same sense as nature, in the Judaeo-Christian scheme of creation, was made for man—hence, the comparisons of women to birds, foxes, and goats in this poem. Given such hierarchy and "natural" inequality, for a man to submissively serve a woman would be as wrong as for animals to rule man.

Donne's discomfort with serving a woman is perhaps most obvious in *Elegy 6*, the opening of which draws a rich, complex analogy between love and politics:[29]

> Oh, let mee not serve so, as those men serve
> Whom honours smoakes at once fatten and sterve;
> Poorely enrich't with great mens words or lookes;
> Nor so write my name in thy loving bookes
> As those Idolatrous flatterers, which still
> Their Princes stiles, with many Realmes fulfill
> Whence they no tribute have, and where no sway.
> Such services I offer as shall pay
> Themselves, I hate dead names: Oh then let mee
> Favorite in Ordinary, or no favorite bee.
>
> (1–10)

Distinguishing himself from others, he rejects in both political and amatory spheres a service in which the lover/suitor is submissive, flattering, and unrewarded, and the woman falsely idealized, made into an idol by her admirer. Instead, Donne offers a different kind of "service," clearly sexual, which "pay[s]" the woman (compare the "tribute" paid into the woman's "purse" in *Elegy 18*) and is in turn rewarded. This kind of service restores male dignity, for it is not servitude but mastery. But mastery is desire rather than accomplishment, for the poem's fictive occasion is the discovery that his mistress is unfaithful.

Recounting their relationship, he represents her as a destructive "whirlpoole" (16) or "streame" (21), himself as the delicate "carelesse" (innocent) "flower" which is "drowne[d]" in the water's "embrace" (15–17). This image of the destructive stream also appears near the end of *Satyre III*, where the stream is explicitly identified with royal power:

> That thou may'st rightly'obey power, her bounds know;
> Those past, her nature and name's chang'd; to be
> Then humble to her is idolatrie;
> As streames are, Power is; those blest flowers that dwell
> At the rough streames calme head, thrive and prove well,
> But having left their roots, and themselves given
> To the streames tyrannous rage, alas, are driven
> Through mills, and rockes, and woods,'and at last, almost

> Consum'd in going, in the sea are lost:
>> So perish Soules, which more chuse mens unjust
>> Power from God claym'd, then God himselfe to trust.
>>> (100–110)[30]

The dating of this satire is uncertain, but the anxiety about royal power (figured as female and identified with the watery female element) would seem to place the poem in the company of those clearly written during the reign of Elizabeth.[31] These complex lines of *Satyre III* articulate both fear of and resistance to royal power, as the speaker, identifying himself with the "blessed flowers" and unjust monarchs with tyrannous streams, rejects idolatrous submission to earthly rulers and hopes to find ultimate (though not necessarily earthly) safety by dwelling at the calm head (God, the source of all power).

In *Elegy 6*, the deceptive mistress, likened to the whirlpool or stream, takes on conventionally "masculine" attributes. She is active, aggressive; he becomes the vulnerable, passive victim. Not the man but the mistress is associated with fire when like the "tapers beamie eye / Amorously twinkling, [she] beckens the giddie flie" to his destruction (17–18). He is the "wedded channels bosome" (24) which she, the "streame" (21), has deserted:

> She rusheth violently, and doth divorce
> Her from her native, and her long-kept course,
> And rores, and braves it, and in gallant scorne,
> In flattering eddies promising retorne,
> She flouts the channell, who thenceforth is drie;
> Then say I; that is shee, and this am I.
>> (29–34)

The cumulative effect of this language, transferring conventionally "masculine" terms (for example, "brave," "gallant") to the woman, is not to question traditional distinctions between male and female but to show her unnaturalness, thereby reinforcing conventional distinctions between the sexes.

These distinctions were being reexamined in medical circles, as Ian Maclean has shown.[32] During the late sixteenth century a limitedly revisionist medical discourse emerged as anatomists and physicians, attacking the Aristotelian idea of woman as imperfect man, argued that women and men were equally perfect in their respective sexes. But in contrast to medical discourses, ethical, legal, theological, and political discourses remained conservative in their view of woman. For all the remarkable innovation of Donne's *Elegies*, they are conservative, even reactionary, in their representations of the sexes. Like Aristotle, Donne presumes clear sex distinctions. Aristotle had justified what he saw as clear sex differentiation among the "higher" animals according to the principle that "the superior one should be separate from the inferior one": "wherever possible and so far as possible the male is separate from the female, since it is something *better* and more divine" (*De generatione animalium*, 2.1 [732a]). In the *Elegies*, Donne like Aristotle is concerned to enforce firm sex distinctions. But whereas Aristotle assumes fixed, stable categories, Donne's poems embody strong anxiety about transgressions of hierarchical distinctions between the sexes—an anxiety understandable in a culture in which those categories, both physiological and social, could no longer be assumed to be fixed or stable. Indeed, Queen Elizabeth herself was effectively destabilizing these clear sex distinctions by publicly cultivating an androgynous image of herself as both a desirable maiden to be courted and a strong, martial ruler who was master of all her subjects and noted for her "masculine" qualities of judgment and prudence.[33]

In Donne's *Elegy 6* the rebellious woman, imaged as both fire and water, has transgressed the supposedly natural, proper boundaries distinguishing the sexes (as did the promiscuous mistress in "Natures lay Ideot," which is, I believe, why the gender changes in the last lines, where the woman is compared to a male "colt," broken in only to be enjoyed by another). The woman's assimilation of "masculine" attributes has effectively "feminized" the man (he is like a flower, or the earth that is the stream's channel). Donne's strategy is first to expose the blurring of gender distinctions as unnatural and then to restore those boundaries and reassert masculine dominance.[34] Once he has exposed her betrayal, the speaker can reassert the "proper" male authority and supremacy as he warns her:

> Yet let not thy deepe bitternesse beget
> Carelesse despaire in mee, for that will whet
> My minde to scorne; and Oh, love dull'd with paine
> Was ne'r so wise, nor well arm'd as disdaine.
> Then with new eyes I shall survay thee,'and spie
> Death in thy cheekes, and darknesse in thine eye.
> Though hope bred faith and love; thus taught, I shall
> As nations do from Rome, from thy love fall.
> My hate shall outgrow thine, and utterly
> I will renounce thy dalliance: and when I
> Am the Recusant, in that absolute state,
> What hurts it me to be'excommunicate?

> (35–46)

His warning effectively gives him control as he suggests that her beauty, and thus her power and authority over him, depends on *him*. Questioning the conventions that idealize the mistress, Donne suggests that the lover empowers the mistress and thus ultimately holds the reigns of control. Perhaps this is all just wishful thinking on the speaker's part, and Donne is just wittily playing with literary conventions; but in this poem which brings together love, religion, and politics, these lines have a dangerous subversive potential. When one returns to the opening analogies between amorous and political service, this ending implies that just as the power of the mistress depends upon the good will of her lover (and the power of the Roman Church depends upon the willing consent of nations), so the power of the queen depends upon her subjects.

Elegy 6 is not the only poem to imply that monarchs can be deposed. In *Elegy 17: Variety*, the speaker rejects constancy for variety in love and invokes political language that suggests that no allegiance is permanent: "I love her well, and would, if need were, dye / To do her service. But followes it that I / Must serve her onely, when I may have choice?" (21–23). Constancy in love entails a loss of man's original "liberty" (62)—it ties him to a single person and makes him subservient to a woman. Rather than being faithful to one woman (and submitting to "opinion" and "honor" [50, 45], which Donne associates with woman in the ideology of courtly love), he chooses to follow a male monarch, making a "throne" (64) for the deposed Cupid. The political implications of this poem, in which worship/admiration of a single woman is replaced by loyalty to a king, would not have been lost on Donne's Elizabethan readers. But the poem might well have been unsettling even after Elizabeth's reign, for by the poem's end the attack on woman's rule has expanded to question the sovereignty of all rulers. Though the speaker proclaims he will now loyally serve the king of love by pursuing a variety of women, eventually even this pursuit will become tiresome and this new loyalty bondage. "But time will in his course a point discry / When I this loved service must deny, / For our allegiance temporary is" (73–75). Paradoxically, continual variety itself will prove boring, so for a change he will become faithful to a single mistress, if he can find one beautiful and worthy. Then the cycle of constancy and change will begin again. Envisioning a succession of allegiances, all of which are provisional and temporary, the poem both explores the psychology of desire and undermines an absolutist interpretation of monarchy.

In their revisions of power the *Elegies* thus have a politically subversive aspect which helps explain why Donne not only did not want his poems published but also in later years apparently regretted having written them (or at least, regretted not having destroyed them). Five elegies (including *Loves Progress* and *To his Mistress Going to Bed*) were refused a license to be published with his other poems in 1633. Probably it was not simply their eroticism that offended. Donne's elegies might have seemed dangerous not just during Elizabeth's reign but even later in James's and Charles I's, when Donne had finally achieved a position of prominence in the church, for repeatedly they imply that allegiances can be withdrawn, that monarchs can be deposed—which was precisely the fate that awaited Charles.

But for all their extended political resonance, I see these poems as distinctly (though not narrowly) the product of, and a reaction to, the historical situation of England's rule by a woman. Donne's anti-Petrarchanism, his debasement of women, his various subversions of women's rule, and his repeated attempts to reassert masculine sovereignty embody both the problematics of male submission to a female ruler and Donne's not unrelated personal sense that male desire requires an element of conflict, a feeling of superiority (however precarious) and the promise of mastery. Participating in the debate about women's rule as they contribute to the development of the love elegy, Donne's elegies embody a central tension: while basically conservative, even reactionary, in their insistence on male superiority and rule, they repeatedly demonstrate woman's unruliness, her subversion of permanent male rule. Thus power (whether in private, interpersonal relations, or in public, social ones) is seen as radically unstable.

The *Elegies* suggest that Donne was deeply disturbed by the sense that the old hierarchical order was threatened by a blurring of gender and sex distinctions (he attacks effeminacy as well as voracious, rebellious, aggressive women), by conventions such as neo-Petrarchan courtly love that seemed to invert the "proper" order in male/female relations, and by rule of a female monarch which seemingly enabled these other disruptions. Clearly, many things in late sixteenth-century English culture besides the presence of the queen on the throne contributed to the unsettling of traditional orders. But even if Queen Elizabeth's reign actually reinforced the existing hierarchies, Donne's *Elegies* are striking evidence that he may have perceived in it a threat to patriarchy, with its assumption of stable, permanent hierarchies. These poems reveal a deep sense of the connectedness of private and political human relations—and a strong sense that hierarchical power relations characterize the most personal and private area of human experience.

Notes

1. See, e. g., Arthur F. Marotti, " 'Love is not love': Elizabethan Sonnet Sequences and the Social Order," *ELH* 49 (1982): 396–428; Louis Montrose's two essays, "Celebration and Insinuation: Sir Philip Sidney and the Motives of Elizabethan Courtship," *Renaissance Drama*, n. s., 8 (1977): 3–35, and " 'Shaping Fantasies': Figurations of Gender and Power in Elizabethan Culture," *Representations* 1 (1983): 61–94; and David Javitch, "The Impure Motives of Elizabethan Poetry," in *The Power of Forms in the English Renaissance*, ed. Stephen Greenblatt (Norman, Okla.: Pilgrim Books, 1982), 225–38. Lauro Martines has suggested similarly complex relationships between courtly love poetry and politics in a paper "The Politics of Love Poetry in Renaissance Italy," given at a conference on "Historical Criticism in an Age of Deconstruction" (University of Illinois at Urbana-Champaign, October 13–15, 1989).

2. Marotti, *John Donne, Coterie Poet* (Madison: Univ. of Wisconsin Press, 1986). Further references to this work will be cited parenthetically in the text. See also John Carey, *John Donne: Life, Mind, and Art* (New York: Oxford Univ. Press, 1981), chaps. 3–4, who similarly argues that "power is the shaping principle in Donne's verse" (117).

3. A. LaBranche, " 'Blanda Elegeia': The Background to Donne's 'Elegies,' " *Modern Language Review* 61 (1966): 357–68, argues that "the study of essential human relationships" is "a principal theme of the love elegy" as developed by Catullus and Ovid and later by Donne (357). LaBranche's argument should make us wary of concluding too narrowly that Donne's concern is only socioeconomic politics.

4. Karl Marx, "Private Property and Communism," in *Economic and Philosophic Manu-*

scripts of 1844, ed. Dirk J. Struik and tr. Martin Milligan (New York: International Publishers, 1973), 134.

5. See Mary Douglas, *Natural Symbols: Explorations in Cosmology* (London: Barrie and Jenkins, 1970), 12, and *Purity and Danger: An Analysis of Concepts of Pollution and Taboo* (New York: Frederick A. Praeger, 1966), chap. 7.

6. Marotti's otherwise excellent reading of *The Anagram*, for example, glosses over the antifeminism when he comments, "The point of the exercise is not to indulge in a virtuoso antifeminism, but to question an entire range of amorous customs and rituals" (*Coterie* [note 2], 48). Other critics simply ignore those poems where the misogyny is difficult to avoid. In *The Metaphysics of Love: Studies in Renaissance Love Poetry from Dante to Milton* (Cambridge: Cambridge Univ. Press, 1985), A. J. Smith, gracefully describing Donne's celebration of mutual love and the interdependency of body and soul, lavishes attention on "The Ecstasy" but nowhere mentions the *Elegies* (chap. 3, "Body and Soul"). Recently, George Parfitt has correctly directed attention to the "reductive," "immature" view of women in the *Elegies* (*John Donne: A Literary Life* [London: Macmillan, 1989], 30–39), but the misogyny of these poems still remains to be historicized and the political implications explored.

7. I have used Helen Gardner's edition of *The Elegies and Songs and Sonnets* (Oxford: Clarendon, 1965) for the texts of the poems, though I refer to the elegies by the numbers assigned to them by Grierson in his 1912 Oxford edition. Specific references are cited parenthetically in the text by line number. I accept Gardner's dating of the *Elegies* as generally belonging to the 1590s (xxxii–xxxiii), though it is possible a few are later. *The Autumnall* has long been assigned a later date. Annabel Patterson, reminding us to be wary of assuming that all the elegies are early, argues that several belong to the period of James I (see "John Donne, Kingsman?," in *The Mental World of the Jacobean Court*, ed. Linda Levy Peck [Cambridge: Cambridge Univ. Press, 1991]).

8. Natalie Zemon Davis, "Women on Top: Symbolic Sexual Inversion and Political Disorder in Early Modern Europe," in *The Reversible World: Symbolic Inversion in Art and Society*, ed. Barbara Babcock (Ithaca: Cornell Univ. Press, 1978), 147–90. Davis's concern is with the symbolism of sexual inversions, especially the image of woman on top, in popular forms of misrule, but her discussion does not extend to Queen Elizabeth and the questions raised by the political rule of a female monarch. This issue has recently been addressed by Constance Jordan, "Woman's Rule in Sixteenth-Century British Thought," *Renaissance Quarterly* 40 (1987): 421–51.

9. Davis (note 8) suggests that in literature, popular festivity and ordinary life, sexual inversions both confirmed women's subjection and offered potential for subversion and change (see, esp. 183). But Montrose (note 1) observes that "because she was always uniquely herself, Elizabeth's rule was not intended to undermine the male hegemony of her culture. Indeed, the emphasis upon her *difference* from other women may have helped to reinforce it. . . . The royal exception could prove the patriarchal rule in society at large" ("Shaping Fantasies," 80). Jordan (note 8) judiciously concludes that the actual presence of a woman on the throne in Britain did not affect social conditions for women but did prompt debate over woman's rule and thus contribute to the general climate of rational inquiry that challenged the notion of fixed, absolute values (424).

10. Jordan (note 8), 421. Jordan examines the writings for and against gynecocracy prompted by the accessions of Mary I and Elizabeth I. Most notorious is John Knox's, *The First Blast of the Trumpet against the Monstrous Regiment of Women* (Geneva, 1558), published the year Elizabeth ascended the throne, though it was written specifically against the Catholic Mary I. Knox insisted that woman's rule is "monstrouse," "repugnant to nature," and a "subversion of good order" (see, for example, 5v, 9r, 12v, 17r, 27v, though his charges are repeated throughout). Knox's diatribe was impelled by his anti-Catholic Protestantism, but the treatise is also an exhausting argument for woman's natural inferiority to man. Knox's treatise was answered by John Aylmer's *An Harborowe for faithfull and trewe Subjectes, against the Late blowne Blaste . . .*

(London, 1559), which in counselling obedience to the queen suggested Knox's position was seditious (B1r, B1v, R2v). On the tensions for men posed by obedience to a female monarch, see also Montrose, "Shaping Fantasies" (note 1), 61, 64–65, 75.

11. Francis Barker, *The Tremulous Private Body: Essays on Subjection* (London: Methuen, 1984), argues that during the seventeenth century the "division between the public and the private [was] constructed in its modern form" (14).

12. See Javitch (note 1), and especially Marotti (notes 1 and 2), "Love is not Love" and *Coterie*, chap. 1.

13. See Mikhail Bakhtin's useful distinction between the "classical" aesthetic and "grotesque realism" as two manners of representing the human body (*Rabelais and His World*, tr. Helene Iswolsky [Bloomington: Indiana Univ. Press, 1984], 18–30). But as Peter Stallybrass and Allon White well point out (*The Politics and Poetics of Transgression* [London: Methuen, 1986], 5–6), Bakhtin idealizes the grotesque when he identifies it with festivity and vitality. Donne's representation of the female body in the *Elegies* betrays a sense of revulsion that contradicts Bakhtin's sense that the bodily element is always "deeply positive" in "grotesque realism" (19).

14. The French ambassador André Hurault, Sieur de Maisse, described her in 1597 as wearing "a great reddish-coloured wig. . . . As for her face, it is and appears to be very aged. It is long and thin, and her teeth are very yellow and unequal. . . . Many of them are missing" (*De Maisse: A Journal of All That Was Accomplished . . . Anno Domini 1597*, tr. G. B. Harrison and R. A. Jones [London: Nonesuch, 1931], 25–26). On Elizabeth's appearance see also J. E. Neale, *Queen Elizabeth I: A Biography* (1934; rpt. Garden City, N.Y.: Doubleday, 1957), 356, and Paul Johnson, *Elizabeth I: A Study in Power and Intellect* (London: Weidenfeld and Nicolson, 1974), 13–14, 374–75. According to Neale, her hair originally had been reddish-gold (28).

15. Marotti (note 2) observes that the "satiric debasement of women" in this poem "could imply a general critique of the cult of female beauty with its prescribed forms of hyperbolic praise" (*Coterie*, 50).

16. There may be yet another glance at the appearance of the aged queen here. The French ambassador De Maisse (note 14) recorded that the queen was given to displaying publicly, and fully, her "somewhat wrinkled" breasts (25, 36).

17. Aristotle, *De generatione animalium {Generation of Animals}*, tr. A. L. Peck, Loeb Library (Cambridge, Mass.: Harvard Univ. Press, 1953), 2.4 [738 b]; cf. 1.2 [716 a]. Further references are cited in the text. Helkiah Crooke's *Microcosmographia: A Description of the Body of Man* (London, 1615), which collects anatomical information from "the best authors" from Aristotle and Galen to Casper Bauhin and André du Laurens, repeatedly cites Aristotle's description of the womb as "the fertile field of Nature" (200, 221, 270). On Aristotelian ideas of sexual difference, see Ian Maclean, *The Renaissance Notion of Woman* (Cambridge: Cambridge Univ. Press, 1980), chap. 3, and Thomas Laqueur, "Orgasm, Generation, and the Politics of Reproductive Biology," *Representations* 14 (1986): 1–41. Galenic medicine follows Aristotle's distinctions between the sexes, though Galen diverged from Aristotle in according women semen.

18. *Symposium*, in *The Dialogues of Plato*, tr. B. Jowett, vol. 1 (Oxford: Clarendon Press, 1892), 580–82; Baldassare Castiglione, *The Book of the Courtier . . . done into English by Sir Thomas Hoby* {1591} (London, 1900), The Fourth Book, 357–63.

19. Alan Armstrong, "The Apprenticeship of John Donne: Ovid and the *Elegies*," *ELH* 44 (1977): 419–42, esp. 433. Armstrong comments that Donne's elegies show "a more aggressive version of the techniques used by Ovid" (434) though the implications and significance of this aggressiveness are not the concern of his important article.

20. L. P. Wilkinson, *Ovid Recalled* (Cambridge: Cambridge Univ. Press, 1955), 44, describes Ovid's continuation of the non-conformist stance in Catullus and Propertius. For the misogynist strain in Juvenal taken up by Donne see especially Juvenal's sixth satire. Though

Ovid depicts love as an art, a game, and a hunt, Wilkinson finds him "a sympathizer with women," with "an unusual inclination to see things from their point of view" (25, 86).

21. On Donne's connection with Essex, see Carey (note 2), 64–69, and especially M. Thomas Hester, "Donne's (Re)Annunciation of the Virgin(ia Colony) in *Elegy XIX*," *South Central Review* 4 (1987): 49–64. Hester argues that the opposition to the dominant court establishment that is inherent in Donne's association with Essex's circle underlies the anti-establishment implications of *Elegy 19*.

22. Neale, 350. On Essex and his relation with Elizabeth, see also Johnson (note 14), 369–74; J. B. Black, *The Reign of Elizabeth 1558–1603* (Oxford: Clarendon Press, 1936), 365–68, 370–73; and Walter Bourchier Devereux, *Lives and Letters of the Devereux, Earls of Essex*, 2 vols. (London: John Murray, 1853). Further references to this work will be cited parenthetically in the text.

23. Neale (note 14), 356.

24. De Maisse (note 14), 11–12. Montrose, who quotes this passage from De Maisse, sees the attempts of Parliament and counselors to persuade the queen to marry as in part motivated by the degradation and frustration men felt with serving a female prince, especially one not subjected to any man in marriage ("Shaping Fantasies" [note 1], 80).

25. Not all readers have stressed these qualities. Marotti (note 2), for example, finds this poem "a curiously antierotic treatment of a sexual encounter" (*Coterie*, 54). Carey's emphasis on Donne's obsession with power leads him to distort the tone of this poem, which he describes as "punitive," revealing a sadistic "urge to dominate" ([note 2], 106, 116, 117, 124).

26. Cf. Essex's curious letter to Queen Elizabeth which reveals an urgent desire for mastery at the same time that he praises her as the object of all his desire: "If my horse could run as fast as my thoughts do fly, I would as often make mine eyes rich in beholding the treasure of my love as my desires do triumph when I seem to myself in a strong imagination to conquer your resisting will" (*Lives and Letters*, [note 22], 1: 292).

Carey (note 2) finds Donne "profoundly excited by the thought of majesty" (113), obsessed by "royalty" (115), but he does not consider that these matters are problematic or subversive. See Hester's (note 21) fascinating discussion of this elegy as a subtle, radical critique of the English colonizing in Virginia, of Sir Walter Ralegh, and (by implication) of Queen Elizabeth.

27. Cf. Montrose's analysis of the seditious political implications of the seductive mastery of a queen ("Shaping Fantasies" [note 1], 62, 65). Marotti (note 2) argues that Donne's seduction poems are vehicles for expressing fantasies of achievement and triumph in the social world (*Coterie*, 89–90). Both Montrose and Jordan ([note 8], 450) recognize that for Elizabeth virginity was a source of power, that to yield to a man in marriage entailed a diminution of her power.

28. Marotti, *Coterie* (note 2), 52–53; also Stanley Fish's paper at the 1987 MLA, "Masculine Persuasive Force: Donne and Verbal Power," which argued that in the *Elegies* Donne and his surrogate speakers can never achieve the control they desire.

29. See Marotti, *Coterie* (note 2), 56–57.

30. For the text of this satire, I have used W. Milgate's edition of *The Satires, Epigrams and Verse Letters* (Oxford: Clarendon Press, 1967).

31. Paul R. Sellin, "The Proper Dating of John Donne's 'Satyre III,'" *Huntington Library Quarterly* 43 (1980): 275–312, questions the traditional dating of this satire as belonging to the 1590s, arguing that the poem grows out of Donne's experiences in the Netherlands in 1619.

32. On the revision of Aristotelian thought, see Maclean (note 17), 43–46.

33. On the queen's androgynous image, see Montrose, "Shaping Fantasies" (note 1), 77–78. Sieur de Maisse (note 14) observes that the queen was "well contented . . . when anyone commends her for her judgment and prudence, and she is very glad to speak slightingly of her intelligence and sway of mind, so that she may give occasion to commend her" (37–38).

34. Douglas, *Purity and Danger* (note 5), 142, suggestively remarks that "beliefs in sex

pollution" are likely to flourish in societies where the principle of male dominance is contradicted by other elements in the social life—which would suggest that misogyny and a reinsistence on female inferiority would flourish if the norm of male dominance in a patriarchal society was threatened by the rule of a female monarch. Donne's interest in sexual inversions, in the crossing of gender boundaries exemplifies her second category of "social pollution": "danger from transgressing the internal lines of the system" (122).

Women among the Metaphysicals: A Case, Mostly, of Being Donne for

JANEL MUELLER*

The so-called metaphysicals trace the origins of their label to an accusation Dryden leveled against Donne's poetic treatment of women.[1] "Not only in his satires," said Dryden, "but in his amorous verses, where nature only should reign," Donne "affects the metaphysics." He "perplexes the minds of the fair sex with nice speculations of philosophy, when he should engage their hearts, and entertain them with the softnesses of love."[2] How shall we evaluate this famous judgment passed by one major male poet of the seventeenth century on another, sixty years his senior? What, more generally, can we say of women as subjects of metaphysical poetry and as readers of it?

In Donne's prose and verse letters to the select women who figured both as subjects and readers of his poetry, we glimpse a dynamics of gender and power quite unlike the one Dryden posits. Crucial initiatives for the production and reception of Donne's poetry rest with these women; they patronize him, not he them. Thus Donne writes to the cultivated Magdalen Herbert, entrusting "the inclosed *Holy Hymns* and *Sonnets* . . . to your judgment, and to your protection too, if you think them worthy of it," since she has bestowed, he says, "all the good opinion" he enjoys.[3] At a later juncture Donne declares as follows of the countess of Bedford, to whom he addressed six of his most "metaphysical" poems. She "only hath power to cast the fetters of verse upon my free meditations." He reserves "for her delight (since she descends to them) . . . not only all the verses, which I should make, but all the thoughts of womens worthiness."[4] Later still, when Donne's complexly motivated *Anniversary* poems on Elizabeth Drury broke into print, the countess of Bedford and the countess of Salisbury were much displeased. They let Donne know this. He quickly bowed to the censures of his two patronesses. A verse letter to each records Donne's struggles to redirect rather than defend the hyperboles he had lavished on a mere slip of a girl. "I confess," run his lines to Lady Bedford.

> Since I had never knowne
> Vertue or beautie, but as they are growne

Modern Philology 87 (1989): 142–51. Reprinted by permission of the University of Chicago Press.

> In you, I should not thinke or say they shine,
> (So as I have) in any other Mine.[5]

For express testimony from a woman regarding the impact of this style of poetry, however, we must look to later in the century and to an area of potential response ignored altogether in Dryden's comments—that of sacred rather than amatory subjects. This woman was a poet herself, who wrote under the name of Orinda.[6] Sometime before her death in 1664 at the age of thirty-two, Katherine Philips addressed Henry Vaughan in a verse epistle that surveyed and saluted his poetic development. Professing hope that her work would mature as his had, she seeks to confirm in Vaughan a recognition she has already reached as a reader and practitioner of his style: "From the charming rigour thy muse brings / Learn there's no pleasure but in serious things!"[7] As we in turn will have occasion to confirm in female readers—critics and one other poet—who have succeeded Orinda, these ringing notes warn usefully against joining Dryden in too narrow notions of how women might relate to or figure in "the metaphysics" in verse.

If he underestimated female capacities for response and judgment, Dryden nevertheless spoke accurately enough for his age in signaling its break with Donne's poetic sensibilities and practice. Donne now stands in our eyes as the last English poet to sustain the force of the great, centuries-old Continental tradition of love lyrics that had celebrated femininity for offering the male poet a privileged access to ideality and divinity as well as a means of grounding his selfhood through intimacy with a person figured to and by this self as other.[8] Among English metaphysicals Richard Crashaw might at first seem a conspicuous exception to the foregoing generalization. In scaling the visionary and affective heights of his best-known poetry, that addressed to women subjects, Crashaw works from a declared conviction that souls in female bodies and social positions, like Teresa of Avila's, are best situated to experience the onset of divine love and to surrender themselves to it. Again and again he urges his little coterie of Englishwomen toward the transcendent inward raptures that are the privilege and the secret of a bride of Christ. The most revelatory example in this vein, "To Resolution in Religion, & to render her selfe without further delay into the Communion of the Catholick Church," was addressed to Crashaw's patroness, the countess of Denbigh. Its octosyllabic couplets pant in serial entreaty:

> Ah linger not, lov'd soul! a slow
> And late consent was a long no,
>
> . . . .
> Choose out that sure decisive dart
> Which has the Key of this close heart,
>
> . . . .
> Unfold at length, unfold fair flowre

And use the season of love's showre,

. . . .

O Dart of love! arrow of light!
O happy you, if it hitt right.[9]

Such elegant double entendres might pass among the small, self-exiled reader-ship of two Paris editions, but the poem displayed too much erotic license to be suitable for London publication without toning-down and retitling as "A Letter from Mr. Crashaw to the Countess of Denbigh." On a biographical and poetic showing alike, Crashaw defines an idiosyncratic extreme in the adoption of Continental modes of sensibility. He finally corroborates far more than he defies the generalization that Donne was the last English poet of the metaphys-ics of heterosexual love.

We confront, then, a spread of primary texts that offer testimony so conflicting as to cry out for analysis and explanation. There is the central figure of Donne—and the eccentric, marginal figure of Crashaw—for whom female subjects and the metaphysical style are inextricably linked. In Andrew Marvell this linkage of subjects and style exhibits an inconstant hold. In Herbert, Vaughan, and Thomas Traherne, the metaphysical style is sustained by displac-ing from female subjects the integrating and spiritualizing functions that had formerly served to anchor the male lover-poet's existence and expression. Why do women figure so divergently across the spectrum of figuration in this style of poetry?

Unless we reckon as integrally with their poetic absence as with their poetic presence, we may settle for a description that falls short as an explana-tion. If we immerse ourselves only in the ranging themes and tonalities that are Donne's great achievement in love poetry, we will be tempted to conclude that he exhausted the potentialities of women as subjects for the metaphysical style and that his successors reacted by turning in other directions. But if we attend, in these successors of Donne, to experiments with other than overtly female constructions of a poetic presence that empowers and validates lyric expression, we will be compelled to attribute more significance to their shift from secular to sacred love themes. Although Donne himself initiated this shift, he does not cast it as a choice between opposed poetic kinds. Later metaphysicals, however—Herbert in the youthful sonnets "My God, where is that ancient heat" and "Sure Lord, there is enough in thee," Vaughan in the prose preface and dedicatory verses of Silex Scintillans, and Marvell in "The Coronet"—repudiate secular ends when they profess sacred ones.

By virtue of chronology and the primacy he accords to female presence, Donne makes the first and longest claims on our attention. As we turn in that direction, we find Dryden, a poet looking closely at another poet's practice, again at our elbow. He points out that Donne, as he "affects the metaphysics," sweeps over the boundary between satire and amorous address and makes it of no account. Dryden's telling observation alerts us to what we soon identify as a constitutive feature—the imperiousness of the subjectivity that utters itself into being in Donne's verse. His poetic discourse is represented as springing from so deeply within the speaker's psyche that the discourse is always for and about that psyche. We owe to women critics of our century some now-classic appreciations of the nuances of thought and feeling that Donne's male discoursers manage to articulate.[10] Self-exploratory and self-revealing in equal measure, the speaker in poem after poem pronounces on the nature of love. Yet in reflecting on the union he seeks or finds or spurns with a female counterpart, the speaker continues to register the reaches and boundaries of his own gendered consciousness, his identity as a man.

Newer feminist readings have begun to show how these speakers' unwittingly negative aspects of self-disclosure can repay close study.[11] Donne acutely delineates a whole range of male attitudinizing about love. Fear of a possibly lasting relationship in "The Indifferent" prompts the fantasy of a Venusian edict against "dangerous constancie" (line 25). Phallic posturings and revulsions belie the speakers' world-weariness in "Loves Alchymie" and "Farewell to Love." Bravado fails to mask longing for a beloved never or only fleetingly possessed in "The Apparition" and "The Curse." A revealing turn at the end of "The Extasie" converts praise of perfect mutuality with a woman to instruction for a male overhearer: "Let him still marke us, he shall see / Small change, when we'are to bodies gone" (lines 75–76). The arrogance of a man who thinks his woman his property is shaken to very different depths in different contexts. "I planted knowledge and lifes tree in thee, / Which Oh; shall strangers taste?" laments the speaker of "Natures lay Ideot" (Elegie 7, lines 26–27). Struggling to confront the prospect of his beloved's death, the speaker of "A Feaver" dissolves his claim in paradoxically sudden and complete self-abandon: "I had rather owner bee / Of thee one houre, than all else ever" ("A Feaver," lines 27–28).

In remarking how Donne "perplexes the minds of the fair sex with nice speculations of philosophy, when he should engage their hearts, and entertain them with the softnesses of love," Dryden rightly realizes that it is the speaker's play of mind—not social contexts, norms, and practices—that determines the roles of the women in Donne's verse. We ourselves note that whatever place Donne's lovers find or make for their love requires them to oppose the world and its concerns ("The Sunne Rising," "The Canonization") or to keep the love secret from a world that is sure to misunderstand ("The Undertaking"). Given the period standards set by the developed realism of the Jacobean theater, Donne, who has so often been termed "dramatic," can so qualify at best in his versifying of speech to reveal the shifts and nuances of a single sensibility, but not in dialogue or full delineation of character. Compared with earlier Renaissance love poetry, Donne's is also odd in eschewing pictorialism and other sensuous effects to convey the allure of a woman's body to a male speaker. Not only must readers of Donne forgo expectations of catching much of the flavor of a woman's personality, they must also learn to "Care lesse, eyes, lips, hands to misse" ("A Valediction forbidding Mourning," line 20). Women remain highly subjectivized presences in this highly subjectivized poetry; as such, as Ilona Bell explains, they prove indispensable to the poetry and to the identities of the discoursing males who are its mouthpieces.[12] Women serve these males' psyches to "ballast"—the verb from "Aire and Angels" (line 15)—and limit what is other than the self, what is otherwise finally the vastness of the world.

In Donne the female other begins to contribute crucially to male selfhood when a speaker registers the onset of desire. This cognizance of specifically sexual attraction impresses a man with his own lack as well as his longing to conjoin to himself all that a given woman has and is. "But this," exclaims the speaker of "The Good-morrow," "all pleasures fancies bee / If ever any beauty I did see, / Which I desir'd, and got, t'was but a dreame of thee" (lines 5–7). To the extent that such desire acknowledges and yearns toward value in its object, it manifests itself as love. By casting desire and love as physical operations actually endured, Donne invigorates stock tropes like the incising of the beloved's image with some new poetic life—as, for example, in "The Dampe," where an autopsy ordered after the speaker's mysteriously sudden death "Will have me cut up to survay each part" and will "finde your Picture in my heart" (lines 3–4). Donne also outgoes every precedent but Spenser's in focusing a number of his lyrics on fulfilled rather than thwarted love, as Lu Emily Pearson was quick to note early in this century's critical vogue of the metaphysicals.[13] But even Spenser does not prepare us to encounter the Donnean male speaker who discourses analytically in these lyrics on the joys of fully reciprocated sexual love to his female counterpart. The yield is an astonishingly exact articulation of what man in Western culture has tended to make of woman and of himself in relation to her.[14]

We find that the onset of love unsettles and even shatters a man by destroying all illusion that he can live in self-containment and self-sufficiency; instead, he discovers that he is contingent, vulnerable, without a center.

> What did become
> Of my heart, when I first saw thee?
> I brought a heart into the roome,
> But from the roome, I carried none with mee,

marvels the speaker of "The Broken Heart" (lines 17–20). Especially disorienting are the concurrent demands that flesh and spirit make, for a man cannot sustain an axiomatic Christian subordination of his body to his soul when he is in love and feels "mixt of all stuffes, paining soule, or sense" ("Loves Growth," line 9). Yet if love is to be, as it is in Donne, the most sublime of human experiences, it must accommodate the "affections" and "faculties" of "sense" as well as "pure . . . soules," since both are tied in "that subtile knot" of our ensouled bodies ("The Extasie," lines 64–66). Once love overwhelms the Donnean male with the complexity and uniqueness of being human, he seeks to reconstitute his identity by obtaining the loving recognition of the woman who is the object of his love: "So thy love may be my loves spheare" ("Aire and Angels," line 25). Insofar as Donne's speakers associate the full mutuality of this human recognition with heterosexual intercourse freely undertaken and enjoyed, they rather strikingly represent the man and the woman as equals in love: "So, to one neutrall thing both sexes fit" ("The Canonization," line 25); "Let us possesse one world, each hath one, and is one" ("The Good-morrow," line 14).

The spiritual counterpart of this equality is the gaze enacted in "The Extasie" and invoked in a number of other lyrics. As the lovers draw close together, face to face, and see themselves reflected in the pupils of one another's eyes, one subjectivity fixes and gives back another subjectivity to itself.[15] In this connection, Aristotle's doctrine that a substance resists change and annihilation through the equal mixture of its elements acquires an emotional and intellectual resonance that brings poetic discourse to a genuinely "metaphysical" level. This doctrine provides the backdrop and perhaps also the stimulus for Donne's remarkable group of lyrics on leave-taking, the event that best verifies because it most severely tests mutuality based in heterosexual love. Of this group, however, only "A Valediction forbidding Mourning" and "A Valediction of Weeping" come close to striking a balance between the forces of the lovers' subjectivities.[16] By contrast, the male speaker of "Sweetest love, I do not go" lapses into self-regard—"'tis best, / To use my selfe in jest / Thus" (lines 6–7)—thus revealing at the critical moment of parting how tenuous an achievement this sexual equality is, how fearsome its counterpulls are. Finally significant are the very few settings Donne offers for his representations of sexual equality. They are limited to the "little roome" that becomes "an every where" or to the "Pregnant banke," a kind of Renaissance lovers' lane ("The Good-morrow," line 11; "The Extasie," line 2). It seems literally inconceivable that such equality might hold elsewhere than in the most intimate aspects of the man's and woman's love.

Thus, what Natalie Davis remarks of Renaissance culture at large applies as well in Donne's poetry generally: to confront the fact of sexual difference is to engage with issues of dominance and subordination, for there seems to be no other reason for the difference to exist.[17] Donne's many cynical and libertine speakers enact their conviction of male superiority, whether or not they finally undercut themselves in what they say. But the lyrics of reciprocated love also inscribe at key points the prevailing asymmetry of outlook and sexual role that casts the male as the persuader and possessor, the female as the persuaded and the possessed: "She's all States, and all Princes, I / Nothing else is" ("The Sunne Rising," lines 21–22). To his personal credit, Donne lends no credence to essentialist views of sexual difference, for his poetry is unmarked by their major premise—that a woman's capacity to bear children defines her and her relation to a man. Yet, conditioned as Donne was to think by the norms for education and conduct in his patriarchal society, he could scarcely at all imagine or figure his analytical, ratiocinative verse as anything but a male prerogative: "my words masculine perswasive force" ("Elegie: On his Mistris," line 4).[18] Even in the poems that figure amorous equality, the male act of representation—"this dialogue of one"—reinscribes the inequality of the sexes ("The Extasie," line 74). Virginia Woolf registers as much in her equivocal tribute to Donne's "power of suddenly surprising and subjugating the reader."[19] Indeed the most conspicuous constant in Donne's verse is the monopoly on discourse enjoyed and exercised by male figures—an aspect of the "phallocentrism" whose "command" of "literary history" is at issue for feminist critics.[20] Within the cultural mainstream—ours no less than Donne's —this monopoly acquires even further valency from the intense, nuanced subjectivities ascribed to these male speakers and the sturdiness of their characterization as active heterosexuals.[21]

If Donne had written only love poetry, the present account of him might end here. After 1607, however, he set to work more or less concurrently in two new genres: religious lyrics and verse letters in praise of prospective or actual patronesses. While there are many obvious differences between them, these two genres proved similar to Donne in an important respect. They brought into question, as inappropriate or wholly inapplicable, the framework of sexual consummation between a man and a woman within which he had located virtually everything he had written about love. This framework had also served as one of two vital props for the compelling naturalism of Donne's poetic representations. The other was provided by the highly developed subjectivity of the male speaking figure, and this figure Donne retained unaltered. But in the new genres this figure had to discourse differently of love, or had to discourse of a different love. It is not always exactly ascertainable how Donne construed his new poetic challenge.[22]

In the Holy Sonnets it proves continuously troubling for the male speaking-figure to do without heterosexual love as a model for ideality. He pursues his self-explorations alone. They leave him overwhelmed with his sins, which he sometimes expressly equates with his former active sexuality now branded as "Idolatry" ("O might those sighes and teares," lines 5–6; "What if this present," line 9). Fear rather than love of God predominates in the Holy Sonnets, where the speaker strains to place this irrepressible reflex in a positive light: "Those are my best dayes, when I shake with feare" ("Oh, to vex me," line 14).[23] Fear persists in the late "A Hymne to God the Father," although there the speaker regards it negatively: "I have a sinne of feare" (line 13). Deprived of the resources of human intersubjectivity, he continually appears at a loss for ways to relate to God as the sole divine Other. Infrequent direct address in very general terms like "God" and "Lord" compounds with expressions of insecurity or bewilderment as this male speaker seeks engagement with his male God.

What options existed for models of personal relationship in the genre of religious lyric? Not the model of single-sex, specifically male friendship that informs Donne's verse letters to male friends, because there could be no second-self or alter-ego relation between the human and the divine in the Christian orthodoxies within which Donne confined his choice of religion.[24] The father-son model carried full biblical and theological sanction, but it is remarkable how rarely and how indirectly the Donnean speaker uses it. Tenaciously figuring his maleness as adult manhood, he evinces the residual force of the sexualized model for love in Donne's religious poetry. Such a speaker cannot posit himself as a child. However, the most strenuous ingenuity proves incapable of adapting the sexualized model to the divine-human relationship without forfeiting the qualities that make this model so valuable and appealing in Donne's secular love poems. This speaker's two experiments along this line produce the "fearful accommodations" of a God who expresses love through torture, rape, and bondage in "Batter my heart" and a spouse who fulfills her role by behaving like a whore in "Show me deare Christ."[25] By contrast, moreover, with their analytic and elucidating functions in the secular love poems, the paradoxes of Donne's religious lyrics remain either paradoxical or blunt to theological commonplace in such characteristic instances as "Thy Makers maker, and thy Fathers mother," "Therefore that he may raise the Lord throws down" ("La Corona. Annunciation," line 12; "Hymne to God my God, in my Sicknesse," line 30).

The same cannot be said of Donne's verse letters to noblewomen and the two *Anniversaries*, which stand to each other as preparatory exercises and masterworks on the symbolic power of femininity. As Barbara Lewalski has discussed in detail, this poetry is nothing if not metaphysical; its trajectories of hyperbole often take us a great distance from any recognizable female presence.[26] Here the Donnean discourser proves capable of displacing the flesh while retaining the spirit at the center of a male-female relationship, and the verse epistles to noblewomen suggest several reasons why. The least of these seems to be the fact that such a relationship tallies in all essentials with the parting and separation—that is, the physical distancing—that figures so crucially as a test of heterosexual love for the male speakers of the love poetry. More important is the readiness shown by this discourser to love his patronesses as authority figures who, through their attentions to him, set the worth of his person and the direction of his life. Of course one can decide to dismiss such "love" as an exaction of Renaissance patronage, but Margaret Mauer has argued cogently for its centrality to Donne's own psychic and social being.[27] Even if we chalk the fact up as a vestige of Marian devotion, it is surely noteworthy that, on the evidence of this poetry, the Donnean male speaker can love a woman much more easily than he can God in a dominating role. Most interesting of all are the reflections offered on femininity. They complete what the love poetry leaves implicit or undeveloped in the Donnean representation of woman as they push to a vanishing point in her the distinction between the human and the divine.

The verse letters go far beyond the love poetry in ascribing to feminine otherness a sweeping ethical force. The judging role of the women in the love poetry is typically confined to the specifics of the argument which the speaker is making about his or their love—for example, in "The Flea" or in "A Valediction of my Name, in the Window." In the verse letters we gain a deepened sense of what the male self seeks in a female other: not just to be acknowledged but also to be wholly ratified by her. The patroness occupies a privileged position in his construction of the world. Her outlook, unclouded (in his casting of the matter) by masculine pursuits and preoccupations, can uniquely reach a true appraisal of his character, his enterprises, and even the quality of his reasoning. Thus an epistle to the countess of Bedford begins:

> Madame,
> You have refin'd mee, and to worthyest things
> . . . now I see
> Rarenesse, or use, not nature value brings.
> (lines 1–3)

In exerting this higher power over the speaker's life, the patroness quickly assumes the aspect of divinity: "Divinity, that's you" ("Reason is our Soules left hand," line 2).

In another epistle to the countess of Bedford, her matchless understanding and practice of virtue are credited to her gender as Donne ingeniously applies pseudologic to establish the sexual double standard as an ethical standard possessed of redoubled force. Since she is a moral agent gendered female, Lady Bedford always has her "honour" to maintain. Her high attainment of goodness results from knowing, as only a lady can, how to unite prudential worldly considerations with heavenly concerns: "Discretion is a wisemans Soule, and so / Religion is a Christians, and you know / How these are one" ("Honour is so sublime perfection," lines 40–42). An epistle to the countess of Huntington also equates her femininity with divinity while disclosing the speaker's adroit manipulation of gender roles and positions. Because Lady Huntington has accepted the (subordinating) involvement with a man that gives her "a wifes and mothers name," she can be trusted not to establish norms inimical to the male speaker: "Vertue having made you vertue, 'is faine / T'adhere in these names, her and you to show" ("Man to Gods image, *Eve*, to mans was made," lines 29, 31–32).

Against this quite innovative backdrop of associations of ideality with the lives and persons of mature married women, the turn to a virgin's body and soul as the locus of all the world's value in *The Anniversaries* both looks and is more conventional. We do not have to agree with Ben Jonson that the poems should have been more conventional still, that if they "had been written of the Virgin Marie" they "had been something." For there is nothing in the poetic transmutation of the fifteen-year-old Elizabeth Drury in *The Anniversa-*

ries that does not tally with traditional attributes of the Virgin at the same age, the age she was supposed to have borne Christ, except for the bearing of Christ. Donne more than makes good any potential deficit in his subject by assimilating the attributes of Christ as well as Mary to what he told Jonson was "the idea of a Woman, and not as she was."[28] The apotheosis of femininity as divinity in the English Renaissance, these poems demonstrate the heights to which male idealization and imagination can rise when the female other is postulated purely as a blank counter. "Her death did wound, and tame thee than," says the speaker of "The First Anniversary," addressing the world— "and than / Thou mightst have better spar'd the Sunne, or Man" (lines 25–26). Donne understood well enough the wire-drawn extremities to which he had pursued virtue in female guise in his *Anniversaries* to see that any defense of them would have to be staked in the world-realizing capacities of the mind— the precincts, from first to last, of all the metaphysicals. In specifically staking out those precincts by demonstrating the centrality of gender relations to the constitution of the mind's capacities,[29] Donne has as strong a claim as he ever did to be considered the definitive poet of the English style that takes its name from his defining practices.

. . . .

Notes

1. I owe to Sidney Gottlieb the idea of undertaking this essay and much encouragement along the way, both of which I gratefully acknowledge. I have my colleagues Joshua Scodel and Richard Strier to thank for their trenchant criticisms of my first draft. Members of the Renaissance Workshop at the University of Chicago—especially Shef Rogers and my colleague John Wallace—and participants in the University of Southern California's Renaissance Conference held in February 1988 have given me questions and comments on a subsequent draft, for which I am indebted. All residual shortcomings are, needless to say, my own.

2. John Dryden, *A Discourse Concerning the Original and Progress of Satire* (1693), cited in A. L. Clements, ed., *John Donne's Poetry* (New York, 1966), p. 106.

3. R. C. Bald, *John Donne: A Life* (Oxford, 1970), pp. 181–82, citing Izaak Walton's excerpt of a letter exchange in his *Life of Mr George Herbert* (1675).

4. John Donne, *Letters to Severall Persons of Honour* (1651), ed. M. Thomas Hester, Scholars' Facsimiles (Delmar. N.Y., 1977), p. 106.

5. "To the Countesse of Bedford. Begun in France but never perfected," lines 11–16; cf. "To the Countesse of Salisbury. August 1614," lines 37–38, both in *The Complete Poems of John Donne*, ed. C. A. Patrides (London, 1985), pp. 302, 307. Subsequent quotations from Donne's poetry are taken from this edition and cited by title and line numbers in my text.

6. Work in progress by Elizabeth H. Hageman documents a guarded, even derivative use of Donne's metaphysical conceits (compasses, exchanged hearts, etc.) in Orinda's lyrics celebrating women's friendship. By contrast, Hageman finds a much more individuated and self-authenticating female voice when Orinda the poet gives place to Katherine Philips the letter-writer. These implications are developed in "Katherine Philips: Private Poetry and Public Letters" (paper presented at the Sixteenth-Century Studies Conference, St. Louis, October 1988).

7. "To Mr Henry Vaughan Silurist on his Poems," lines 37–38 (Catherine Cole

Mambretti, ed., "A Critical Edition of the Poems of Katherine Philips" [Ph.D. diss., University of Chicago, June 1979], p. 121).

8. Still authoritative discussions are offered by J. B. Broadbent in *Poetic Love* (London, 1964); and by N. J. C. Andreasen in *John Donne: Conservative Revolutionary* (Princeton, N. J., 1967).

9. "To the Noblest & best of Ladyes, the Countesse of Denbigh," lines 13–14, 33–34, 43–44, 49–50 (L. C. Martin, ed., *The Poems of Richard Crashaw*, 2d ed. [Oxford, 1957], p. 237).

10. See Joan Bennett, "The Love Poetry of John Donne: A Reply to Mr. C. S. Lewis," in *Seventeenth-Century Studies Presented to Sir Herbert Grierson* (Oxford, 1938), pp. 85–104; the introduction, notes, and appendices to John Donne, *The Elegies and the Songs and Sonnets*, ed. Helen Gardner (Oxford, 1965); Roma Gill, "*Musa locosa Mea*: Thoughts on the *Elegies*," in *John Donne: Essays in Celebration*, ed. A. J. Smith (London, 1972), pp. 47–72; and Barbara Hardy, "Thinking and Feeling in the *Songs and Sonnets*," in Smith, ed., pp. 73–88.

11. Lois E. Bueler, "The Failure of Sophistry in Donne's Elegy VII," *Studies in English Literature* 25 (1985): 69–85; Janel M. Mueller, "'This Dialogue of One': A Feminist Reading of Donne's 'Extasie'," *Association of Departments of English Bulletin* 81 (1985): 39–42.

12. Ilona Bell, "The Role of the Lady in Donne's *Songs and Sonets*," *Studies in English Literature* 23 (1983): 113–29.

13. Lu Emily Pearson, "John Donne's Love Lyrics," in her *Elizabethan Love Conventions* (Berkeley, 1933), pp. 223–30.

14. The fullest inventory of cultural constructions remains that of Simone de Beauvoir in her magisterial *Le deuxieme sexe: 1—Les faits et les mythes* (Paris, 1949), abridged in H. M. Parshley's translation, *The Second Sex* (New York, 1953).

15. See Wilbur Sanders's sensitive discussion of this recurring moment in *John Donne's Poetry* (Cambridge, 1975), pp. 66–72.

16. For detailed analyses that support this generalization, see William Empson, "A Valediction of Weeping," in *John Donne: A Collection of Critical Essays*, ed. Helen Gardner (Englewood Cliffs, N. J., 1962), pp. 52–60; John Freccero, "Donne's 'Valediction: Forbidding Mourning,'" in *Essential Articles for the Study of John Donne's Poetry*, ed. John Roberts (Hamden, Conn., 1975), pp. 279–304; and Avi Erlich, "Ambivalence in John Donne's 'Forbidden Mourning,'" *American Imago* 36 (1979): 357–72.

17. Natalie Zemon Davis, "Women on Top," in her *Society and Culture in Early Modern France: Eight Essays* (Stanford, Calif., 1975), pp. 124–51, esp. p. 128.

18. Though frameworks of explanation vary, the denomination "patriarchal" characterizes Donne's era in such diverse accounts as Roberta Hamilton, *The Liberation of Women: A Study of Patriarchy and Capitalism* (London, 1978); Lawrence Stone, *The Family, Sex and Marriage in England, 1500–1800* (London, 1977); and Keith Wrightson, *English Society, 1580–1680* (London, 1982).

19. Virginia Woolf, "Donne after Three Centuries," in her *The Second Common Reader* (New York, 1932), pp. 22–37, quote on p. 24.

20. Hélène Cixous, "Sorties," in *New French Feminisms: An Anthology*, ed. Elaine Marks and Isabelle de Courtivron (New York, 1981), pp. 90–98, quote on p. 92. Also see Luce Irigaray, *This Sex Which Is Not One*, trans. Catherine Porter (Ithaca, N.Y., 1985), chaps. 2, 4, 5.

21. Donne's "Breake of Day" and "Confined Love" are short, slight exercises. Only in "Sapho to Philaenis" does a Donnean woman speaker sustain discursive and imaginative force comparable to a male's in addressing the object of her passion. It cannot be accidental that she is also an imperious poetic talent. Her lesbianism, equally, cannot be accidental; see my essay, "A Letter from Lesbos: Utopian Homoerotics in Donne's 'Sapho to Philaenis'," in *Sexuality and Gender in Early Modern Europe—Multidisciplinary Essays*, ed. James Grantham Turner (Cambridge, England, 1993), pp. 182–207.

22. For a sympathetic highlighting of such continuities as can be discerned in the earlier

and later phases of Donne's poetry, see Kitty Datta, "Love and Asceticism in Donne's Poetry: The Divine Analogy," *Critical Quarterly 19*, no. 2 (1977): 5–25.

23.   For discussion of the theological sources and implications of this Donnean fear, see Richard Strier, "John Donne 'Awry and Squint,'" *Modern Philology* 86 (1989): 357–84.

24.   For an influential reading of Donne in which his exchange of the Roman for the English Church becomes a self-determining act of apostasy, see John Carey, *John Donne: Life, Mind and Art* (New York, 1981).

25.   See William Kerrigan's incisive essay, "The Fearful Accommodations of John Donne," *English Literary Renaissance 4* (1972): 337–63.

26.   Barbara Kiefer Lewalski, *Donne's Anniversaries and the Poetry of Praise: The Creation of a Symbolic Mode* (Princeton, N. J., 1973); cf. my review article, "Death and the Maiden: The Christian Symbolism of Donne's *Anniversaries*," *Modern Philology* 70 (1973): 280–86.

27.   Margaret Mauer, "The Real Presence of Lucy Russell, Countess of Bedford, and the Terms of John Donne's 'Honor is So Sublime Perfection,'" *ELH* 47 (1980): 205–34. For further probing of Donne's self-cognizance regarding the transactional character of his maneuverings for patronage and position, see Judith Scherer Herz's "'An Excellent Exercise of Wit That Speaks So Well of Ill': Donne and the Poetics of Concealment," in *The Eagle and the Dove: Reassessing John Donne*, ed. Claude J. Summers and Ted-Larry Pebworth (Columbia, Mo., 1986), pp. 8–14.

28.   Ben Jonson, *Conversations with Drummond of Hawthornden* (1618–19), excerpted in Clements, ed., *John Donne's Poetry*, p. 103.

29.   For further suggestive discussion, see Nancy Chodorow, *The Reproduction of Mothering: Psychoanalysis and the Sociology of Gender* (Berkeley and Los Angeles, 1979); Dorothy Dinnerstein, *The Mermaid and the Minotaur: Sexual Arrangements and Human Malaise* (New York, 1976); and Carol Gilligan, *In a Different Voice: Psychological Theory and Women's Development* (Cambridge, Mass., 1982).

The Lyric in the Field of Information: Autopoiesis and History in Donne's *Songs and Sonnets*

Richard Halpern*

Racine and Donne looked into a good deal more than the heart. One must look into the cerebral cortex, the nervous system, and the digestive tracts.
—T. S. Eliot, "The Metaphysical Poets"[1]

"It is surely not the smallest charm of a theory that it is refutable; this precisely attracts the subtler minds. . . . Someone always comes along who feels strong enough to refute it once more."[2] The charmingly refutable theory of which Friedrich Nietzsche speaks here is the autonomy of the will, but for a variety of post-New Critical theorists, the autonomous *lyric* has offered an equally, almost hypnotically tempting target: someone always comes along who feels strong enough to deconstruct the lyric poem, or historicize it, once more. Poetic closure has, indeed, been elevated to the uncomfortable and paradoxical status of most-favored victim; no one believes in it any more, yet it is sustained in a kind of half-life, like a comatose patient, only in order to be wheeled out and beaten as occasion demands. Marxists, new historicists, and poststructuralists have all challenged the formal closure of lyric, whether in the name of a social totality, a general textual economy, or contiguous fields of cultural and social practice. In every case there is an "outside" to the text which corrodes the boundaries of lyric—even if the outside is only more text, and hence no outside at all. Opposition to lyric closure is a metaposition on which even antagonistic approaches can agree; it forms the common ground for a variety of methods fashionable in the humanities today.

Marxist criticism has devoted relatively little attention to the lyric, compared with narrative and dramatic modes, but its arguments against literary formalism go back to the days of Trotsky, Bakhtin, and Medvedev, and contemporary Marxist critics who have turned to lyric insist that a poem's formal closure must be punctured in order to release its historical meaning. Frank Lentricchia, opening his book *Ariel and the Police* with a virtuoso reading

The Yale Journal of Criticism 6 (1993): 185–215. Reprinted by permission of the author and Blackwell Publishers.

of Wallace Stevens' "Anecdote of a Jar," writes: "The advantage of beginning with this odd little anecdotal lyric in the practice of Wallace Stevens is that we are forced at the outset into confronting the inadequacy of the modernist literary theory of aesthetic autonomy (inadequate but possessed of many more than nine lives) and its corollary critical stance of trying to situate and contain all commentary within the text's formal boundaries."[3] For Lentricchia, lyric closure is little more than an ideological ruse of modernism, one that artificially encloses the poem in an atemporal realm. Only with the recognition that the poem "will not cohere"[4] can formalism be banished, and Stevens's "Anecdote of a Jar" opened to historical and social meaning. Lyric poems, like the bleeding trees of romance, can speak only after being wounded; they recount their own histories only when their formal integrity has been violated. In his important reading of Blake, John Brenkman likewise insists that "The utopian power of poetry can only lie in its concrete connections, as a language practice, with its relevant social contexts rather than in its capacity either to separate itself from those contexts or to set itself above them."[5]

One important exception to Marxism's suspicions regarding lyric autonomy would seem to be the work of Theodor Adorno. In his famous essay on "Lyric and Society," Adorno depicts the autonomy of lyric not as a modernist illusion but as a utopian strategy on the part of lyric itself, by means of which it attempts to carve out an oppositional space within reified culture: "The more heavily social conditions weigh, the more unrelentingly the poem resists, refusing to give in to any heteronomy, and constituting itself purely according to its own particular laws. . . . The idiosyncrasy of poetic thought, opposing the overpowering force of material things, is a form of reaction against the reification of the world, against the rule of the wares of commerce over people which has been spreading since the beginning of the modern era."[6] Adorno's rhetoric emphasizes the fragility of lyric form and the pathos of its brave though increasingly precarious effort to fend off the logic of capitalism. Yet for Adorno the lyric must also overcome what he calls the subject's "naked, isolated opposition to society," which is as much an effect of reification as is its apparent opposite, the subordination of the subject to a merely instrumental reason.[7] The lyric resists heteronomy, then, not so as to enclose itself in a protective shell but so as to emerge into a redeemed and utopian collectivity represented by language itself. "From a condition of unrestrained individualism, the lyric work strives for, awaits the realm of the general."[8] Stephen Georg's poetry, as read by Adorno, effects a "transformation of . . . a tremendously exaggerated individuality to self-annihilation."[9] As if gripped by the Freudian death-drive, the autonomous lyric fends off destruction from without, yet does so in order to specify its own path to extinction.[10] While Adorno grants lyric autonomy a real social and historical weight, the utopian work of lyric nevertheless requires it to transcend its own boundaries in order to become "the voice of men between whom the barriers have fallen."[11] For Marxist theory, then, the lyric has only to choose the means by which its closure will be dissolved. The poem may find its space effracted by the bustle of a reified world; it may generate a concrete utopia through its internal contradictoriness as text, and through its connections with other fields of practice; it may produce or await a more abstract utopian moment in which its mode of utterance is universalized and thus transfigured; or finally, it may discover that its closure was never anything but a delusion of modernist and New Critical theory, much as Alice in *Through the Looking Glass* comes to doubt whether she isn't really just a dream of the Red King.

This essay will attempt to re-pose the question of lyric autonomy by invoking a theoretical framework which has become increasingly influential in the natural and social sciences but not, as yet, in the humanities: I mean the theory of autopoietic or self-referring systems.[12] The theory of autopoiesis was formally mapped out in the 1970s by two Chilean neuroscientists, Humberto Maturana and Francisco Varela, and since that time has spread beyond the biological sciences to such fields as psychology, sociology, and law.[13] Its claim to enfold both the natural and human sciences will doubtless provoke some skepticism among critics who worry about the ideological effects of applying biological models to cultural phenomena. Yet autopoietic theory does not impose organic metaphors onto culture; if anything, it draws the field of the living into a paradigm whose terms, while novel and surprising, are not the least incompatible with critical apparatuses already in play. Promising to deconstruct the boundaries between the "two cultures," autopoietic theory offers a paradigm whose scope exceeds even that of the structuralist revolution of the 1950s and 1960s.[14] Yet its universalizing aspirations are also balanced by an antitotalizing impulse. As a "grand theory" of nontotalization, it provides a possible third way beyond the current impasse between Marxist theory, on the one hand, and the new historicists' refusal to theorize, on the other. At the same time, it offers a model of language and culture radically different from that of poststructuralism.

The first part of this essay will introduce the concept of autopoiesis and try to indicate its distinctive features. The second part will explore the ways in which a theory of autopoietic systems can shed new light on the question of lyric autonomy, focusing on issues raised by the historical reading of the Renaissance love lyric; in particular, it will attempt to situate Donne's *Songs and Sonnets* within a history of sexuality which at once respects the formal boundaries of the lyric and questions some of the assumptions behind a Foucauldian understanding of sexuality. The third and final section will return to the role of lyric autonomy within Marxist criticism, and will try to locate those areas in which autopoietic and Marxist theory can achieve, if not harmony, then at least a productive conflict.

I

In the most basic sense, an autopoietic system can be understood as a self-reproducing one. Maturana and Varela define an autopoietic machine as a network of processes of production of components—components which, through their interactions and transformations, regenerate and realize in their turn the network of processes that produced them in the first place. They thus constitute the autopoietic machine as a concrete unity within the topological domain of its realization as a network.[15] The concept of autopoiesis provides, among other things, a definition of living organisms—or, as Maturana and Varela call them, "physical autopoietic machines"—but it is by no means limited to or fully derivative of a biological domain.

Self-reference is, essentially, the recursive process in which relations of production create the components by which they are in turn produced. It is not a structuralism, for it entails not a maintenance of static patterns, nor the reproduction of structural relations among elements, but rather a relation among dynamic processes which constantly produce new and ephemeral components, such as behaviors or communications.[16] Nor, in the case of living systems, should autopoiesis be conceived of as a *drive* toward self-reproduction, along the lines of Freudian self-preservative instincts. Systems are either autopoietic or not; self-reference is not a goal but a condition.

As a result of their recursive functioning, autopoietic machines are informationally closed systems: they do not receive or process input from their environments, nor do they produce output of any kind, nor do they admit of heteronomy. Though born of cybernetics, autopoiesis is in effect an anticybernetic theory. Maturana and Varela's work principally involves the nervous system, which perfectly exemplifies the informational closure of autopoiesis. Neurological systems, including those of human beings, are incapable of either receiving or storing information from their environments. "All that is accessible to the nervous system at any point are states of relative activity holding between nerve cells, and all that to which any given state of relative activity can give rise are further states of relative activity in other nerve cells."[17] Individual neurons cannot process qualitative information; they can only receive and transmit quantities of energy that produce internal states of difference. As a result, "the phenomenology of the changes of state of the nervous system is exclusively the phenomenology of the changes of state of a closed neuronal network; that is, for the nervous system as a neuronal network there is no inside or outside."[18] Reactions in the nervous system, as in any autopoietic system, can be "triggered but not specified by the circumstances of their interactions" with other entities.[19] What the "anatomical and functional organization of the nervous system secures," then, is "the synthesis of behavior [of the organism itself], not a representation of the world [it inhabits]."[20]

Recognizing that the nervous system is a closed, self-referring system does not lead either to solipsism or idealism. It does not deny the perceptual and phenomenal richness of human experience, or refuse to recognize that things such as learning, memory, and communication occur. But it does radically redefine our understanding of these things. Learning, for instance, does not involve retrieving previously stored information about the environment. It arises rather, from an organism's recursive processing of its own behavior, which produces a "blind" adaptation to its surroundings. A helpful though imperfect analogy here is biological evolution, in which the recursive application of random variations in a species modifies its capacity to survive and cope in a given context. To an observer over time (a Lamarckian, for instance), it might wrongly appear that the species itself somehow "perceived" the features of its environment and mutated as a purposeful response to what it had learned.[21] Similarly, autopoietic machines such as the nervous system seem to adapt, remember, and communicate with their environments, yet they do so through the recursive generation of what the cybernetician Heinz von Foerster calls "eigenbehaviors,"[22] by means of which they "learn those operations which are valid in coping with their environment, to which they have no direct access."[23] It may appear to an observer that an autopoietic machine receives, processes, or transmits information, but this is only, as Maturana and Varela put it, "an artifice of . . . description."[24]

The theory of autopoiesis has radical implications for conceptions of language and communication. While a transfer of information between closed systems is out of the question, Maturana argues that organisms can couple their behaviors in such a way that a change in one organism becomes a source of deformation (N. B.: not information) for the other, and the other's compensatory behavior in turn becomes a source of deformation for the first. Through the recursive application of behavioral coupling something like a mutual orientation in an environment is achieved, even though neither organism can specify a predefined change in the other.[25] Language is, in this view, consensual, not informational—connotative, not denotative—even though the behavioral coupling which constitutes communication may *appear* to an observer as a transfer of information.[26]

Maturana himself has employed the concept of autopoiesis to evolve a decidedly left wing, radically egalitarian theory of society.[27] But the growing influence of autopoiesis in the human and social sciences is due primarily to the work of the prolific and more politically conservative German sociologist Niklas Luhmann. For Luhmann, the specialized social systems which constitute modern, industrialized societies—legal, political, economic, and cultural systems—are essentially autopoietic or self-referring communicative networks. Luhmann regards these systems as cognitively open to one another but normatively closed.[28] The legal system, for instance, can receive messages from other systems, but it always filters them through its own system of norms, on which its decisions and interpretive procedures will necessarily be based.[29]

For Luhmann, the information that a system receives from its environment is not determined by a transfer of data but by the system's own internal principles of selectivity, which limit an otherwise overwhelming flood of messages by specifying which will count as meaningful. As social systems become more fully differentiated, their principles of selectivity will become more restrictive, more exactingly determined by the internal needs of the system's functioning, and consequently less open to communication with other systems. As Luhmann aphoristically puts it, "complexity enforces selection."[30]

Luhmann's theory of social systems entails a distinctive and rather grim narrative of modernity. "The transition from traditional to modern society," he writes, "can be conceived of as the transition from a primarily stratified form of differentiation of the social system to one which is primarily functional."[31] Premodern society, in other words, is divided by traditional forms of social stratification such as class or caste, while in modern society the predominant mode of differentiation is by social function, resulting in the increasing autonomy of specialized systems. The transition from stratified to functional differentiation does not, however, mean that social differences of class and gender are progressively eroded in the name of functional efficiency. On the contrary, traditional or stratified systems tend to hold social differences within stable boundaries, while functional differentiation feeds on even small differences and multiplies them without limit. Moreover, social differentiation produces increasingly closed and self-referring systems which find it ever more difficult to communicate. Society divides into distinct and incommensurable epistemic regions, with the result that democratic control of society as a whole becomes increasingly difficult.[32]

This rather long excursus was necessary in order to convey the distinctiveness of the concept of autopoiesis. Luhmann's theory of social systems, with its emphasis on closed communicative networks, is congenial with certain versions of postmodernism, but radically incompatible with both poststructuralist notions of unbounded textual circulation and Marxist notions of society as an overdetermined totality.[33]

Before a theory is either attacked or defended, it ought to prove itself to be "charmingly refutable" in Nietzsche's sense; that is to say, it must first produce results which are interesting or compelling enough to merit its being entertained in the first place. In this essay, then, I do not propose to offer either a formal endorsement or a formal critique of Luhmann's narrative of modernity. Instead I shall provisionally entertain a theory of social autopoiesis in order to see whether it can enrich the historical reading of lyric. My test case here will be John Donne's *Songs and Sonnets*, but even before turning to Donne we can see how a theory of autopoiesis begins to resituate the terms of the relation between history and lyric autonomy. For as the very name "autopoiesis" suggests, Luhmann's conception of social systems takes on the very properties of closure and self-reference formerly associated with the lyric poem. The notion that an historical reading can refute or dissolve lyric autonomy becomes more complex if social systems themselves begin to assume lyric is thus itself a form of historical and social testimony—and in Donne's case it is explicitly so.

It would be misleading, however, to suggest that Donne's "pretty rooms" are exclusively aesthetic spaces. For they are also spaces of love and sexuality. Love, after all, is what "makes one little room an every where," as Donne puts it in "The Good Morrow." It is for love or sexual passion that Donne claims, in "The Canonization" and elsewhere, to sacrifice wealth and worldly power. And finally, it is love that, at least occasionally in Donne's verse, provides a utopian realm of mutuality among persons, contrasting with the litigiousness of civil society and the tyranny of the political realm. Thematically, at least, the autonomy of Renaissance lyric is strongly bound up with the autonomy of love and sexuality. Some recent new historical work has challenged both halves of this relation by claiming that the rhetoric of love in the Elizabethan lyric is primarily a way of encoding political discourse. Thus Arthur Marotti entitles his influential essay on the politics of Elizabethan sonnet sequences "Love is Not Love."[40] By demonstrating how Elizabethan love poetry provided an acceptable expression for political and social criticism, Marotti attacks the notion of poetic autonomy precisely by undercutting the autonomy of love; and thus he demonstrates, in a negative fashion, how closely these two issues are tied together. In what follows I will be arguing, somewhat tautologically, that love *is* in fact love, and I will employ this (now strangely controversial) idea to offer an anti-Foucauldian reading of Donne's place within the history of sexuality.

The basis for such a reading is supplied by Niklas Luhmann's book *Love as Passion*, the argument of which I will summarize here because it provides an illuminating context for Renaissance love poetry in general. Luhmann situates his treatment of love within his larger narrative of modernity and its effects on the individual person. The evolving differentiation of social systems, Luhmann argues, inhibits the ability of any given system to select information from others. Social systems become less receptive to their environments, leading to a breakdown of communication unless institutional countermeasures are taken.[41] What Luhmann calls "generalized symbolic media" attempt to make improbable communications between social systems possible.[42] Such media attempt, in effect, to create a common world or semantic space through which self-referring systems can communicate.

Among other distinctions produced by the transition from stratified to functional differentiation of society, argues Luhmann, is that between personal and social systems. "This is the case because with the adoption of functional differentiation individual persons can no longer be firmly located in one single subsystem of society, but rather must be regarded a priori as fundamentally displaced."[43] As increasingly isolated and dislocated systems, individual persons suffer the general fate of decreasing receptivity to one another and to the other social systems that constitute their environments. Love, argues Luhmann, is a compensatory mechanism which surmounts mutual indifference among

the texture and contours of lyric. The historical field begins paradoxic‹
mirror the very object it is meant to situate.

II

In the critical reception of John Donne's poetry one can trace the
decline of modernist aesthetics. Praised by T. S. Eliot for their difficulty
he saw as prefiguring that of modernist poets, Donne's *Songs and Son*
served Cleanth Brooks as a test case for the thesis that poetic meaning
entirely in a poem's total immanent structure.[34] More recently, and
reaction to his enshrinement by critical modernism, Donne has also
attention from poststructuralist and new historical critics. Arthur
important book, *John Donne: Coterie Poet*, helped inspire a spate of
readings by focusing on what he calls Donne's "context-bound vers‹
announcing his intention "to view Donne's poems as coterie social tra
rather than as literary icons."[35] Restoring Donne's *Songs and Sonne*
original positions within the poet's total *oeuvre* and its socioliterary
Marotti clearly enriches both their historical and literary meanings.
dure in what follows differs so strongly from Marotti's that it may ‹
construed as a critique of his work and of more recent historical
Annabel Patterson, David Norbrook, and others.[36] I want to in
outset, then, that there is no contradiction between a poem's be
self-referring and context-bound.[37] Autopoiesis and allopoiesis, aut
heteronomy, are not contradictory states but simply inhabit differ‹
tive domains. Far from being an impediment to historical criticisn
of lyric autonomy can reveal different modes of historical labor and ‹

Part of his appeal to a critic like Brooks doubtless arose fr
strong and explicit claims, in several of the *Songs and Sonnets*, to
a poetic space or domain sealed off from the rest of society. "W
sonnets pretty rooms" is perhaps the most famous line in "The C‹
a poem which vigorously insists on poetic and erotic autonomy.
claims tend to obscure the social and institutional forces which sl
Donne's verse, they also offer historical evidence of a different
declaring the birth of a literary space distinct from other social sp
poem attests indirectly to a more general if incipient process of so
ation which, for Luhmann, characterizes modernity in its broa
constructing a world which blocks out others, Donne registers
fragmentation that results from the modernizing process. My
that Donne's "pretty rooms" ultimately signify neither a utopi
from society nor a pseudoaristocratic refusal to engage in busine
even if they do both or either of these things, they also be‹
growth of social complexity which they help to produce. Th

persons. In his view, love is a generalized symbolic medium of communication; its role is to establish a personal sphere of mutual receptivity in contrast with a public world which to the individual appears increasingly indifferent and incomprehensible.

In the seventeenth century, argues Luhmann, love is codified in a way which renders it at once more unified and more strictly differentiated from other systems. It develops a ramifying set of differences which are meaningful only within its own field and thus approaches a condition of autopoiesis or self-reference even though, paradoxically, its function is to bridge the space between other closed systems. Love's temporality, for example, increasingly detaches itself from other kinds. Earlier Renaissance love poetry tended to assert the eternity of love, thus protecting it from the mutability and decay of mundane things. Donne often follows suit, but sometimes, as in "The Broken Heart" or "Farewell to Love," he claims that love is, by contrast, an ephemeral, even momentary state. Commenting on this latter notion, Luhmann writes: "Love inevitably ends, *and indeed faster than does beauty*, in other words, *faster than nature*; its end is not accorded a place in the general decline of the cosmos, but is self-determined."[44] In Donne, the ephemerality of love is thus a sign of fragility but also of strength. Only love can kill love; love dies according to its own temporality, and its absolute power is the power to dispose of itself. In this way the ephemerality of love is identical to its eternity; though opposed in content, both render love immune to external or mundane temporalities. The paradoxical incorporation of suffering into the experience of love—another recurrent theme of Renaissance lyric—also feeds the self-reference of the code. "Even its negative value is part of love in such a way that it cannot be outbid by values of a different order."[45] If love is suffering rather than pleasure, it cannot enter into a calculus with other pleasures or values but determines its own value.

But it is above all in the discourse of *passion* that this autonomizing labor is carried out. As its etymology suggests, "passion" indicates a subjection to something outside of oneself, "something unalterable and for which one cannot be held accountable."[46] Descriptions of love as disease, folly, madness, miracle, or religious ecstasy, all common in Renaissance love lyric, participate in this discourse. Donne's lyric "The Canonization" is typical in portraying passion as that which transgresses social convention. The demands of civil society— demands that one earn a living, that one meet one's obligations, that one find a vocation or course in life—give way to an all-consuming demand which negates all the others. Passion manifests itself precisely in the violation of other social norms. Its very excessiveness, as Luhmann points out, abrogates the older medieval conception of love as feudal contract, with its attendant services, duties, rewards, and so forth. "Love only comes into being when one exceeds what can be demanded and prevents a legal entitlement to love from ever coming about."[47] In Donne's lyrics as in Shakespeare's, juridical language paradoxically insists on the incompatibility of passion with any social contract—above all, with the contract of marriage. In Donne, as in the Renaissance love lyric generally, the female partner occupies the position of mistress, not wife; even those lyrics which Donne seems to have written for Ann More after their marriage—including "The Canonization"—contain no hint of domesticity or any indication that the addressee of the poem might be the writer's spouse. The "pretty rooms" of Donne's songs and sonnets are most definitely not part of a household; they require neither dusting nor duty. They are, rather, the space of a seemingly autonomous eros which resists institutionalization.[48] In the discourse of passion, lovers are no longer defined by their places in the social order; they are in effect rebaptized as lovers and enclosed in a quasi-religious state of seclusion from the secular world.

In "The Canonization," love claims to establish just such a private, autonomous domain predicated on the abandonment of civil society, however real or effective we may judge this domain to be. In fact, the poem's opening stanzas describe the public realm not as a unified field but as a plurality of alternative professions and institutions: commerce, the arts, law, the court, the church.

> For God's sake hold your tongue, and let me love,
>   Or chide my palsy, or my gout,
> My five grey hairs, or ruined fortune flout,
>   With wealth your state, your mind with arts improve,
>   Take you a course, get you a place,
>   Observe his honour, or his Grace,
>   Or the King's real, or his stamped face
>   Contemplate; what you will, approve,
>   So you will let me love.
>
> (1–9)

Offering an array of options at once bewildering and unappealing, the exterior world seems to answer to Luhmann's vision of differentiating social systems whose dislocating effect pushes Donne into yet another, private system—that of love, which establishes at once mystical unity between the lovers and their complete separation from the world. Love is not a reaction to this or that social system but to the ramifying distinctions among them. In "The Good Morrow," Donne writes: "Let sea-discoverers to new worlds have gone, / Let maps to others, worlds on worlds have shown, / Let us possess one world, each hath one, and is one" (12–14). Here again the opposition is not between two worlds—public and private—but between a dizzying multiplication of worlds on the one hand, and a single, unifying world on the other.[49] This multiplicity renders the social environment as a whole unmappable; but by withdrawing into its own space, love attempts to bestow on its environment a kind of negative unity, in that everything else can now be grasped under the rubric of "not-love." This early attempt at what Fredric Jameson has called "cognitive mapping"[50] bears its fruits in the final stanza of "The Canonization," where the external world in all its immensity and multiplicity is reduced and epitomized in the mutually gazing eyes of the two lovers. Love masters that from which it previously fled, and assimilates that which it previously expelled. Withdrawing from the social world, love then seemingly reproduces it as a manageable microcosm.

"The Canonization" thus figures love as a generalized symbolic medium of communication, one which by means of its own self-reference attempts to overcome or compensate for the differentiated closure of other social systems and the resulting dislocation of the individual subject. Yet this project is always necessarily paradoxical. Because its presumed capacity to map its environment depends on its self-referential closure, the code of love is just one more autopoietic system added to the others. Love does not occupy an Archimedean point from which it can grasp the whole of a social terrain; rather, its attempt to produce an exterior domain simply extends the chain of subsystems, because autonomy is not the same as exteriority. Even religious hermitage, which "The Canonization" takes for its model, does not really renounce the social world but occupies a well-defined space within the Church and its system of religious observances. The language of paradox which suffuses "The Canonization" may thus be regarded as a local instance or symptom of the larger cognitive paradox which governs the poem's utterance.[51]

To say all this, of course, involves accepting the fictional premises of Renaissance love poetry; and it seems to result in a commentary which looks less like a critical analysis than a rather credulous restatement. The antidomestic autonomy of Donne's eros, one might reasonably argue, cannot be taken at face value; it at once encodes a recognizably gendered fantasy and at the same time denies the historical fact that love and sexuality were deeply embedded in—indeed, deployed by—a social system of class, property, and political alliance. Donne's pretty rooms enact at best a utopian denial of the fact that love and marriage are socially determined; and they mask their resistance by coding action as passion or passivity, freedom as subjection to desire.[52] Such objections, while legitimate, seem to me to pose the issue misleadingly. For the dichotomy "fictive-real" obscures the fact that the literary system and its semantics are as "real" as any other. The autonomy of the sexual emerges at first in the literary realm, and its effects are no more utopian than those produced by social differentiation in general. Donne's lyric poems generate a real politics even if we entertain their arguments instead of immediately puncturing them. Hence I choose to take Donne at his word; and in doing so I am simply adopting the anti-hermeneutic stance which, in Foucault's view, should govern the description of any discourse.[53]

In Donne's love poetry, eros claims to occupy a closed, private domain cut off from the rest of society; and the closure or self-reference of eros seems connected, in a way as yet obscure, with the formal autonomy of lyric. To some degree these assumptions govern all of Renaissance love lyric from

Petrarch on; hence it will be useful, before proceeding further, to specify some of Donne's departures from the Petrarchan tradition. Donne's anti-Petrarchan strain manifests itself formally in his rejection of the sonnet, and thematically in his amalgamation of the Petrarchan scenario or stance with Ovidian and libertine elements.[54] Donne's speakers are not chaste, idealizing, and sexually frustrated; nor are his love lyrics, with a few exceptions, attempts at sexual seduction. Rather, they are generally cast as the utterances of speakers—male or female—who already enjoy or have enjoyed a sexual relationship. In "The Canonization," as in most of Donne's love poems, sexuality is fully incorporated into love. As a result, the fictional space of the poems does not coincide with that of an isolated speaking subject. Donne's poems do not inhabit the lonely if often sublime interiority of the Petrarchan speaker; often, the scene is a bedchamber or other secluded space occupied by two lovers in conversation. Consequently, the privacy or interiority of the poems is decidedly *not* that of the individual. The erotic space is, rather, one which the poetic speaker can enter, leave, or return to, whether to pursue other business or because of boredom or dissatisfaction with the partner. The pretty rooms of love remain standing even when abandoned; hence they are not merely an effect or projection of an inhabiting consciousness or subjectivity but an independent social domain. They are "private" not in the sense that they hide within the unreachable depths of the subject but simply in the etymological sense of "privacy" as privation or emptying out of everything which is not love. Thus it is that love, intended as a substitute home for the socially dislocated subject, can itself become alienated from or closed to that subject.

In describing Donne's difference from an earlier tradition I am not, of course, necessarily indicating his uniqueness; he seems representative, in some respects, of broader changes within the code of love. Yet if, as Luhmann argues, this code reveals a greater semantic closure in the seventeenth century than it did earlier, still nothing has yet been said about the social mechanisms by which such closure is achieved. How do love and sexuality detach themselves from their social matrix so as to achieve a state of autopoiesis? And how does this transform the nature of their interactions with a social environment? In pursuing these questions I hope eventually to move also from a merely thematic reading of Donne's love poetry to a more rhetorical and figurative—in other words, a more specifically literary—one.

To ask, "How did sexuality become autopoietic?" is no small question, for it is in effect to ask, "When does the history of sexuality begin? When, that is, does sexuality gain *its own history*, which is not merely an effect of some other history—of the economy, say? How is it that sexuality came to define an apparently independent domain, so that, for instance, a science of psychoanalysis developed which took sexuality as its distinctive field?" Michel Foucault, of course, has done the most to transform our way of posing questions about the history of sexuality. Like Luhmann, Foucault looks to the seventeenth century as a crucial period of transformation. But while Foucault has insisted that the history of sexuality cannot be grasped as a mere effect or reflex of other histories—say, that of the modes of economic production—his approach is nevertheless opposed to any conception of sexuality as a closed or self-referring domain.[55]

An alternative history to Foucault's, I believe, can be derived from within psychoanalysis itself—specifically, from the work of Jean Laplanche. Laplanche's book *Life and Death in Psychoanalysis* does in fact offer a compelling "history of sexuality," even though this history is strictly ontogenetic.[56] Laplanche, moreover, is concerned precisely with those mechanisms through which sexuality detaches itself from the vital order and becomes autopoietic, thus establishing, at one stroke, an independent topology which also defines the scientific boundaries of psychoanalysis. Laplanche's exposition begins with the Freudian concept of anaclisis or "propping," wherein sexuality initially emerges as dependent on the self-preservative instincts. In the infant, sexual pleasure begins as a marginal phenomenon attendant on nursing; but sexuality as such arises in what Laplanche calls a "derivation from the vital order." Only when the aim of the instinct is metaphorized (here, when the nutritive ingestion of food is replaced by fantasmatic introjection) and the object of instinct is metonymized (here, when milk is displaced by the breast as part-object) does sexuality begin to define an independent domain separate from the instincts of self-preservation. "Sexuality appears as a drive that can be isolated and observed only at the moment at which nonsexual activity, the vital function, becomes detached from its natural object or loses it. For sexuality, it is the reflexive (*selbst* or *auto-*) moment that is constitutive: the moment of a turning back towards self, or "autoeroticism" in which the object has been replaced by a fantasy, by an object *reflected* within the subject."[57] Once the sexual object has become fantasmatic, its significance is determined by its place within the subject's own system of representations, and not by the objective characteristics of the real object that corresponds to it. "Insofar as the object is that 'in which' the aim finds its realization, the specificity or individuality of the object is, after all, of minimal concern; it is enough for it to possess certain *traits* which trigger the satisfying action; in itself, it remains relatively indifferent and contingent."[58] What Laplanche describes here, in virtually so many words, is the relation between an autopoietic system and its environment.[59] External objects can trigger, but not specify, a reaction within the sexual field; they are a source of deformation, not information. Likewise, in the Renaissance love sonnet, the mistress as loved object tends to become a mere triggering device whose specific characteristics are increasingly irrelevant.[60] For Laplanche—and, if we accept his argument, for Freud as well—sexuality is constitutively autopoietic, and its (ontogenetic) history is thus necessarily the history of its self-reference.[61]

Through a "metaphorico-metonymic displacement" of the kind he describes, Laplanche's own reading of Freud can, I believe, be usefully mapped onto the field of history in its larger, social sense. For sexuality in the early modern period emerges from a state of what might be called social anaclisis, embedded not in a vital order but in an economic, social, and political one. Love and sexuality, in other words, "prop up" and—even more fundamentally—are in turn propped up by a varied set of social functions: property transfer, political alliance, the reproduction of kinship and domestic relations. Yet sexuality does not so much "invest" or energize these social functions as it is determined by them, to the degree that it cannot as yet claim an independent or self-referring dynamic. Sexuality as such can emerge only by detaching itself from its instrumental role in a social matrix, which it does at first in socially illicit or transgressive forms: adultery, fornication, prostitution, masturbation, homosexuality, etc. It would be naive, of course, to assume that an activity serves no social function simply because it is proscribed. Adultery, for instance, in the form of courtly love, was a means of sustaining, not subverting, property-based marriage;[62] and prostitution is obviously a profitable economic activity. Yet in these illicit forms, the production of sexual pleasure becomes at least provisionally an end in itself. In prostitution, sexuality *is* the commodity, rather than just a conduit for other commodities. It is worth noting here that Donne's erotic verse, though not directly composed for publication or sale, both draws upon and reflects a burgeoning market in literary and pictorial erotica that arose in England in the late sixteenth century.[63] Both thematically, and in the actual experience of reading that the poems create, Donne's erotic lyrics at least allude to a sexuality which is autonomous and for that reason socially suspect. In both content and performance, Donne's love poems prise sexuality free from a functionally subordinate role within a social matrix. The tendential result of this process is not that sexuality will decisively throw off its extraneous social functions but that increasingly it will fulfill them through and by means of its own self-reference.

"The Canonization" enacts in an unusually dense yet lucid way the movement whereby sexuality detaches itself from a condition of social anaclisis or propping and achieves a state of autopoietic closure. It does so, moreover, not only in its thematic and semantic registers but in its figural and rhetorical work. The poem, it has plausibly been argued, was composed around 1603, following the catastrophic consequences of Donne's secret marriage to Ann More.[64] I don't believe that an interpretation of the poem necessarily hinges on this dating or its biographical significance; yet Donne's ill-fated marriage strikingly illustrates the penalty someone of his social class might pay for placing love and sexuality above considerations of property and patronage. John and Ann Donne did indeed "at their own cost die," as the sexual pun in stanza 3 of "The Canonization" suggests; but it is from the ashes of their social death that the phoenix known as sexuality is born.

"The Canonization" stages the social unpropping of sexuality in two phases, in a kind of protonarrative. The first phase occurs in stanza 2:

> Alas, alas, who's injured by my love?
> What merchant ships have my sighs drowned?
> Who says my tears have overflowed his ground?
>   When did my colds a forward spring remove?
>   When did the heats which my veins fill
>   Add one more to the plaguy bill?
> Soldiers find wars, and lawyers find out still
>   Litigious men, which quarrels move,
> Though she and I do love.
>
> (10–18)

Here Donne's irony grants love a utopian force. The poet claims merely that loving does not *harm* civil society by interfering with its work; but he clearly suggests that the aggressive competitiveness and litigiousness of that society would *benefit* from contamination by love. In this sense, then, Donne's love *does* injure the world by withdrawing from it. Yet this is true not only in the utopian sense which underwrites the stanza's irony. Donne's marriage to Ann More, for example, may not literally have sunk merchant ships or flooded ground, but it *did* interfere with the workings of commerce and landed property by denying George More his accepted right to dispose of his daughter's hand in an economically and politically expedient manner. Thus Donne's and Ann More's sexual desires *did in fact* upset the business of the world; and in this respect the stanza is disingenuous.

Donne obscures the social transgression of his love, however, by converting a causal or metonymic relation into a merely reflective or metaphoric one. Sexual desire no longer plays a role of "propping" with regard to an economic and political order; but in abandoning its productive contiguity with civil society, love then substitutes for this a metaphoric resemblance. At the very moment that sexuality ceases actually to be a form of cargo or wares, its sighs become *like* the winds that propel (or sink) a merchant's ship.[65] The Petrarchan metaphors that ramify in this stanza mark the absence of the metonymic ties for which they now substitute.[66] Sexuality detaches itself from a state of social anaclisis or "propping" by undergoing at once a metonymic contraction and a metaphoric exfoliation.

We have now arrived at one of the leading paradoxes of Donne's work: at the level of argument, his erotic poems define a private space set off from the social world. Yet his metaphors often reintroduce the very world he claims to want to exclude. The languages of law, mercantile exploration, and monarchy inhabit the figural register of the poems, thus apparently undercutting or ironizing the movement towards privacy, exclusion, or detachment. Yet this seeming contradiction dissolves once we grasp the fact that for Donne, resemblance is a way of negating causality, metaphor a way of fending off metonymy or continuity. Dr. Johnson's famous description of the metaphysical conceit as "the most heterogeneous ideas . . . yoked by violence together" captures the precise dynamic of Donne's metaphors, in which the conjunction of vehicle and tenor serves to drive the two apart, generating the semantic equivalent of a repulsive force. The Donnean conceit is a structure of absolute difference or separation generated paradoxically through the medium of resemblance.

What is probably Donne's best-known conceit perfectly illustrates this mechanism. In "A Valediction Forbidding Mourning," Donne famously compares the lovers' two souls with "stiff twin compasses." This simile generates as many differences as it does resemblances: differences between the incorporeality of souls and the rigid materiality of the compasses, between the elevation of the spiritual realm and the banality of a mechanical instrument, and not least between the internalized privacy of the lovers' world and the exterior, public world of navigation, exploration, and commerce represented by the compasses. The twin compasses, moreover, comprise a kind of meta-conceit, because they represent not only the poem's two lovers but also Donne's manner with metaphor. Connecting at one end solely to insure their constant separation at the other, Donne's twin compasses are like the two terms of his conceits. In Donne the metaphoric vehicle is held at a rigid distance from the tenor, troping around it but never actually approaching it. Indeed, it inscribes a kind of protective circle around the tenor, which never partakes of its orbit but can only be inferred as a kind of virtual point, at once central yet invisible. And if we now recall that Donne's conceits in the *Songs and Sonnets* invariably pertain to love or eros, we can see that the protective circle of the compasses defines the boundaries of love's autopoiesis, cutting it off from the public world as social environment. Metaphor, in other words, does not work here as a window which allows us to peer voyeuristically into love's pretty rooms; it is, rather, a mirrored surface which simply reflects the public world back onto itself. Or again, it resembles the eye in the last stanza of "The Canonization" which "epitomizes" the world in the tiny reflective mirror of the pupil. Once it becomes autopoietic, sexuality involutes; once the metonymic accessibility of *linkage* is broken, only the play of environmental surfaces remains. The emergence of sexuality is thus at one with its disappearance.

Drawing a firm boundary between sexuality as autopoietic or self-referring system and its social "environment" might seem to foreclose any possibility for a political reading of Donne's verse. Yet it does not in fact do so, any more than the autopoietic nature of the neurological system forbids us to speak of perception, memory, or communication. The point is simply that sexuality's linkage with other social systems cannot be conceived of in terms of direct exchange or transfer but rather as a kind of adaptive coupling carried out through the autopoiesis of each system. Questions of gender, for instance, manifest themselves within the poems' internal system of differences. Indeed, women are threatening to Donne insofar as they represent a possible blurring of the lines of difference; that is to say, insofar as they represent the Kristevan "abject" or the collapse of a firm symbolic grid.[67] Conversely, homosexuality—

both male and female—is represented in the verse by a principle of identity or consonance among terms, which is now coded not as abjection but rather as purity, transparency, or cleanliness.

The broadest political reading of Donne's erotic verse, however, would seem to develop along Foucauldian lines. For what is the Renaissance love lyric if not a form of confessional discourse? What does it do if not implant sexuality as the truth of the subject, which seems of its own will to seek expression in language? Indeed, the Renaissance love lyric seems to reflect what is, for Foucault, a crucial shift in confessional practice, whereby emphasis on particular sexual *acts* is replaced by an interest in accompanying states of mind: thoughts, desires, fantasies, delectations, appetites, etc.[68] Support for a Foucauldian reading can be found in Donne himself—for instance, in his "Valediction: Of My Name in a Window," in which he writes: "'Tis much that glass should be / As all-confessing and through-shine as I" (7–8). In his elegy on Donne, affixed to the 1633 edition of the poems, Sir Thomas Browne tries to defuse the embarrassingly "promiscuous" mixture of erotic and religious verse in that collection by explaining the former as acts of confession.[69] Donne's *Songs and Sonnets* seem to fit comfortably within Foucault's history of sexuality, and to respond most readily to an analysis based on the politics of surveillance.

The theory of autopoietic systems, and particularly the work of Luhmann, allows us to forestall, or at least question, such a reading by pointing to what we might call a "cybernetic hypothesis" in Foucault's work. For Foucault, power is frequently predicated upon information and transmitted or circulated as data. Sexuality, for instance, emerges as a confessional practice whose results are transferred among, and routed through, various mechanisms of surveillance and discipline. Yet the capacity for linkage (*agencement*) among the various micromechanisms of power relies silently on the assumption of cybernetic transparency: it assumes, in other words, that the information produced by one social agency will be legible or useful to another. More fundamentally, it assumes that something like a transfer of information occurs in the first place. A theory of autopoietic systems will, by contrast, postulate a fundamental limit to informational linkage, because as social mechanisms become increasingly complex and differentiated, their principles of selectivity will render them increasingly closed to one another. The discourse of sexuality, for instance, will become less and less legible to other systems as its own semantics becomes more fully developed and differentiated. Or rather, sexuality actually becomes more and less legible at once. More, when a form of psychoanalytic listening develops whose specialized function is to "hear" and decode sexuality; less, because the increasing complexity and differentiation of psychoanalysis renders its results more opaque to other social systems, such as the law.[70] This is not, I should add, the result of any kind of resistance to, or struggle against, surveillance; it is, rather, an inevitable systemic necessity which nevertheless produces the happy result of limiting coordination among mechanisms of social power.[71]

If John Donne's poetry seems to participate in the ominous history of sexuality described by Foucault, it also resists this history and questions some of the assumptions that underlie it. First of all, the *Songs and Sonnets* do not implant sexuality as the latent truth of the subject because, as I argued above, Donne's erotic space does *not* coincide with that of subjectivity; it is, rather, a social sphere or domain to which the subject tries to repair in a paradoxical and ultimately self-frustrating attempt to escape the effects of social differentiation. Second, and more important, the emergence of sexuality as an autonomous and self-referring domain renders its semantics increasingly opaque. In Donne's *Songs and Sonnets*, the opacity of the sexual is a persistent thematic refrain. Donne repeatedly portrays love as mystical, esoteric, impenetrable, uncommunicative. In "The Ecstasy," for instance, he writes:

> This ecstasy doth unperplex
> (We said) and tell us what we love,
> We see by this it was not sex,
> *We see, we saw not what did move.*
> (29–32)

Even for the lovers themselves, passion can be obscure, inarticulate. Luhmann argues that the code of love is transformed in the seventeenth century through the incorporation of sexual passion into it. Yet passion and pleasure fit awkwardly into Luhmann's conception of love as communicative medium. As he admits: "taken on its own, *plaisir* is not actually a medium of communication because it is not affected by the problem of acceptance or rejection."[72] Figured in the Renaissance as a kind of death or loss of self, sexual climax resists the transmission of meaning.

Yet informational poverty or semantic closure is less striking as a thematic concern in Donne's work than as a textual effect. From the beginning, Donne's critical reception has largely been governed by the issue of his *difficulty*. Ben Jonson complained to Drummond that "Donne himself for not being understood would perish," and in the eighteenth century Lewis Theobald called Donne's poems "a continued Heap of Riddles."[73] Donne does not simply portray eros as incomprehensible; he produces it as such. In "The Canonization," this fact is represented somewhat emblematically in the movement between the poem's second and third stanzas. If stanza 2 represents the poem's metonymic contraction from the world, stanza 3 represents its metaphoric exfoliation:

> Call us what you will, we are made such by love;
> Call her one, me another fly,
> We are tapers too, and at our own cost die,
> And we in us find the eagle and the dove,
> The phoenix riddle hath more wit

> By us; we two being one, are it.
> So to one neutral thing both sexes fit
> We die and rise the same, and prove
> Mysterious by this love.
>
> (19–27)

Arthur Marotti surveys the critical commentaries on this notoriously complex stanza and concludes: "Religious, Neoplatonic, alchemical, as well as Petrarchan and other literary sources are possible aids to interpretation, but it would seem that for the coterie reader these metaphors, finally, would have been multivalent, ambiguous, and fundamentally *resistant* to interpretation."[74] Donne's poetry installs sexuality in an inaccessible domain, either by adopting an esoteric closure, or by assuming a transparency which allows one to look *through* sexuality but not *into* it, or else by mirroring the public world back onto itself. Yet paradoxically, difficulty is conjoined in Donne's verse with a kind of intimacy. Donne's love lyrics often invite the reader into the bedchamber or other private space, but then cancel this gesture of admission by generating a fog of obscurity.[75] We might vary Luhmann's phrasing and say that Donne's *Songs and Sonnets* are voyeuristically open but informationally closed. Yet it is this contradictory double-coding, this apparent clash of form and content, which constitutes sexuality as a self-referring domain. Donne's erotic poetry does its historical work not only by participating in a confessional discourse, then, but by frustrating it as well.[76]

Literary history has ironically reversed Ben Jonson's prediction that Donne would perish for not being understood. For the difficulty of Donne and the other metaphysical poets was what attracted figures such as Cleanth Brooks and T. S. Eliot, who saw in Donne an important precursor of the modernist aesthetic. In his essay entitled "The Metaphysical Poets," Eliot writes: "Our civilization comprehends a great variety and complexity, and this variety and complexity, playing upon a refined sensibility, must produce various and complex results. The poet must become more comprehensive, more allusive, more indirect, in order to force, to dislocate if necessary, language into his meaning. . . . Hence we get something which looks very much like the conceit—we get, in fact, a method curiously similar to that of the 'metaphysical poets', similar also in its use of obscure words and of simple phrasing."[77] For Eliot, as for Luhmann, modernity is marked by "great variety and complexity." And the difficulty of the modernist poem arises from trying to condense this discursive variety within a single form. Something like the metaphysical conceit arises when the modernist poet attempts to bridge distinct epistemic regions, to combine or bind together closed autopoietic domains. This project is rendered paradoxical, moreover, because the literary sphere which envisions this binding is itself a specialized cultural system. Hence the modernist poetic idiom increasingly becomes closed to all but a relatively small elite of academics and connoisseurs.[78] It is suggestive that Northrop Frye, himself a pillar of

Anglo-American critical modernism, chooses to render *melos*, the Greek word for lyric poem, as "babble."[79] "Babble" suggests a kind of pleasantly meaningless utterance; it comports as well with extreme simplicity as with difficulty, but it alludes with special force to the discursive closure of the modern lyric. Roland Barthes betrays a similarly modernist bias in claiming that the essential aim of literature is to "inexpress the expressible."[80] But his phrasing suggests that literature, in the modern period, may play a role precisely opposed to Luhmann's concept of a "generalized symbolic medium of communication." Rather than attempting to relink closed autopoietic domains in a common semantic field, literature—and above all the lyric—may serve to express in an especially vivid way the discursive fragmentation of modern society. Reversing Luhmann, we may say that lyric poetry makes improbable communications still less probable, and thereby comes to represent the cybernetic barrier *as such*. Or again, inverting Heinz von Foerster's famous principle of "order from noise," we may suggest that the modern lyric tends to produce noise from order.[81] Donne's literary significance, judged correctly by the modernists, thus consists largely in his creation of *difficult* poems, full of cybernetic noise. And his role in helping to produce sexuality as a closed discursive domain results from a kind of constructive interference with his more "proper" labor as lyric poet. In Donne, the discursive walls of lyric enclose the "pretty rooms" of eros.

III

I began by considering the role of lyric autonomy within Marxist literary theory, and here I want to conclude by returning to this issue, now that the theory of autopoiesis has been laid out. Luhmann himself has offered a critique of Adorno's theory of art, arguing that the autonomous artwork does not stand in simple *opposition* to society; rather, "art shares the fate of modern society precisely because it seeks to find its way as an autonomous system."[82] Luhmann's approach saps art of its utopian force of resistance by making the emergence of the aesthetic realm into just one more symptom of social differentiation. Yet his emphasis on art as system does locate the absence of this crucial mediating term in Adorno's theory. In his essay on lyric, Adorno posits a dualism between the autonomous poem and a reified society without taking into account the role of literary systems or institutions. In doing so, he reduces the concept of reification by eliminating Lukács's crucial category of the "partial system." For Lukács, capitalism fragments and reorganizes social functions on a rationalized basis in the same way that it breaks down and reorganizes commodity production to make it more efficient. The result is a set of seemingly autonomous "partial systems" such as law, politics, culture, economy, and so forth, which operate in blind indifference to one another yet rely on the quantifying logic of the commodity. Only the eruptions of generalized economic crises reveal the underlying connection of the commodity-structure uniting what seemed to be independent systems. Lukács's account of German philosophy since Kant in part two of his essay on "Reification and the Consciousness of the Proletariat" treats philosophy as just such a partial system, formally independent of capitalist production yet homologous with it.[83] Likewise, the emphasis on genre in his literary criticism places the individual work within a framing literary system.

If Lukács and Luhmann begin to sound alike in some respects, this results from a shared problematic, inherited from Weber, in which modernity is equated with rationalization. Yet from this common starting point, two very different paths emerge. For Lukács, the formal autonomy of partial systems is contradicted by their shared logic of quantification. Elements of the bureaucratic state may operate in an isolated and uncoordinated fashion, but the same rationalizing impulse underlies each. The autonomy of partial systems is thus necessarily provisional; it can be undermined accidentally and temporarily, by economic crisis, or intentionally and permanently, by abolishing generalized commodity production.

Luhmann, however, regards autopoietic systems as generating truly incommensurable semantics which do not simply conceal an underlying homology. As a result, he forecloses the possibility of a totalizing movement—effected by, say, the proletariat as universal class—which would restore a full communicative matrix among social systems. The conservative thrust evident in Luhmann results not from any attempt to legitimate capitalist society but rather from an attempt to delegitimate the search for anything beyond it: "We cannot seriously want to change the condition of modern life; we cannot imagine an alternative to its mode of primary system differentiation; and in any case, we cannot plan to change the types of differentiation of our society."[84] Planning large-scale social change, Luhmann argues, falls prey to the difficulty of managing the whole of a system by part of that same system.[85] Above all, one cannot plan to reduce social complexity, because any planning depends on a simplified description of society, and "this will only produce a hypercomplex system that contains within itself a description of its own complexity."[86] In Luhmann's view, modern society can only *evolve* in unplannable ways, and it will always evolve in the direction of greater, not lesser, complexity and differentiation.

Some aspects of Luhmann's theory are not entirely incompatible with certain strands of post-Marxist thought—for instance, with Laclau and Mouffe's insistence that a socialist society cannot be conceived of as abolishing social antagonism and difference, or with Alec Nove's argument that a socialist economy would have to be more, not less complex than a capitalist one.[87] Indeed, Luhmann's quietism does not strike me as a necessary consequence of his theory. What he shows, rather, is that the movement from a capitalist to a post-capitalist society cannot be conceived of as a reduction of the complex to the simple, or of the differentiated to the unified. Rather, a workable socialist alternative would involve a movement towards greater social complexity, even hypercomplexity, and could not base itself either on a universalizing class or on a bureaucracy of planners. Luhmann and Lukács might be partially reconciled by suggesting that generalized commodity production does in fact promote the differentiation of social systems, but that once under way, the growth of social complexity is not easily halted or reversed.

We may seem to have strayed rather far from the lyric poem, but for Marxism the fate of aesthetic autonomy is inseparable from the question of society as a whole. For Adorno, as we have seen, the autonomy of lyric is invested with a certain pathos by virtue of its social fragility. The lyric is always about to disappear, either being swallowed by reification or anticipating a utopian transcendence of its own boundaries—though one that is constitutively deferred. Adorno does not simply invent this pathos, of course; he derives it, rather, from the tradition of lyric itself, which frequently announces the delicate beauty of its own products: in Donne's well-wrought urn, for example, which seems so eminently perishable next to the granite bulk of "half-acre tombs." It seems reasonable to inquire, indeed, whether the more recent critical assault on lyric autonomy doesn't in some sense internalize the lyric's own rhetoric of vulnerability.

But what if the rhetoric of pathos in which lyric so readily clothes itself turns out to be disingenuous? Perhaps the autonomous lyric is sturdier than it seems, or makes itself out to be. The boundaries of lyric cannot simply be ground down by reified culture if the literary system in which it forms an element is itself the product of reification. And lyric cannot promise a utopian dissolution of its semantic barriers if the post-capitalist condition demands an increase in social complexity. If poetic closure figures the self-reference of the literary system, then the apparent death-drive which Adorno locates in the lyric may turn out to be a ruse. In this case the historical testimony of modern lyric may better be extracted not through the violation of its autonomy but through a recognition of its unexpected resilience. Somehow, to put it crudely, the lyric is still always *there* even after its autonomy has been refuted. The situation is not unlike that described by Donne in *The Anniversaries*, where the death of Elizabeth Drury apparently causes the cosmos itself to fragment: "'Tis all in pieces, all coherence gone; / All just supply, and all relation" (213–14). Yet, despite the departure of its unifying force, the world persists, even within its dissolution: Donne is still there to anatomize it, and we are still here to read his anatomy. Likewise, the autonomous lyric somehow survives its own apparent death; it announces the fragmentation of the social world into self-referring systems, but derives from this fact a curious sustenance. The historical meaning of lyric thus results from its status as a miraculous corpse which continues to walk about, strangely unaware of its own demise.

Notes

1. *Selected Prose Works of T. S. Eliot*, ed. Frank Kermode (New York: Harcourt Brace Jovanovitch, 1975), 66.

2. Friedrich Nietzsche, *Beyond Good and Evil*, trans. Marianne Cowan (Chicago: Henry Regnery, 1955), 19.

3. Frank Lentricchia, *Ariel and the Police: Michel Foucault, William James, Wallace Stevens* (Madison: The University of Wisconsin Press, 1988), 6.

4. Lentricchia, *Ariel and the Police*, 10.

5. John Brenkman, *Culture and Domination* (Ithaca: Cornell University Press, 1987), 108.

6. Theodor Adorno, "Lyric and Society," *Telos* 20 (Summer 1974), 56–71. Quotation from page 58.

7. Adorno, "Lyric and Society," 63.

8. Adorno, "Lyric and Society," 57.

9. Adorno, "Lyric and Society," 71.

10. On pages 60–61 of his essay, Adorno discusses the lyric with respect to the moment before sleep or death: "Warte nur balde / Ruhest du auch" and "Ach, ich bin des Triebens müde" are lines which Adorno chooses as representative of the Romantic lyric.

11. Adorno, "Lyric and Society," 71. In John Brenkman's essay on Blake, which both extends and critiques Adorno's view of lyric, this utopian moment of self-annihilation is even more concretely imagined. Speaking of the lyrics "A Poison Tree" and "London," Brenkman writes that "each of these poems enacts the hope for conditions of existence and experience which would make its own speaking unnecessary" (137).

12. An important attempt to apply the theory of autopoiesis—and, more broadly, of self-organizing systems—to literary theory is William R. Paulson, *The Noise of Culture: Literary Texts in a World of Information* (Ithaca: Cornell University Press, 1988). Paulson discusses issues on autopoiesis and literary autonomy on pp. 121–144. My differences with his treatment of the topic are more a matter of emphasis than of substance. However, I do believe that his discussion of literary texts as "artificially autonomous objects" tends at points to turn Maturana and Varela's epistemology into an ontology of the text; and I dissent from his claim that treating texts as self-referring tends to isolate them from cultural or social contexts. Indeed, the value of autopoietic theory, in my view, is its capacity radically to transform the apparent opposition between textual and contextual analysis, formalism and historicism.

13. Humberto R. Maturana and Francisco J. Varela, *Autopoiesis and Cognition: The Realization of the Living*, Boston Studies in the Philosophy of Science, vol. 42 (Dordrecht and Boston: D. Reidel, 1980). See also Frank Benseler, Peter M. Heijl, and Wolfram Köck, eds., *Autopoiesis, Communication and Society: The Theory of Autopoietic Systems in the Social Sciences* (Frankfurt and New York: Campus Verlag, 1980); Wolfgang Krohn, Günter Küppers, and Helga Nowotny, eds., *Selforganization: Portrait of a Scientific Revolution* (Dordrecht and Boston: Kluwer Academic Publishers, 1990); Gunther Teubner, ed., *Autopoietic Law: A New Approach to Law and Society* (Hawthorne, N. Y.: De Gruyter, 1987).

14. See especially the introduction to Krohn *et al., Selforganization*.

15. Maturana and Varela, "Autopoiesis: The Organization of the Living," in *Autopoiesis and Cognition*, 78–79.

16. Maturana and Varela, "Autopoiesis," p. 79; Niklas Luhmann, *Essays on Self-Reference* (New York: Columbia University Press, 1990), 9–10.

17. Humberto R. Maturana, "The Biology of Cognition," in Maturana and Varela, *Autopoiesis and Cognition*, 22.

18. Maturana and Varela, "Autopoiesis," 128.

19. Humberto R. Maturana, "Science and Daily Life: The Ontology of Scientific Explanations," in Krohn *et al., Selforganization*, 13.

20. Maturana, "The Biology of Cognition," 22.

21. At the same time, according to Maturana and Varela, the environment cannot specify evolutionary mutations within a given species. Rather, species and their environmental niches engage in a pattern of structural coupling within the process of "evolutionary drift." See Humberto Maturana and Francisco Varela, *The Tree of Knowledge: The Biological Roots of Human Understanding*, rev. ed., trans. Robert Paolucci (Boston and London: Shambhala Publications, 1987), 94–117.

22. See Heinz von Foerster, "Objects: Tokens for (Eigen-)Behaviors," in *Observing Systems* (Seaside, CA: Intersystems Publications, 1984), 273–286.

23. Gunther Teubner, "How the Law Thinks: Toward a Constructivist Epistemology of Law," in Krohn *et al., Selforganization*, 94.

24. Maturana and Varela, "Autopoiesis," 86.

25. Maturana and Varela, "Autopoiesis," 120.

26. Maturana, "The Biology of Cognition," 32.

27. See Humberto R. Maturana, "Man and Society," in Benseler *et al., Autopoiesis, Communication, and Society*, 11–31, and the introduction to "Biology and Cognition," xxiv–xxx.

28. Luhmann insists that the concept of autopoiesis resolves arguments in systems theory about whether systems are open or closed. Autopoietic systems, he states, are open systems, and their openness is a function of their self-reference or closure. Despite the elegance of this formulation, however, the emphasis of Luhmann's work is clearly on the closure of systems.

29. Luhmann, *Essays on Self-Reference*, 229. See also Gunther Teubner, "How the Law Thinks: Toward a Constructivist Epistemology of Law," in Krohn *et al., Selforganization*, 87–113; and Teubner, ed., *Autopoietic Law*.

30. Luhmann, *Essays on Self-Reference*, 81.

31. Niklas Luhmann, *Love as Passion: The Codification of Intimacy*, trans. Jeremy Gaines and Doris L. Jones (Cambridge: Polity Press, 1986), 5.

32. Jürgen Habermas, *The Philosophical Discourse of Modernity: Twelve Lectures*, trans. Frederick G. Lawrence (Cambridge, Mass.: MIT Press, 1990), 368–385.

33. For Luhmann, the barriers between social systems operate at a semantic level; hence even if signs flow freely, this does not insure that communication will take place. Data, in other words, are not the same as information.

34. Cleanth Brooks, *The Well Wrought Urn: Studies in the Structure of Poetry* (New York: Harcourt Brace Jovanovitch, 1974), 3–21. Brooks's approach to the reading of poetry is compatible in many respects with the theory of autopoiesis and ought to be reexamined in light of it. For instance, his insistence that "the poet is most truthfully described as a *poietes* or maker, not as an expositor or communicator" (75) shifts critical emphasis from the information conveyed by a poem to its immanent semantic structure. Like Maturana, Brooks is especially interested in calling attention to the connotative aspects of language (8–9). Finally, his notion that poetic meaning cannot be localized through paraphrase but inheres in the poem's total structure offers intriguing analogies to Maturana's position that memories are not stored as engrams at specific locations in the neuronal system but inhere in the total relational structure of that system. (Maturana, "Biology of Cognition," 36–38, 45; see also Heinz von Foerster, "Memory without Record," *Observing Systems*, 91–138).

35. Arthur F. Marotti, *John Donne, Coterie Poet* (Madison: The University of Wisconsin Press, 1986), 3, 19. [Reprinted in part in this volume.]

36. David Norbrook, "The Monarchy of Wit and the Republic of Letters: Donne's Politics," in Elizabeth D. Harvey and Katharine Eisaman Maus, eds., *Soliciting Interpretation: Literary Theory and Seventeenth-Century English Poetry* (Chicago: University of Chicago Press, 1990), 3–36; Annabel Patterson, "All Donne," in Harvey and Maus, 37–67.

37. W. Ross Ashby points out that the concept of "good" self-organization has meaning only in the context of the adaptive coupling of one system to a second, which serves as an environment for the first. W. Ross Ashby, "Principles of the Self-Organizing System," in Heinz

von Foerster and George W. Zopf, Jr., eds., *Principles of Self-Organization* (New York: Macmillan, 1962), 255–278.

38.   All quotations of Donne's verse are taken from *John Donne: The Complete English Poems*, ed. A. J. Smith (Harmondsworth: Penguin, 1971).

39.   These are, respectively, Empson's and Marotti's positions. See Norbrook, "The Monarchy of Wit," 15.

40.   Arthur F. Marotti, " 'Love is Not Love': Elizabethan Sonnet Sequences and the Social Order," *ELH* 49 (1982), 396–428.

41.   Luhmann, *Essays on Self-Reference*, 33.

42.   Luhmann, *Love as Passion*, 18.

43.   Luhmann, *Love as Passion*, 15.

44.   Luhmann, *Love as Passion*, 70.

45.   Luhmann, *Love as Passion*, 65.

46.   Luhmann, *Love as Passion*, 26.

47.   Luhmann, *Love as Passion*, 67–68.

48.   The depiction of marriage in Donne's *Epithalamion Made at Lincoln's Inn* is suggestive. The poem nervously deflects all economic motives onto the "Daughters of London" in stanza 2 and avoids any suggestion that the bride is a token to be exchanged in an economic and political network; rather, it portrays the wedding as the culmination of the bride's own sexual maturity: "Today put on perfection, and a woman's name," runs the refrain. Focusing on autotelic development, rather than paternal law, the poem struggles to disentangle sexuality from its social environment.

49.   The specifically semantic dimension of this problem emerges in Donne's *Satire 4*, where the poet is plagued by a begging, bragging courtier. Among his other accomplishments, the courtier boasts a mastery of places and languages:

> This thing hath travelled, and saith, speaks all tongues
> And only knoweth what to all states belongs,
> Made of th'accents, and best phrase of all these,
> He speaks one language; if strange meats displease,
> Art can deceive, or hunger force my taste,
> But pedant's motley tongue, soldier's bombast,
> Mountebank's drugtongue, nor the terms of law
> Are strong enough preparatives, to draw
> Me to bear this, yet must I be content
> With his tongue: in his tongue, called compliment.
>
> (35–44)

Here the "worlds on worlds" of which society consists become semantic worlds: knotted bundles of professional jargon. The courtier who has travelled widely and tasted all these tongues pretends to meld them into one language, "made of th'accent, and best phrase of these." Yet this new hybrid is, for Donne, the most unendurable of all.

50.   Fredric Jameson, "Cognitive Mapping," in Cary Nelson and Lawrence Grossberg, eds., *Marxism and the Interpretation of Culture* (Urbana, Illinois: University of Illinois Press, 1988), 347–357.

51.   See Luhmann: "Generally speaking, codes of generalized symbolic communicative media function to secure an adequate degree of probability for the reception of improbable expectations. In the end, it is always *this* socio-structural paradox which is transposed into the semantics and then expressed as an inherent paradox (in the essence of religion, of insight, of love)" (*Love as Passion*, 55).

52.   Luhmann, *Love as Passion*, 60.

53.   Michel Foucault, *The Archaeology of Knowledge*, trans. A. M. Sheridan Smith (New York: Pantheon Books, 1972), esp. 21–30, 118–125.

54. This discussion of Donne's anti-Petrarchan elements is indebted to Anne Ferry, *The "Inward" Language: Sonnets of Wyatt, Sidney, Shakespeare, Donne* (Chicago: University of Chicago Press, 1983), 218–237. Though unlike Ferry I prefer to detach the privacy of Donne's lyrics from the question of the subject, I find her book extremely suggestive on many counts.

55. Michel Foucault, *The History of Sexuality, Volume I: An Introduction*, trans. Robert Hurley (New York: Vintage Books, 1980).

56. Jean Laplanche, *Life and Death in Psychoanalysis*, trans. Jeffrey Mehlman (Baltimore: The Johns Hopkins University Press, 1976).

57. Laplanche, *Life and Death in Psychoanalysis*, 88.

58. Laplanche, *Life and Death in Psychoanalysis*, 12.

59. From the perspective of autopoietic theory, one of the points of interest of Laplanche's book must be the way in which he has restored theoretical respectability and pertinence to Freud's early neurological speculations, especially in the *Project for a Scientific Psychology*. Compare, for instance, Laplanche's summary of Freud with the views of Maturana and Varela:

> A mnemic system is a system of memory or memories, but with a remarkable characteristic: *nothing qualitative is directly inscribed in it*. What is in question, of course, is a construct capable of registering "engrams," but the Freudian engram is absolutely unassimilable to "image" or an "analogon" of the perceived object. The entire originality of a given engrammatic inscription lies solely in the specificity of the paths followed by the circulating quantity. And that specificity is limited solely to the difference between two paths as to the succession of differences. . . . It is thus *the structure of the whole*, the *sequence of these "choices" in a series of bifurcations*, that forms by itself, for each memory, a unique constellation.
>
> (36–37)

Freud's biological theories were strongly influenced by Gustav Theodor Fechner (1801–1887), whose work prefigures twentieth-century concepts of self-organizing systems. See Michael Heidelberger, "Concepts of Self-Organization in the Nineteenth Century," in Krohn *et al.*, *Selforganization*, 170–180.

60. See Luhmann: "Furthermore, incorporating the other's freedom into the reflexion of the social relationship necessarily undermines the erstwhile orientation toward the *specific characteristics* of the partner. Rather, the orientation is replaced by one toward the partner's *love*" (Luhmann, *Love as Passion*, 52). This contrasts with the courtly tradition in which love is determined by the supposed perfections of the loved object.

61. The self-reference of the sexual field enables Laplanche to eject everything else from the "art of psychoanalytic listening" (see footnote 43); yet this does not mean that sexuality is definitively cut off from its environment. Rather, the sexual and vital orders engage in a kind of adaptive cleavage or mutually compensatory deformation which for an observer of both systems can look like communication, but which for a psychoanalyst, who is by definition concerned with sexual autopoiesis, simply does not exist.

62. See Joan Kelly, "Did Women Have a Renaissance?," in *Women, History and Theory: The Essays of Joan Kelly* (Chicago: University of Chicago Press, 1984), 19–50.

63. On erotica and pornography in the English Renaissance see David O. Franz, *Festum Voluptatis: A Study of Renaissance Erotica* (Columbus: Ohio State University Press, 1989); Robert P. Merrix, "The Vale of Lilies and the Bower of Bliss: Soft-Core Pornography in Elizabethan Poetry," *Journal of Popular Culture* 19.4 (Spring 1986): 3–16; Wendy Wall, "Disclosures in Print: The 'Violent Enlargement' of the Renaissance Voyeuristic Text," *SEL* 29.1 (Winter 1989): 35–59. See especially Wall's suggestive remarks on the "erotics of commodification" (56).

64. Marotti, *John Donne: Coterie Poet*, 137, 138, 147.

65. Describing sexuality as "cargo" or "wares" may recall the kinds of commodified

sexuality I discussed above, whereas in fact I want to distinguish between the two. In property-based marriage, it is not sexuality but property itself which is exchanged. Sexual rights to the partner are purely subsidiary to this primary function, and as a result, love or sexual satisfaction are hoped for but neither expected nor generally achieved. In this sense sexuality is hardly the primary "cargo" of the merchant's ship; yet Donne's figure is meaningful if we read it as suggesting that sexuality is *carried* along inertly, rather than charting its own course. In certain respects this situation provides a social analogue to Laplanche's argument that sexuality is at first a "marginal effect" of the vital order, arising as a subsidiary pleasure attendant on other kinds of excitation—nursing, for instance, or auto-aggression. It is only when sexuality detaches itself from the vital functions that it can then, at a later stage, reinvest those functions by means of sublimation. At this point sexuality becomes the wind that drives the ship; it "props up" the vital (or social) order instead of merely leaning *on* it. In sublimation, sexuality "returns" to the non-sexual realm, but does so by means of its own autopoiesis.

66.　In the lines "When did the heat which my veins fill / Add one more to the plaguy bill?", a metaphoric "causality" again substitutes for a metonymic one. Donne's conceit asks whether the Petrarchan "heats" of his love raise the city's temperature enough to promote spread of the plague. But this outlandish suggestion at once invokes and denies a more obvious connection between sexual "heat" and the "plague" of venereal disease.

67.　See Julia Kristeva, *Powers of Horror: An Essay in Abjection*, trans. Leon S. Roudiez (New York: Columbia University Press, 1982). For Donne's most outrageous portrayal of women as embodying the abject, see his elegy "The Comparison." For more on the symbolic destabilization effected by women in Donne's poems, see Stanley Fish, "Masculine Persuasive Force: Donne and Verbal Power," in Harvey and Maus, *Soliciting Interpretation*, 223–252; and Thomas Docherty, *John Donne, Undone* (London and New York: Methuen, 1986), 51–87.

68.　Foucault, *The History of Sexuality*, 63.

69.　Arthur Marotti, "John Donne, Author," *Journal of Medieval and Renaissance Studies* 19.1 (Spring 1989):74.

70.　See Teubner, "How the Law Thinks."

71.　Here I think it is important to distinguish between the policing of sexuality and the policing of sex—i.e., of sexual acts. In the latter case, semantic barriers present relatively little problem. It is only when sexuality becomes discourse, and hence a question of truth in discourse, that difficulties arise. A suggestive instance from Renaissance literature occurs in act 2, scene 1 of Shakespeare's *Measure for Measure*: when Pompey is interrogated about an insult apparently given to Elbow's wife in a bawdyhouse, his "testimony" is so abundant and inconsequential that his interrogators can neither assimilate nor construe it. Angelo finally breaks off the proceedings, complaining: "This will last out a night in Russia / When nights are longest there" (I.2.127–128). This episode amusingly illustrates the breakdown of a confessional apparatus, and it suggests that the putting of sexuality into discourse can overload attempts at surveillance through the production of cybernetic "noise."

72.　Luhmann, *Love as Passion*, 89.

73.　Quoted in Marotti, *John Donne: Coterie Poet*, 20.

74.　Marotti, *John Donne: Coterie Poet*, 163. Author's emphasis.

75.　Writing on Donne's elegy, "To his Mistress Going to Bed," Marotti comments on Donne's transformation of his Ovidian model: "Ovid focuses entirely on the erotic space, but Donne fills his poem with metaphoric distractions, using the mistress's clothes and body as occasions for witty metaphors" (*John Donne: Coterie Poet*, 83–84).

76.　Here it is necessary to distinguish more carefully than I have hitherto between two very different kinds of resistance to confessional discourse. The third stanza of "The Canonization" generates a kind of symbolic overdetermination familiar in both psychoanalytic and literary-critical realms. As such, it corresponds to what Foucault calls sexuality's "principle of latency" (*History of Sexuality*, 66). While this latency seems to hide sexuality from surveillance, it also—as Foucault points out—becomes a lure for interpretation, and indeed constitutes sexuality as *that which is to be interpreted*, i.e., as the object of a *scientia sexualis* which eventually decodes its mysteries. Thus Donne's "esoteric" qualities do not, as such, constitute a barrier to a Foucauldian reading. The real point of resistance emerges when this localized obscurity reproduces itself at a more global level—which it does because a specialized *scientia sexualis*, at the very moment that it uncloaks sexuality, finds that its own discourse becomes less and less legible to other social systems. It is at the level of this *semantic* barrier, rather than the more localized *symbolic* one, that Foucault is open to critique.

In *John Donne, Undone*, Thomas Docherty writes that "Donne's texts produce a 'catholic' spirit of guilt in their reading, together with a necessity, but impossibility, of confession to some crime" (10).

77. Eliot, *Selected Prose*, 65.

78. Adorno complains that in Baudelaire, "the contradiction of poetic to communicative language grew extreme," thereby inhibiting the lyric's utopian work of anticipating the realm of the general (Adorno, "Lyric and Society," 63). Adorno's choice of example here bodes ill for his whole theory, since Baudelaire is generally recognized as the father of poetic modernism.

79. Northrop Frye, *Anatomy of Criticism: Four Essays* (Princeton: Princeton University Press, 1957), 275.

80. *Essais Critiques* (Paris: Seuil, 1964), 15. Quoted in Christopher S. Braider, "Chekhov's Letter: Linguistic System and its Discontents," in Krohn *et al., Selforganization*, 156.

81. Von Foerster, "On Self-Organizing Systems and their Environments," in *Observing Systems*, 2–22.

82. Luhmann, *Essays on Self-Reference*, 193.

83. Georg Lukács, "Reification and the Consciousness of the Proletariat," in *History and Class Consciousness: Studies in Marxist Dialectic*, trans. Rodney Livingstone (Cambridge, Mass.: The MIT Press, 1968), 83–222. For the partial system, see 92–110. For Lukács' reading of German idealist philosophy, see section two, "The Antinomies of Bourgeois Thought," 110–149.

84. Luhmann, *Essays on Self-Reference*, 181.

85. Luhmann, *Essays on Self-Reference*, 172.

86. Luhmann, *Essays on Self-Reference*, 179–180.

87. Ernesto Laclau and Chantal Mouffe, *Hegemony and Socialist Strategy: Towards a Radical Democratic Politics* (New York and London: Verso, 1985); Alec Nove, *The Economics of Feasible Socialism* (London, 1983).

Donne as Social Exile and Jacobean Courtier: The Devotional Verse and Prose of the Secular Man

Arthur F. Marotti*

Donne's religious poems, particularly those pieces he composed in the decade preceding his ordination, were fundamentally coterie texts. He gave sacred verse to such friends as Sir Henry Goodyer, George Garrard,[1] and Magdalen Herbert. The appearance of religious poems in Rowland Woodward's manuscript collection suggests that such work went through processes of transmission similar to those of the *Elegies* and *Satires*. Donne even expected this poetry to help him win patronage: he sent six "Holy Sonnets" to the new (and notoriously extravagant) Earl of Dorset along with a brazenly flattering introductory sonnet.[2] The poems express Donne's private psychological, religious, and moral struggles, but they were also, to a great extent, witty performances designed for an appreciative readership. Donne wrote in "A Litanie," "When wee are mov'd to seeme religious / Only to vent wit, Lord deliver us" (188–89), suggesting his awareness of some of the less edifying motives that led him to compose religious verse. The divine poems of the preordination period certainly represent a mixture of secular and religious intentions; after all, when he composed them he was vigorously pursuing worldly advancement by all available means.

The context of the religious verse was not only that of Donne's personal desires and private relationships with friends, patrons, and patronesses; it was also the more general one of Jacobean culture. Under the new monarch religious literature took on greater importance than it had in the Elizabethan era for a number of reasons including the King's own interests as well as the increasingly heated national and international polemical atmosphere. In *both* Tudor and early Stuart times religious poetry served as a way for courtier-careerists to express slight or serious political disappointment: Wyatt's penitential psalms and many subsequent religious lyrics expressing a contempt for worldly involvement and success were composed as responses to setbacks to or failures of secular ambitions.[3] The Psalm translations done by Sir Philip

*From *John Donne, Coterie Poet* (Madison and London: University of Wisconsin Press, 1986), 246–68, 326–46. Reprinted by permission of the publisher. Minor revisions have been added by the author.

Sidney with his sister, poems admired by Donne for their artistry,[4] were probably read along with Sidney's other work in the context of the myth of his glorious political failure. Such cultural encoding of sacred poetry carried over into the Jacobean era, as the example of Donne himself testifies. But from the start of James's reign, religious verse also assumed a higher place in the hierarchy of genres within the literary system as other genres, such as the love poetry that flourished in Elizabethan times, declined sharply in importance. For a politically sensitive courtier like Fulke Greville, who wrote poetry during both reigns, the change was dramatic: his Elizabethan love lyrics suddenly gave way at the start of the Jacobean period to religious poems reflecting both his political poor fortune during the first half of James's reign and the new changes in the literary system.[5] Donne, too, responded to the changed sociocultural conditions in turning to the composition of religious verse, just as he did in writing controversial prose.[6] The very act of composing sacred verse in the reign of a monarch who had himself written religious poetry and especially favored pious and polemical writing was a political gesture.[7] By authorizing the composition of religious works, King James created a situation in which religious poetry could, paradoxically, both continue to signal the frustration of ambition (with a consequent sense of alienation from the world of power and wealth) and express active suitorship in an officially sanctioned literary vocabulary. It didn't take a conversion experience to move a politically active Jacobean courtier-poet to compose religious literature. Even in private circulation, such work was responsive to the changed sociocultural environment.

In *La Corona* (and in his other religious verse) Donne accepted the poet's role. He refers to his Muse (*LC* 1.6 and 7.13) in a serious way, whereas, for the most part, he earlier used the term quite negatively or ironically. To a significant degree, this acceptance of *poetic* authority was possible because King James himself had written sacred poetry and, therefore, sanctioned such activity as proper for the politically active man. While, in an Elizabethan situation, religious verse was the recourse of courtly losers and an indirect form of social protest by recusant Catholics (like Constable and Southwell),[8] in Jacobean England, despite retaining its effectiveness as the expression of sociopolitical frustration, it was more assuredly establishment literature. . . . In penning religious verse, Donne officially (if not actually) followed the example of the king himself. He felt no need, therefore, in *La Corona*, to apologize for playing the poet.

Donne's personal feelings connected with his search for employment and advancement in the early Jacobean period intruded into his religious verse. Court politics and personal ambition account for some of the language and metaphors Donne utilized for both the conscious and the unconscious connections he made between the religious and the political. In the sonnet to Magdalen Herbert sent along with the *La Corona* sequence, for example, Donne chose the politically encoded term "advance" (3) to apply to Mary Magdalen's salvation. Although in *La Corona* and the other religious poems he portrayed private spiritual struggle as separate from the secular environment in which men pursued worldly success[9] (just as he earlier set the private sphere of mutual lovers apart from the larger public world), the two orders overlapped for him. The grief and despair with which Donne's early religious poems are preoccupied (particularly the *Holy Sonnets*) seem to have been rooted, as the letters to Goodyer indicate, in *both* personal piety and secular needs.[10] And so, when Donne confessed that "vehement griefe has beene / Th'effect and cause, the punishment and sinne" (1635 *HS* 3.13–14),[11] he expressed himself in an idiom he used elsewhere to discuss his economic and political misfortunes. In mentioning that "Kings pardon . . . punishment" (*HS* 7.10), Donne may have been expressing his wish that James would forgive him his past indiscretions and accept him into royal service. Conversely, courtiership, like amatory courtship, provided Donne with a scheme for his relationship with God: "I durst not view heaven yesterday; and to day / In prayers, and flattering speeches I court God. / To morrow'I quake with true feare of his rod" (W-*HS* 3.9–11). While Donne seems to have made divine favor the object of his suits and to have thought of the raising of his Muse by the Holy Spirit (*LC* 7) as a much greater benefit than courtly advancement, his political consciousness betrayed itself. Through contrasts as well as analogies between the monarchical and the divine, the courtly and the heavenly, Donne reinforced the connection between the political and the religious in his sacred poetry. Even when he depicted "tyrannies" (*HS* 4.6) and "kings" (*HS* 6.9) as evil and destructive, he signaled, by the use of such terms, his insistent awareness of the political order.

Written probably in late 1608[12] at a time Donne was sick in body, mind, and fortune, "A Litanie" is a good example of this politically encoded religious verse. Lewalski claims that this poem, and the later "A Hymn to God the Father," "transpose public forms into private devotions," exemplifying the Protestant practice of applying religious truths to the self.[13] While this is certainly true, it is also the case that Donne used the poem to comment, for a knowledgeable audience, on his sociopolitical condition as well as on his private spiritual state. It functioned, in many respects, as social verse. Donne, we know, sent a copy of the poem to his friend Goodyer, with the explanation that, though it was an exercise in a form originally designed for "publike service in . . . Churches," it was aimed primarily at a restricted readership, "for lesser Chapels, which are my friends" (*Letters*, p. 33). He offered the work "for a testimony of that duty which I owe to your love, and to my self, who am bound to cherish it by my best offices" (*Letters*, pp. 33–34): it was, therefore, like the prose letters, part of an ongoing self-revelatory private communication with a receptive audience. Donne relied on his coterie reader's ability to understand "A Litanie" in the context of its author's personal situation. The "ruinous" (4) state and susceptibility to "dejection" (5) Donne mentions, then, were not simply the adverse conditions of the representative Christian's tormented soul; they were the particular contemporary circumstances about which Donne constantly complained at this low point in both his private and public life.

Donne admitted in this poem, as he did four years later in the *Essays in Divinity*, that he had "wasted" himself "with youths fires, of pride and lust" (22); he saw in his restless thirst for knowledge and in his indulgence in versifying culpable "excesse / In seeking secrets, or Poetiquenesse" (71–72). He prayed to be delivered

> From being anxious, or secure,
> Dead clods of sadnesse, or light squibs of mirth,
> From thinking, that great courts immure
> All, or no happinesse. . . .
>
> (127–30)

He thus characterized his own behavior and interests as those of a witty, depressed, ambitious but frustrated careerist seeking preferment at the Jacobean court. He even admitted that his "Pietie" might have been "intermitting" and "aguish" (209), more the product of sickness and poor fortune than of a steady religious commitment. So, too, he retrospectively considered his own attraction to "learning" (235), "beauty" (237), and "wit" (239) as sinful, dangerous, and debilitating.

In referring, in stanza 26, to his being criticized and slandered by others, he alluded to the burden of the bad reputation he bore, which apparently still kept him from being entrusted with a position of responsibility in the government. Ostensibly addressing God, Donne seems to have had King James in mind as well:

> That living law, the Magistrate,
> Which to give us, and make us physicke, doth
> Our vices often aggravate,
> That Preachers taxing sinne, before her growth,
> That Satan, and invenom'd men
> Which well, if we starve, dine,
> When they doe most accuse us, may see then
> Us, to amendment, heare them; thee decline;
> That we may open our eares, Lord lock thine.
>
> (226–34)

Donne autobiographically claimed that political authority and envious competitors magnified the seriousness of his sins and errors, stating that public disapproval beneficially led to "amendment." This is his contention in those letters he wrote to people in power in which he distinguished his mature self from his indiscreet younger (but not much younger) one.[14] In praying that "Lord lock" his ears to the voices of his critics and slanderers, however, Donne probably hoped that the human monarch, James, would admit him into service despite his past mistakes.

Throughout "A Litanie" Donne conflates spiritual and secular monarchical authority, God and King—something he does also in his controversial prose. This strategy reinforced the Jacobean ideology of divinely sanctioned kingship. In the poem the language of courtly relationships describes spiritual affiliations: men are "in Wardship to [God's] Angels" (47), and heaven has "faire Palaces" (48). Donne's defense of wealth in stanza 18 looks suspiciously like an apology for the extravagance of James's court:

> . . . through thy poore birth, where first thou
> Glorifiedst Povertie,
> And yet soone after riches didst allow,
> By'accepting Kings gifts in th'Epiphanie,
> Deliver, and make us, to both waies free.
>
> (158–62)

Donne conspicuously omitted the biblical commonplace of the rich man and the eye of a needle, as he took pains to suggest that the wealthy have as easy moral access to heaven as the poor. Stanza 25 asserts that some "bold wits jest at Kings excesse" (223), but Donne suggested, in defending James, that mocking the monarch was only one step away from mocking God, "majestie divine" (224). It suited his purpose, as the last term indicates, to mix royalty and divinity, as Jonson did in his masques. For, whatever his spiritual needs, as an importunate courtly suitor Donne wanted James's favor to make him prosper.

"A Litanie" is a text parallel to many of the contemporary letters to Sir Henry Goodyer. The religious and the political, the private and the public are merged in both kinds of writing. Both literary genres assume the existence of sympathetic and knowledgeable readers able to understand the nuances of Donne's writing. In asking for the acceptance of his prayer-poem by God, Donne in effect once again called for the competent receptivity of his coterie audience (even as he fantasized a similar benevolence on the part of the King). Such well-wishing was for Donne a precondition for the very act of communication: "Heare us, for till thou heare us, Lord / We know not what to say" (203–4). The relationship portrayed between the speaker and God in the poem thus reflects the desired poet-reader transaction.

In the 1590s, when the fashion was at its height, Donne avoided composing an amorous sonnet sequence, probably largely because such an activity bespoke professional authorship and/or the search for artistic patronage.[15] He did use the sonnet form for epistolary exchange, but he cast his love lyrics in other shapes that were, at once, more formally complex and more affectedly casual. In Jacobean England, nevertheless, Donne felt free to turn to the sonnet for sacred verse—partly because the King wrote some holy sonnets himself, and partly because the religious sonnet was not stigmatized, as was the love sonnet, by being associated with importunate suitorship.

Like Donne's other coterie writings, the *Holy Sonnets* are witty performances that exploited a knowledgeable audience's awareness of their author's personal situation and history. Just as Donne expressed religious ideas in his letters to Goodyer specifically in relation to his immediate social circumstances, in his *Holy Sonnets* and other religious verse he presented the themes of despair and hope, spiritual pride and humility, sin and redemption in ways that signaled specific personal, social, and political coordinates for these typical preoccupations of a devout Christian. He self-consciously referred to his past life (and verse)—for example, in mentioning his erotic "idolatrie," his "mistresses" (*HS* 9.9–10), and his "humorous" "prophane love" (*W-HS* 3.5–6). He also allowed his current secular concerns with ambition and preferment to intrude upon—or rather to be translated into the language of—his sacred verse. It took a conversion to Roman Catholicism to make Henry Constable into a religious sonneteer, but no such dramatic change in Donne accounts for his divine poems. He might have been deeply bothered about his apostasy, as John Carey has argued,[16] and he might have expressed abiding interests in religion and in the welfare of his soul, but, at least when he wrote his early Jacobean religious poems, Donne was no saint and his energies and desires were directed toward worldly success. As late as 1614, Lady Bedford, who obviously thought she knew the kind of man he was, was astonished that someone with Donne's unedifying personal history had decided to enter the ministry.[17]

By Donne's own standards, the religious sonnets and other preordination sacred verse were contaminated by self-interest. In a letter to Goodyer in which he discussed prayer, he named thanksgiving and praise, rather than petition, as the properly selfless purpose of true devotion: "I had rather [devotion] were bestowed upon thanksgiving then petition, upon praise then prayer; not that God is indeared by that, or wearied by this; all is one in the receiver, but not in the sender: and thanks doth both offices; for, nothing doth so innocently provoke new graces, as gratitude. I would also rather make short prayers then extend them, though God can neither be surprised, nor beseiged: for, long prayers have more of the man, as ambition of eloquence, and a complacencie in the work, and more of the Devil by often distractions . . ." (*Letters*, pp. 111–12). Insofar as they request or demand divine help or become self-aggrandizing performances, the religious poems veer away from this devotional ideal.

Whatever the circumstances of their original composition (perhaps as an exercise in private devotion), the coterie transmission of the *La Corona*[18] sonnets to Magdalen Herbert exemplifies the social uses of religious verse. There survives a prose letter accompanying the poems from Donne to Mrs. Herbert, whose acquaintance he had made and whose patronage he was securing in the years 1607–9:

Madam,

Your Favours to me are every where; I use them, and have them. I enjoy them at *London*, and leave them there; and yet, find them at *Micham*: Such Riddles as these become things unexpressible; and, such is your goodness. I was almost sorry to find your Servant here this day, because I was loth to have any witness of my not coming home last Night, and indeed of my coming this Morning: But, my not coming was excusable, because earnest business detain'd me; and my coming this day, is by the example of your St. *Mary Magdalen*, who rose early upon *Sunday*, to seek that which she lov'd most, and so did I. And, from her and my self, I return such thanks as are due to one to whom we owe all the good opinion, that they whom we need most, have of us—by this Messenger, and on this good day, I commit the inclosed *Holy Hymnes* and *Sonnets* (which for the matter, not the workmanship, have yet escap'd the fire) to your judgment, and to your protection too, if you think them worthy of it; and I have appointed this inclosed *Sonnet* to usher them to your happy hand.

> *Your unworthiest Servant,*
> *unless your accepting him*
> *have mended him.*
> JO. DONNE (*Selected Prose*, pp. 124–25)

He used the formally deferential language of client-patroness relations in this piece, addressing himself to a woman he knew took devotional practices quite seriously and who might, thus, welcome a set of religious poems.[19] Taking the verse into her "protection" involved strengthening her social bond with the poet. In the case of a patroness and friend like Mrs. Herbert, religious language could serve as a medium of social intimacy. In the dedicatory poem prefixed to the *La Corona* sequence Donne relates "Mrs. Magdalen Herbert" to "St. Mary Magdalen" as a way of complimenting the addressee for her piety even as he chose her as a proper recipient for what he had written, work he supposedly refrained from burning only because of its edifying "content." After playing with the Magdalen Herbert–Mary Magdalen association, Donne asked this coterie reader to "Harbour" the "*Hymns*" he sent her.

The language of *La Corona* is that of the religious transvaluation of the secular. The personal depression Donne experienced at the time—largely because of his lack of an "occupation"—appears in the poems as a "low devout melancholie" (*LC* 1.2). The secular rewards symbolized by the various crowns such as the laurel wreath (of poets and military victors) are subordinated to the "crowne of Glory" (*LC* 1.8) won by a Christ who wore a "thorny crowne" (*LC* 1.7). In the religious context of Scriptural meditation on Christ's life, Herod, a model of bad kingship, is "jealous" (*LC* 3.8) of the virtuous Christ, a reversal of a frustrated political inferior's resentment of the great. So too, in the poems, evil "ambitious" (*LC* 5.3) men express "envie" (*LC* 5.2) of a suffering Christ with whom the poems' speaker identifies, another inversion of Donne's own social and political situation. The "sparks of wit" (*LC* 4.3) Donne praises in the fourth sonnet of the sequence are the wisdom of Christ, not the skeptical, riddling, or paradoxical utterances of a man whose poetry proclaimed an ambivalence toward established authority. In *La Corona,* salvation and glorification replace advancement and preferment as the objects of desire. Generally, then, the conversion of secular into religious values represents an attempt to reaffirm self-worth and regain a measure of control in the most unfavorable of social circumstances.

In the *Holy Sonnets* Donne relocates in a religious framework the conflict between autonomy and dependence he expresses in his encomiastic verse. These emotionally charged and intellectually tortuous poems enact personally and socially the contradictory attitudes of assertion and submission that were basic to Donne's temperament, but that were heightened by the desperateness of his ambition in the early Jacobean period.[20] The social and political dimensions of this conflict are highlighted by a number of related features of the sonnets: the portrayal of male authority, the rhetorical elaboration of the struggle of spiritual pride and humility, the subversive indecorum of particular works, and the general transformation of a (religiously expressed) passive aggression into an aesthetically sadomasochistic relationship with his readers.

One way the religious verse noticeably differs from the earlier secular poetry is in its changed attitude toward male authority. Whereas fathers and other authority figures are portrayed negatively, often derisively, in Donne's erotic and satiric verse (the major exception being *Satire* 3), in the divine poems the basic attitude is changed. In the fourth "penitential" sonnet, Donne imagines the father who died in his early childhood benevolently looking down from heaven on his spiritual triumphs:

> If faithfull soules be alike glorifi'd
>   As Angels, then my fathers soule doth see,
> And adds this even to full felicitie,
> That valiantly I hels wide mouth o'rstride. . . .
>   (*1635-HS* 4.1–4)

Such a figure functions psychologically as what Roy Schafer has called the "loving and beloved superego,"[21] sanctioning behavior that satisfies the individual's ideals. More typically in the *Holy Sonnets,* Donne depicts a paternal deity with whom he wishes to come to terms and whose love he wishes to enjoy. He expresses some angry, resentful, and rebellious feelings, but he capitulates before a God who seems, in some ways, to have been for him a lost father found.[22]

The sudden serious interest in fathers and the depiction of paternal deity reveal Donne's preoccupation with powerful authority and his relationship to it. John Carey has observed that Donne's primary emphasis in his later *Sermons* is upon God's power, rather than His love: "It is Power that does all" (*Sermons,* 8:128).[23] So, too, in the *Holy Sonnets,* the Donne who felt neglected and abused by secular authorities, including the king, portrayed a paradoxically hurtful and helpful God whose power he both resisted and felt drawn to. Not only is the angry, judgmental Old Testament God whose "sterne wrath . . . threatens" (HS 5.8) present in his poems, a deity whose violent punishment the speaker masochistically calls upon in "Batter my heart," but also Christ himself, usually portrayed as loving and merciful, is seen (in HS 9) as gruesomely frightening, his redemptive act primarily one of power: "Christs blood" has "might" (HS 2.13). The Beatific Vision does not evoke a sense of radiant love and comfort, but rather an image of "that face, / Whose feare already shakes my every joynt" (HS 3.7–8). In the Incarnation, a powerful God became "weake enough to suffer woe" (HS 7.14), but "weaknesse" (HS 8.7) is associated with God's creatures generally. The language of courtly suitorship is drawn into the Holy Sonnets to define the Christian's relationship to a strong kingly God, which suggests that behind Donne's theological preoccupation with strength and weakness lay his experiences in the secular world. Holy Sonnet 11, for example, imagines "God the Spirit, by Angels waited on / In heaven" (2–3) in the way King James was attended at Court. This poem presents the fantasy of being made "by adoption / Coheire to'his glory" (7–8) and Holy Sonnet 12 deals with getting part of a "double interest" in his "kingdome" (1–2) in language that suggests the economic benefits of royal patronage. When Donne in a later sermon reflected on the idea of enjoying the "friendship" of a "King" (Sermons 1:210–14), he elaborately developed just such analogies. In the light of this material, the statement "Thou lov'st mankind well, yet wilt not chuse me" (HS 1.13) sounds like a translation of a neglected client's complaint from a political into a religious context.

The conflict between assertion and submission is enacted in the Holy Sonnets in the thematic and rhetorical interplay of spiritual pride and humility. This familiar devotional material (portrayed, as Herbert later handled it, as the individual Christian's resistance, then capitulation, to God's grace and love) is developed throughout the series of poems—at least through the first twelve that have been considered as a structured sequence.[24] Holy Sonnet 1, for example, seems more concerned with blaming God than with loving Him, with complaining about ill treatment rather than with humble petitioning for grace. When the speaker cries out "Why doth the devil then usurpe in mee? / Why doth he steale, nay ravish that's thy right?" (9–10), he does so petulantly, accusingly, as though it were God's fault that he is plunged in sin. He seems to deliver God a moral ultimatum: "Except thou rise and for thine owne worke fight, / Oh I shall soone despaire" (11–12). The speaker arrogantly puts all the responsibility on God, having, in the first part of the poem, set out in lawyerlike terms the contractual relationship of creature and Creator, sinner and Redeemer. The problem of spiritual attitude in this poem is one that must be solved in the succeeding sonnets. A number of the other lyrics do dramatize the speaker's coming to terms with it by adopting the piously affectionate humility that is a precondition to receiving divine grace. Holy Sonnet 4, for example, self-consciously pulls back in the sestet from the tone and tenor of the octave, in which the speaker, in effect, has usurped God's role as the initiator of the Apocalypse:

> At the round earths imagin'd corners, blow
>   Your trumpets, Angells, and arise, arise
> From death, you numberlesse infinities
> Of soules, and to your scattred bodies goe,
> All whom the flood did, and fire shall o'erthrow,
> All whom warre, dearth, age, agues, tyrannies,
> Despaire, law, chance, hath slaine, and you whose eyes,
> Shall behold God, and never tast deaths woe.
> But let them sleepe, Lord, and mee mourne a space,
> For, if above all these, my sinnes abound,
> 'Tis late to aske abundance of thy grace,
> When wee are there; here on this lowly ground,
> Teach mee how to repent; for that's as good
> As if thou'hadst seal'd my pardon, with thy blood.

This poem's sharply contrasting attitudes of prideful assertion and humble submission are made into a structural balance. Analogously, *Holy Sonnet* 5 is divided into an accusatory, disputatious octave and a self-consciously meek sestet. But the scheme of spiritual pride overthrown and replaced by proper religious humility does not adequately account for what Donne is doing with the interplay of assertion and submission in these poems. There is something intractably boastful and self-advertising about the works that remains despite the gestures of self-effacement. Repeatedly, especially in poems like "Oh my blacke Soule" (*HS* 2), "This is my play's last scene" (*HS* 3), and "Spit in my face yee Jewes" (*HS* 7), Donne pridefully *over*dramatizes the self. As Lewalski and others have noticed, Donne legitimately employed the Protestant devotional technique of "application to the self" in both his poems and sermons,[25] but this does not explain the impression of boastfulness some sonnets create. Whereas a religious poet like George Herbert repeatedly expressed embarrassment over just such a tendency in himself, Donne seems to have reveled in it.

Meditative practice might have sanctioned vivid imagery and emotional heightening in devotional acts of the imagination, but the octave of a poem like *Holy Sonnet* 2 has an aura of self-consciously witty melodrama about it:

> Oh my blacke Soule! now thou art summoned
>   By sicknesse, deaths herald, and champion;
> Thou'art like a pilgrim, which abroad hath done
> Treason, and durst not turne to whence hee's fled,
> Or like a thiefe, which till deaths doome be read,
> Wisheth himselfe delivered from prison;

> But damn'd and hal'd to execution,
> Wisheth that still he might be imprisoned. . . .
>
> (1–8)

Similarly, the chain of epithets in the first quatrain of *Holy Sonnet* 3 is less functional than wittily overdramatic:

> This is my playes last scene, here heavens appoint
>   My pilgrimages last mile, and my race
> Idly, yet quickly runne, hath this last pace,
> My spans last inch, my minutes last point. . . .
>
> (1–4)

The poetic act of intensification is as much one of self-reflexive performing as of emotional scene-setting.

  Holy Sonnet 6 may rest on sound theological grounds and on the conventional devotional sharing in Christ's victory over death through the redemption, but Donne seems to have formulated religious truth in this poem in a particularly self-aggrandizing manner; joyful confidence in the power of the redemption and arrogant boasting are hard to disentangle. Likewise, in *Holy Sonnet* 7, Donne creates the impression—at least in the octave—that the speaker is engaging as much in an act of shockingly witty self-assertion as in a gesture of repentance:

> Spit in my face yee Jewes, and pierce my side,
>   Buffet, and scoffe, scourge, and crucifie mee,
> For I have sinn'd, and sinn'd, and onely hee,
> Who could do no iniquitie, hath dyed:
> But by my death can not be satisfied
> My sinnes, which passe the Jewes impiety:
> They kill'd once an inglorious man, but I
> Crucifie him daily, being now glorified.
>
> (1–8)

The last phrase of this passage contains a (perhaps unconscious) grammatical ambiguity. Is the subject of "glorified" Christ or the self-assertive speaker? Lewalski's remark that "the speaker seeks to arrogate to himself all the elements of Christ's passion"[26] points to the problem of tone in this poem. The self in performance and the self in humble devotion seem here, and throughout the *Holy Sonnets*, to be intractably, if creatively, at odds. In the religious lyrics Donne's fascination with the experiencing self produces a form of that self-conscious poetic performing in which he habitually engaged before his coterie readers.

  Donne's presentation of the self's conflicts between assertion and submission included the acts of witty indecorum to which he called attention in the

Holy Sonnets. In the performative context of the poems, Donne used shocking indecorum as a metacommunicative device to signal the emotional ambivalences at the heart of his religious verse, thus extending into a new genre a technique he had employed in his prose paradoxes, his amorous verse, and his complimentary poetry. Just as in his encomiastic epistles and lyrics Donne used calculated violations of decorum to express conflicts related to the situation of patronage, so too, in the divine poems, he seems to have restated the problem, but in a new thematic context. William Kerrigan has discussed some of those shocking elements of the religious verse that cannot be explained by references to the intellectual-historical or literary-historical precedents—such features as the sexualization of the speaker's relationship to God. Kerrigan is right to notice that such indecorum is a means of simultaneously assaulting the self and the reader in an attempt to express spiritual and psychological conflicts in a forceful manner.[27] But there are further (social) implications to the technique having to do both with Donne's relationship with his coterie audience and with his attitudes toward the political establishment.

Because the models of sonnet sequences were basically amorous ones and because Donne's own lyrics had been love poems, he turned to the language of love and to familiar erotic conventions to express religious desire in his *Holy Sonnets,* enlivening and testing the rhetoric of prayer and meditation as he alluded to his own past amorous experiences. In one of his sermons, Donne later spoke of Solomon in an autobiographical way: "*Salomon*, whose disposition was amorous, and excessive in the love of women, when he turn'd to God, he departed not utterly from his old phrase and language, but having put a new, and a spiritual tincture, and form and habit into all his thoughts, and words, he conveys all his loving approaches and applications to God, and all Gods gracious answers to his amorous soul, into songs, and Epithalamions, and meditations upon contracts, and marriages between God and his Church, and between God and his soul . . ." (*Sermons* 1:237).

Donne's eroticized spirituality manifests itself in *Holy Sonnet* 9 ("What if this present were the worlds last night?") where he explicitly connects his amorous wooing with his religious suitorship in addressing the figure of the crucified Christ:

> . . . as in my idolatrie
> I said to all my profane mistresses,
> Beauty, of pitty, foulnesse onely is
> A signe of rigour: so I say to thee,
> To wicked spirits are horrid shapes assign'd,
> This beauteous forme assures a pitious minde.
> (9–14)

Such analogizing between the erotic and the spiritual—present in another form in the secular verse—has been explained in terms of the conversion experience Donne was supposed to have undergone (an Augustinian transformation of the unholy amorist into the holy Christian). There are, of course, biblical and other precedents for erotic spirituality, such as the one Donne cites in the sermon passage. And it is certainly possible to associate Donne's practice with that of other Mannerist and Baroque artists. This last context has been used to account for the strategy of shock and excess adopted by Donne in the erotic metaphors and other techniques of the *Holy Sonnets*.[28] And yet such erotic material is basically indecorous and Donne presumably knew what he was doing with it. In the lines just quoted, for example, Donne does not simply connect the general terms of Petrarchan amorousness with his spiritual solicitation of Christ. Since the "pitty" sought from "mistresses" in his secular lyrics (if not in his life) was specifically sexual yielding, the opposite of "rigour," the analogy between the erotic and the religious seems to have been shocking by design.

A similar indecorum is to be found in the erotic spirituality of *Holy Sonnet* 10 ("Batter my heart")—a poem whose cry for "Divorce" (11) may, incidentally, express Donne's deep misgivings about his marriage. Kerrigan discusses this poem in terms of the tradition of "accommodation" and of Donne's imaginative testing of the limits of theological anthropomorphism.[29] But the holy rape the speaker of this sonnet invites—"I / Except you'enthrall mee, never shall be free, / Nor ever chast, except you ravish mee" (12–14)— seems to reveal more than the intensity of spiritual yearning. Through its rhetorical aggressiveness, it also calls attention to the *sadistic* undercurrent in the poet-reader relationship expressed through the *masochistic* formulations of the verse. The indecorous sexualization of the individual's relationship to God is only one way in which the rhetorical sadomasochism of the *Holy Sonnets* operates, the extreme communicative circumstances in which Donne again enacts his conflict of assertion and submission in the poems.

Of all the *Holy Sonnets*, "Batter my heart" best illustrates some of the aspects of the change in sociopolitical codes from the Elizabethan to the Jacobean periods. The sexualization of the speaker's relationship to God at the end of the sonnet is shocking partly because it has the shape of a passive homosexual fantasy. Assuming a homologous relationship among the religious, political, and sexual orders, Donne makes the connection, in *Pseudo-Martyr*, between sodomy and preferment; here he homoerotically sexualizes salvation. The cultural logic underlying both associations was not simply that of devotional topoi or of polemical scurrility; it was, in Jacobean England, in the reformulation of the heterosexual metaphor of Petrarchan amorousness into a (more or less sublimated) homosexual one suited both to male-male patron-client transactions generally (as in Shakespeare's *Sonnets*) and to Jacobean courtier-King relationships specifically. Being loved in the spiritual homoerotic context of "Batter my heart" corresponded to being favored in the political order. In the early Jacobean period, then, Donne's metaphoric capitulation to a divine lover took a peculiarly Jacobean form.

The rhetoric of the religious poems, particularly these *Holy Sonnets*, operates in interesting ways. Donne utilizes the "symbolic I"[30] of Protestant meditation and preaching as a way of forging a bond with an audience by means of which personal religious experience and insight, communal piety and general truths, can be joined. In contrast to most of his earlier verse, in which the reader was often overtly treated as an antagonist, the divine poems emphasize the collective "we" and the representativeness of the speaker to affirm an emotional-intellectual bond between speaker and listener, poet and reader.[31] There are, however, also opposite gestures of aggression toward the listener and the reader by means of which the poet, as in the complimentary verse, asserted his intellectual and literary authority in the very midst of his expressions of personal vulnerability and need. The strong language, the violent and shocking metaphors, the poems' sudden changes of thought and turns of development characteristically proclaim Donne's individuality and aesthetic superiority in ways that seem to undercut the stance of humble piety and communal spokesmanship.

In style and manner, then, Donne expressed his basic conflict between assertion and submission, alternately sharing deep spiritual experience with his readers and assaulting them aesthetically by various means. One final remark needs to be made about the rhetoric of the *Holy Sonnets* and of the religious poetry in general. Since this verse only really acknowledges one hierarchical relationship—that between man and God—and posits a communal equality of all Christians, it offered Donne the opportunity to treat any reader—friends like Sir Henry Goodyer and George Garrard, as well as Mrs. Herbert and the Earl of Dorset—with the kind of familiarity impossible in complimentary poetry, where the social distinctions were emphasized. Just as, in his controversial prose Donne assumed the kind of authority that allowed him (as he put it in one of his *Problems*) to satisfy "an *Ambition* . . . to speake *playnly* and *fellowly* of Lords and Kings" (p. 28), so too in the sacred poems he exercised the kind of religious authority he enjoyed in his later preaching, acting as a master of a discourse within which individuals from all social strata were theologically leveled. The only deference he needed to express was toward God. Hence, in such verse he could imaginatively escape the social conditions that generated conflicts between assertion and submission in the first place.

   As Gardner, Martz, Lewalski, and others have noted, the *Holy Sonnets* are private meditations utilizing a variety of conventional devotional techniques.[32] The sonnets no doubt satisfied some of Donne's personal emotional and intellectual needs at the time he composed them, offering within a religious sphere ways of dealing with anxieties and struggles that were less manageable in his actual social life. But, in both their thematic design and in their coterie "publication," these poems were attuned to the religious and political realities of Jacobean England. Whatever personal spiritual conflicts Donne experienced in the eight or so years preceding his ordination, he expressed them in relation to his career ambitions in the Jacobean environment. Although I am suspicious of any scheme that has Donne moving gradually toward a serious religious commitment (since, for example, as late as 1614 he was still vigorously pursuing secular preferment), his experience as a religious apologist,[33] his continued failure to find political advancement in the court of a king ready only to grant him ecclesiastical preferment, and his private study and agonized meditation all certainly led him to the inevitable acceptance of a religious vocation.

Donne obviously thought deeply about the decision to take orders, even though he resisted making it for a considerable time. Falling sometime between the time of composition of the early religious verse and the *Anniversaries* and that of the poetically valedictory "Obsequies to the Lord Harrington" and his ordination, that strange prose work later published as his *Essays in Divinity* records some of Donne's vexed thinking about the possibility of an ecclesiastical career. Usually viewed as a devotional exercise written with no particular audience in mind,[34] this work can, like the earlier *Holy Sonnets* and the subsequent (?) "Goodfriday, 1613. Riding Westward," fruitfully be read not only as private religious acts of meditation and prayer but also as coterie literature laden with both specific and general sociopolitical significance. Like his other coterie prose writing, the *Essays in Divinity* can help us to read Donne's contemporary poetical texts with a better sense of their contextual implications.

The *Essays in Divinity* is a mixed-genre work: a piece of mock-or comical-scholarship, parodying the methods of scriptural exegesis and mystical writing, a religiopolitical commentary in which Donne took advantage of his position as an amateur theologian and political outsider to comment on both the secular and religious spheres of activity, an exercise in private meditation and devotion experimenting with the rhetorics of prayer and preaching. Donne engages in both straightforward and paradoxical arguments, simultaneously valorizing the rational faculties as the means to truth and driving them into nonsensical helplessness. He treats learning, particularly theological tradition, as both magisterially authoritative and intellectually absurd. By mixing trivial and serious matters, important with insignificant authors, he disorients the reader, creating a vexing perplexity from which state, he suggests, only the intuitions of faith can rescue both the writer and the reader from a condition of intellectual and emotional impasse. In its rhetorical strategies, erratic thematics, and intellectual mischievousness, this work extends the manner and some of the matter of coterie prose pieces like *Biathanatos* and the *Paradoxes* and *Problems*— if not also of the polemical *Pseudo-Martyr* and *Ignatius His Conclave*. But, especially in its prayer sections, Donne engaged in a kind of writing that characterizes his mature religious poetry and prose, a form of devotional rhetoric that attempts to transcend intellectual perplexity by means of both plain and metaphoric perception grounded in faith and the material of Revelation.

In their intellectual convolution, Donne's *Essays in Divinity* signals a crisis of motive, belief, and commitment. It devastates its own intellectual materials and, in the process, also assaults the forms of order and value that are sanctioned in the public world. Donne's comments about secular authority, worldly success, and the pretensions of earthly monarchs (like Milton's in *Paradise Lost*) bespeak a bitter personal disillusionment, if not a pained cynicism—here the kind of rhetorical violence found in *Biathanatos* is aimed more frequently outward at nameless, faceless objects than it is at the masochistic self. *Essays in Divinity* is a text whose powerfully satiric force has not been properly acknowledged—partly because in it, as in the *Anniversaries*, satire and earnest idealization are combined in a way that directs attention toward positive intellectual, moral, and spiritual values. But here, as assuredly as in the other prose and poetical works of the previous decade of his life as a frustrated careerist, Donne reveals his preoccupation with the sociopolitical world even as he abstracts himself from it devotionally.

Within the work, the contexts of Donne's allusions to secular political power are those of his desire for forgiveness and renewal and of his ambivalence about his future secular or ecclesiastical career choices. Treating his personal suffering (implicitly attributed to his poor fortunes in the public world) as the instrument of God's healing power,[35] Donne contemplates the possibility of a "Vocation . . . to serve God" (p. 71), works toward the *contemptus mundi* gesture of the final prayer section, yet, because of yet-unrenounced political ambitions, clearly expresses envy toward the politically successful and criticism of the political establishment. In a section dealing with God's justice, he asks a rhetorical question, for example, in which his resentment of those who have benefited from royal patronage shows through:

> will any favorite, whom his Prince only for his appliableness to him, or some half-vertue, or his own glory, burdens with Honours and Fortunes every day, and destines to future Offices and Dignities, dispute or expostulate with his Prince, why he rather chose not another, how he will restore his Coffers; how he will quench his peoples murmurings, by whom this liberality is fed, or his Nobility, with whom he equalls new men; and will not rather repose himself gratefully in the wisdom, greatness and bounty of his Master?
>
> (p. 87)

At the end of the first decade of Jacobean rule, such a comment satirically alludes to some of the most powerful charges leveled at James by Parliamentarians, dissatisfied nobles, and the general populace.

In a section discussing miracles, Donne calls James's exercise of royal power into question through a particularly subversive use of the God/King analogy: "*Nature* is the *Common law* by which God governs us, and *Miracle* is his *Prerogative*. For Miracles are but so many *Non-obstantes* upon Nature. And Miracle is not like prerogative in any thing more then in this, that no body can tell what it is" (p. 81). In the context of the Commons-Crown argument over the relative strengths of common law and royal prerogative, Donne expressed, at the least, a skeptical attitude toward the Jacobean expansion of the legal scope of kingly power. In this particular discussion, he finally obliterates the Nature-Miracle contrast by explaining that "Miracles . . . produced to day were determined and inserted into the body of the whole History of Nature . . . at the beginning, and are as infallible and certain, as the most Ordinary and customary things" (p. 81). This solution to the problem does not really do away with the suggestion he makes that royal prerogative constitutionally conflicts with a normative common law his contemporaries were trying to systematize, just as "*Miracle* is against the whole *Order* of Nature" (p. 81). Several pages later, he makes a comment that confirms this impression: ". . . multiplicity of laws . . . is not so burdenous as it is thought, except it be in a captious, and entangling, and needy State; or under a Prince too indulgent to his own Prerogative" (p. 94).

Donne earlier refers to earthly monarchs in the context of a discourse on "*Nothing*" (p. 27): "And, oh ye chief of men, ye Princes of the Earth . . . know ye by how few descents ye are derived from Nothing? you are the Children of the Lust and Excrements of your parents, they and theirs the Children of *Adam*, the child of durt, the child of Nothing" (p. 30). Or, again referring to kings, Donne asks: "But alas, what are these our fellow-ants, our fellow-dirt, our fellow-nothings, compared to that God whom they make but their pattern?" (pp. 35–36). In the same place in the work, Donne's preoccupation with his poor sociopolitical status takes the form of a set of reflections just preceding the first prayer section, in which he seems to be in competition with royalty rather than in a stance of clientage:

A prince is Pilot of a great ship, a Kingdome; we of a pinnace, a family, or a less skiff, our selves: and howsoever we be tossed, we cannot perish; for our haven (if we will) is even in the midst of the Sea; and where we dy, our home meets us. If he be a lion and live by prey, and wast amongst Cedars and pines, and I a mole, and scratch out my bed in the ground, happy in this, that I cannot see him: If he be a butterfly, the son of a Silkworm, and I a *Scarab*, the seed of durt; If he go to the execution in a Chariot, and I in a Cart or by foot, where is the glorious advantage? If I can have (or if I can want) those things which the *Son of Sirach* calls principall, water, fire, and iron, salt and meal, wheat and hony, milk, and the blood of grapes, oyle, and clothing; If I can *prandere Olus*, and so need not Kings; Or can use Kings, and so need not *prandere Olus*: in one word, if I do not *frui* (which is, set my delight, and affections only due to God) but *Uti* the Creatures of this world, this world is mine; and to me belong those words, *Subdue the Earth and rule over all Creatures*; and as God is proprietary, I am *usufructuarius* of this Heaven and Earth which God created at the beginning. And here, because *Nemo silens placuit, multi brevitate*, shall be the end.

(p. 36)

It is in the context of the kind of envy and dissatisfaction expressed in this passage that Donne in the *Essays* takes a *contemptus mundi* stance and portrays his conversion from secular to religious values.

Applying to his own life the meaning of the deliverance of the Israelites from Egypt, Donne interprets his personal suffering as God's schooling him through affliction to make a break with worldly values to which he was still, nonetheless, attached:

> Thou hast delivered me, O God, from the Egypt of confidence and presumption, by interrupting my fortunes, and intercepting my hopes; And from the Egypt of despair by contemplation of thine abundant treasures, and my portion therein; from the Egypt of lust, by confining my affections; and from the monstrous and unnaturall Egypt of painfull and wearisome idleness, by the necessities of domestick and familiar cares and duties. Yet as an Eagle, though she enjoy her wing and beak, is wholly prisoner, if she be held by but one talon; so are we, though we could be delivered of all habit of sin, in bondage still, if Vanity hold us but by a silken thred.
>
> (p. 75)

That "silken thred" continued to keep the ambitious Donne connected to the world of secular preferment, even as he felt pushed toward the acceptance of the king's call to Church service. The final gesture of rejecting worldly values toward which *Essays in Divinity* moves looks more like an act Donne would like to have made rather than one he actually felt ready to make with a full sense of new commitment:

> We renounce, O Lord, all our confidence in this world; for this world passeth away, and the lusts thereof: Wee renounce all our confidence in our own merits, for we have done nothing in respect of that which we might have done; neither could we ever have done any such thing, but that still we must have remained unprofitable servants to thee; we renounce all confidence, even in our own confessions, and accusations of our self . . . yea we renounce all confidence even in our repentances. . . . We have no confidence in this world, but in him who hath taken possession of the next world for us.
>
> (pp. 98–99)

This devotional prose work records a stage in Donne's career in which he felt ambivalent both about his further search for courtly advancement and about the possibility of taking orders.

Donne no doubt used the occasion of writing the *Essays* to put his conflicted thoughts down on paper for his own benefit, but there are some signs that he intended the work to be read by a receptive, if quite limited, coterie audience also. Although he characterized the *Essays* as "solitary Meditations" (p. 41), or, as he put it elsewhere, "Sermons, that . . . have no Auditory" (p. 41), he suggests that he is writing "a Meta-theology, and super-divinity

. . . but to my equals" (p. 59)—that is, composing a form of lay theology that metacommunicatively examines some of the premises and methods of the forms of theological and devotional discourse the work both enacts and parodies. In asking rhetorically, at one point, ". . . do not many among us study even the Scriptures only for ornament?" (p. 40), he seems to be addressing fellow men of fashion. The rationale he offers for God's allowing contradictions in Scripture is similar to the one implied by some of his own paradoxical coterie prose: "To make men sharpe and industrious in the inquisition of truth, he withdrawes it from present apprehension, and obviousness. For naturally great wits affect the reading of obscure books" (p. 56). Just as the *Paradoxes* and *Problems* were used by Donne as "alarums to truth" for a witty readership willing to work through intellectual perplexity, so too it is likely that Donne directed his *Essays in Divinity* to a similarly receptive coterie familiar with his "intemperance of scribbling" (*Letters*, p. 228).

In one of the final prayers, Donne suggests that he was composing the *Essays* in rural exile—possibly in the country house of one of his friends, if not in France during his Continental sojourn with Sir Robert Drury: "And thou hast put me in my way towards thy land of promise, thy Heavenly *Canaan*, by removing me from the Egypt of frequented and populous, glorious places, to a more solitary and desart retiredness, where I may more safely feed upon both thy Mannaes, thy self in thy Sacrament, and that other, which is true Angells food, contemplation of thee" (p. 96).[36] At times, Donne implies the existence of an audience other than himself—in a phrase such as "let me observe to you" (p. 88), for example. He sometimes, especially in the formal prayer sections, utilizes the communal "we" for whom the writer speaks like a typical Protestant preacher: "Behold us, O God, here gathered together in thy fear, according to thine ordinance, and in confidence of thy promise, that when two or three are gathered together in thy name, thou wilt be in the midst of them, and grant them their petitions" (pp. 97–98). The work was clearly not intended for print, but Donne might have shown it to friends. It probably belonged to socioliterary circumstances similar to those of the religious lyric with which it seems to have intellectual and emotional affinities, "Goodfriday, 1613. Riding Westward."

Two related sets of terms are contrasted with one another in the Good Friday poem: 1) "Pleasure" and "businesse" (7) vs. the retreat from the secular world into the sphere of religious piety; 2) prideful rationality vs. humble intuitive faith. With regard to the first of these, the coterie context can help to focus the issues involved. If, as seems likely, "Goodfriday, 1613. Riding Westward" was composed en route from Sir Henry Goodyer's Polesworth estate to Sir Edward Herbert's Montgomerey Castle,[37] its circumstances of composition and of initial reception were properly incorporated thematically in the poem in specific ways. Given some of the values and interests Donne shared with both friends—in particular the courtly ambitions and fondness for witty intellectuality—the poem was particularly adjusted to the receptivities of a primary audience and its immediate circumstances, moving from a visit to one friend to enjoy the hospitality of another. One of the argumentative tasks Donne undertakes in this religious lyric is the reconciliation of worldly involvement with devotional obligations or of secular with religious goals. Initially the two orders are opposed: riding westward, in the specific metaphor of moral movement Donne employs, indicates a turning away from God toward the world that conflicts with the obligation to move eastward toward the theological Orient symbolized by the crucified Christ.[38] The speaker's strategy of splitting himself into a body riding westward on horseback and a soul bending devotionally toward the East is wittily presented as a rationalization that does not solve the problem posed by the conflict of allegiances. By the end of the poem, however, moving westward is redefined as a necessary condition of worldly existence that is a penitential preparation for facing that God whose bright image, according to traditional doctrine, can only be confronted in Heaven.

The solution Donne poses is based on an equation that is implicit also in the *Essays in Divinity*: worldly suffering = spiritual penance. Just as, in the *Essays in Divinity*, Donne interpreted his "idlenesse," his sociopolitical disappointments, and his consequent "despair" (p. 75) as the afflictions through which he could be redeemed, so, in the poem, he portrayed the fixation of his heart on worldly success (paradoxically) as the means by which he could turn toward God. What this redefinition of suffering permits, then, is the reconciliation of the two commitments opposed in the Good Friday poem. Moving westward becomes a penitential experience through which the man of the world makes himself available (here consciously, in Donne's life unconsciously or ironically) to God's loving, yet violent, ministrations. By having the speaker invite punishment, Donne imaginatively assumes control not only of what God will do to him to make him worthy of salvation, but also of what is happening and what has happened to cause him pain all along, all those griefs he has endured, especially in the decade prior to the poem's composition:

> I turne my backe to thee, but to receive
> Corrections, till thy mercies bid thee leave.
> O thinke me worth thine anger, punish me,
> Burne off my rusts, and my deformity,
> Restore thine Image, so much, by thy grace,
> That thou may'st know me, and I'll turne my face.
> (37–42)

The call for punishment is also, however, Donne's way of asking that some agency outside himself decide between a secular and a religious commitment for him. God's striking St. Paul off his horse to recruit him to His service seems a close analogue to Donne's request for divine action to change him (from an ambitious courtier to a devout Churchman).

The second contrast in the Good Friday poem—between rational and intuitive acts, or reason and faith—is related to the first: Reason is to worldly commitment as Faith is to spiritual commitment. As Donald Friedman has argued in his fine essay on this lyric: "The poem . . . illuminates a current of Donne's thought that became central to his sermon practice; it criticizes the rationalism that regards itself as self-sufficient, and demonstrates the rejection of that kind of devotion that believes it can comprehend the mysteries of faith by being 'reasonable.' Like many of the sermons the poem enacts a discovery of the inadequacy of such paltering mechanics of the mind; but it does this by transcending the concept-making skills of the intellect, not by discarding them."[39] Friedman's analysis of the rhetorical development of the poem, especially his account of the function of its opening ten lines, is convincing: one can see how the speaker of the poem moves through intellectually strained conceits (1–10) and the recitation of smugly pat paradoxical formulae (11–14) to a more emotionally and imaginatively charged response to the crucifixion and his own sinfulness (15–34) and to an affectionately pious (if masochistic) colloquy.

Friedman notes that " 'Goodfriday, 1613. Riding Westward' proceeds towards its spiritual discovery by way of mockery and self-parody,"[40] but such features characteristically mark it as a coterie work that is a religious lyric as well as a metapoetic commentary on its poetic materials and on the implied relationship of poet and audience. The private agonizing over personal commitments figured in the poem is enacted for readers able to relate the lyric's self-reflexivity to the private and sociopolitical contexts in which it is set. Although I agree with the basic analysis of the poem's rhetorical development that Friedman offers, I think there is something wrong with his explanation of Donne's intentions. To say that this lyric was meant to serve as "a vehicle of conversion for Donne's audience"[41] is to ignore the poet's presentation of the crisis of commitment and the need for (violent) change as his own. In order to support his claim, Friedman has to argue that the poem "foreshadows both the purpose and the designs of many sermons Donne was to preach in later years."[42] The preacher-congregation situation, however, does not really fit a lyric in which, as in the *Anniversaries* and the *Essays in Divinity*, personal struggles and disappointments, doubts about the future, and a crisis of purpose are expressed through vexed intellectuality, emotional masochism, and idealistic yearning. In "Goodfriday, 1613" Donne was less confidently in control—intellectually, emotionally, rhetorically—than he was in his later sermons, and the instability or uncertainty of this lyric, like that of the *Holy Sonnets*, accounts for much of its power. All the biographical evidence suggests that at the time Donne composed this poem, he was still unable to accept the ecclesiastical service toward which the King had beckoned him. He was still unwilling to relinquish his aggressive pursuit of secular preferment: in the context of his actual behavior, the religious thematics of "Goodfriday, 1613" and of the other preordination religious and philosophical poetry were rendered deeply problematic, and would have been perceived as such by a knowing coterie readership.

Notes

1. Garrard, who shared lodgings with Donne at the time he composed many of the religious poems, probably had some of this verse in mind when he referred to the "very transcendent" poems of Donne he had read in manuscript and copied out for his own use (quoted in *John Donne: The Critical Heritage*, ed. A. J. Smith [London and Boston: Routledge & Kegan Paul, 1975], p. 109). In this essay I use the following editions of Donne's poems and prose: *The Divine Poems of John Donne*, ed. Helen Gardner, 2nd ed. (Oxford: Clarendon Press, 1978); *The Elegies and The Songs and Sonnets*, ed. Helen Gardner (Oxford: Clarendon Press, 1965); *Letters to Severall Persons of Honour (1651)*, a facsimile reproduction with an introduction by M. Thomas Hester (Delmar, NY: Scholars' Facsimiles & Reprints, 1977); *Paradoxes and Problems*, ed. Helen Peters (Oxford: Clarendon Press, 1980; *Pseudo-Martyr*, a facsimile reproduction with introduction by Francis Jacques Sypher (Delmar, NY: Scholars' Facsimiles & Reprints, 1974); *Essays in Divinity*, ed. Evelyn M. Simpson (Oxford: Clarendon Press, 1952); *The Sermons of John Donne*, ed. George R. Potter and Evelyn Simpson, 10 vols. (Berkeley: University of California Press, 1953–62); *Selected Prose*, chosen by Evelyn Simpson, ed. by Helen Gardner and Timothy Healy (Oxford: Clarendon Press, 1967).

2. See Gardner, *Divine Poems*, pp. xlviii–ix. The Earl, who succeeded to the title in February 1609, was hastily married to Lady Anne Clifford (with whom Donne was acquainted through Lady Bedford) two days before his father's death to avoid becoming a ward to the Duke of Lennox. He was one of the most extravagant spenders among the aristocracy, someone to whom authors could look for patronage (Lawrence Stone, *The Crisis of the Aristocracy, 1558–1641* [Oxford: Clarendon Press, 1965], pp. 213, 582–83).

3. See Stephen Greenblatt, *Renaissance Self-Fashioning: From More to Shakespeare* (Chicago and London: Univ. of Chicago Press, 1980), pp. 115–56, for a discussion of Wyatt's penitential psalms in relation to their political context. The Elizabethan and Jacobean courtier Sir John Harington, who composed in his last years a treatise based on Petrarch's *Life of Solitude, The Prayse of Private Life*, wrote of the futility of his own courtly striving: "I have spent my time, my fortune, and almoste my honestie, to buy false hope, false friends, and shallow praise;— and be it remembered, that he who castethe up this reckoning of a cowrtlie minion, will set his summe like a foole at the ende, for not being a knave at the beginning. Oh, that i could boaste with chaunter Davide, *In te speravi Domine*" (*Nugae Antiquae*, 3 vols. [1779; reprint, Hildesheim: G. Olms, 1968]: 2:212).

4. Since these poems were not printed until the nineteenth century, Donne knew them in manuscript and composed his late poem about them, "Upon the translation of the Psalmes by Sir Philip Sidney, and the Countesse of Pembroke his Sister."

5. Like Donne, Greville was out of office from about 1604 to 1614. The poems in the last part of *Caelica* (82, 84–109), an anthology of philosophical and religious verse, were probably composed in this period. Some of them express his political frustration and resentment over the success of others. *Caelica* 91, for example, demystifies the honors and titles dispensed by royalty, referring to "*Nobilitie*" as "*Powers golden fetter*" (7) and expressing a hatred of "subiection" (8). *Caelica* 95 is preoccupied with the forces responsible for "scornfull wrong or . . . suppressing merit" (9).

6. In the Preface to *Pseudo-Martyr*, Donne explained to the King the composition of the work in the following way: "The influence of those your Maiesties Bookes, as the Sunne, which penetrates all corners, hath wrought vppon me, and drawen vp, and exhaled from my poore Meditations, these discourses: Which with all reuerence and deuotion, I present to your

Maiestie" (p. A3ʳ). In his sixth Problem, with the Jacobean context in mind, Donne clearly attributed secular motives to an intellectual interest in theology, suggesting that "perchance when wee study it by mingling humane respects, it is not divinity" (p. 28). Sir John Harington talked theology with the King. *The Letters and Epigrams of Sir John Harrington*, ed. Norman E. McClure [Philadelphia: Univ. of Pennsylvania Press, 1930], p. 110)

7. King James, of course, was well known as a religious poet himself. He translated DuBartas's *Uranie* into English, invited the author to visit him in Scotland in 1587, translated Psalms (that were published posthumously), and wrote other religious verse: see the discussion in Lily B. Campbell, *Divine Poetry and Drama in Sixteenth-Century England* (Cambridge: Cambridge Univ. Press and Berkeley and Los Angeles: Univ. of California Press, 1959), pp. 74–83. Campbell says of the religious sonnet sequence of Henry Lok, who came to the Scottish Court as Elizabeth's secret agent, that it was "literary work which would win favour with the Scottish King, who was probably in a similar exercise himself" (p. 131). She notes also that "Sir John Harington ... during the reign of King James undertook to translate the Psalms and sent them to the King for criticism" (p. 54). It is not surprising that Ben Jonson began the collection of largely secular poems in *Under-wood* with three religious lyrics.

8. In the context of the "cult of Elizabeth," which had appropriated to itself both the language of Petrarchan amorousness and some of the features of Catholic Mariolatry, Southwell's elevation of religious over secular poetry (a traditional gesture on the part of a sacred poet) and Constable's choice of the Virgin Mary rather than the sonnet mistress or the Queen as the object of praise are both indirect forms of political protest.

9. See, for example, *La Corona* 5.

10. See, for example, *Letters*, pp. 48–54, 137–39.

11. I refer by number to the twelve sonnets printed as a set by Gardner, but use "1635-HS" to designate the four additional sonnets printed in the 1635 edition and "W-HS" to refer to the three poems found in the Westmoreland MS.

12. Gardner (*Divine Poems*, p. 81) suggests the autumn of 1608 as a date of composition.

13. Barbara Kiefer Lewalski, *Protestant Poetics and the Seventeenth-Century Religious Lyric* (Princeton, N. J.: Princeton Univ. Press, 1979), p. 260.

14. See, for example, the 1608 letter to Lord Hay (quoted in R. C. Bald, *John Donne: A Life* [New York and Oxford: Oxford Univ. Press, 1970], pp. 161–62).

15. See my discussion of these topics in " 'Love is not love': Elizabethan Sonnet Sequences and the Social Order," *ELH* 49 (1982): 407–18.

16. John Carey, *John Donne: Life, Mind, and Art* (Oxford: Oxford Univ. Press, 1980), pp. 15–59.

17. In a letter to Goodyer, Donne described her reaction to his announcement that he intended to take orders: ". . . she had more suspicion of my calling, a better memory of my past life, then I had thought her nobility could have admitted" (*Letters*, p. 218).

18. Gardner (*Divine Poems*, p. 152) suggests 1608 as the year of composition, while Novarr estimates "late in 1608 or early in 1609" (*Disinterred Muse*, p. 93).

19. For Donne's relationship with Mrs. Herbert, see Gardner, *Elegies and Songs and Sonnets*, pp. 251–55; Bald, *Life*, pp. 180–84; H. W. Garrod, "Donne and Mrs. Herbert," *Review of English Studies* 21 (1945): 161–73; and the four letters printed in Gosse, 1:164–67. In describing Mrs. Herbert's household at Charing Cross, where she generously entertained many friends, Amy Charles uses Donne's funeral sermon for her to emphasize the piety that was mixed with her hospitality: "Not only did Mrs. Herbert see to it that prayers were conducted morning and evening in her home, but Donne tells us, she herself went to church for daily offices: 'From this I testifie her holy *cheerfulnesse*, and a *Religious alacrity*, (one of the best *evidences* of a *good conscience*) that as shee came to this place, God's house of *Prayer*, duly not onely every *Sabbath* . . . but even in those *weeke-dayes*' " (*A Life of George Herbert* [Ithaca and London: Cornell Univ. Press, 1977], p. 42). The verse letter Donne sent Mrs. Herbert in 1608 (before her second marriage, to the much younger Sir John Danvers), bespeaks an easy social familiarity. In it,

Donne uses encomiastic topoi in a comically teasing manner. He humorously alludes to his own clientage (in which he vied with, as well as enjoyed the company of, other "noble'ambitious wits" [35] who gathered socially about Mrs. Herbert in her "Cabinet" [34]). He contrasts this healthy vying for her favor with the vicious competition of the larger world. In this smaller context, she is like a "Prince" (11) but lacks princely "faults" (11); she "dares preferre" "Truth" (12), rather than evil men—the kinds of "wicked" (8) political scramblers for "great place" (6) whose success Donne resented. The speaker's feigned envy of her fiancé, whose writings are portrayed as competing with his and others' for her affectionate attention, finally turns into a compliment as the poem's speaker declares "so much I doe love her choyce, that I / Would faine love him that shall be lov'd of her" (51–52). The poems Donne sent to her to read might have included such occasional pieces as "The Crosse" and "Upon the Annunciation and Passion falling upon one day. 1608." The former poem, identified by Gardner as a work that seems "more like a Verse-Letter than a Divine Poem" (*Divine Poems*, p. 92), defends the cross as a religious artifact against the kind of radical Protestant criticism to which King James responded in the 1603 Hampton Court Conference (Gardner, *Divine Poems*, p. 92), but, despite the public issue involved, Donne probably used the work to express his own belief in the legitimacy of using the cross for devotional purposes, communicating this attitude to someone who, like Mrs. Herbert, would have agreed with him.

20.   Gardner dates the first six *Holy Sonnets* between February and August of 1609 (*Divine Poems*, p. xlix) and the second six, along with the four penitential sonnets between 1609 and the writing of *The Second Anniversarie* (*Divine Poems*, p. 1). Of the Westmoreland sonnets, the first two ("Since she whome I lov'd" and "Show me deare Christ") seem clearly to have been written after Donne's ordination, and the third ("Oh, to vex me, contraryes meete in one") probably belongs to the same period.

21.   Roy Schafer, "The Loving and Beloved Superego in Freud's Structural Theory," *The Psychoanalytic Study of the Child* 15 (1960): 163–88.

22.   Donne lost his father at the age of four and he grew up with Dr. John Syminges as a stepfather (see Bald, *Life*, pp. 36–38).

23.   Carey, *Donne: Life, Mind, and Art*, pp. 122–25.

24.   I agree with the analysis of these twelve poems as the enactment of a process of discovery in Carol Marks Sicherman, "Donne's Discoveries," *Studies in English Literature* 11 (1971): 84–87.

25.   See the discussion of the *Holy Sonnets* in Lewalski, *Protestant Poetics*, pp. 264–75.

26.   Lewalski, *Protestant Poetics*, p. 270.

27.   William Kerrigan, "The Fearful Accommodations of John Donne," *English Literary Renaissance* 4 (1974): 337–63.

28.   See, for example, Murray Roston, *The Soul of Wit: A Study of John Donne* (Oxford: Clarendon Press, 1974), pp. 163–84.

29.   Kerrigan, "Fearful Accommodations," pp. 351–56.

30.   Lewalski (*Donne's* Anniversaries *and the Poetry of Praise: The Creation of a Symbolic Mode* [Princeton: Princeton Univ. Press, 1973], p. 105) uses this term.

31.   Earl Miner is right, but only in a limited sense, when he says of the religious poems: ". . . there is almost none of that antagonism of the secular poems against his audience" (*The Metaphysical Mode from Donne to Cowley* [Princeton: Princeton Univ. Press, 1969], p. 173).

32.   By now the emphasis on the importance of Ignatian meditation for Donne's religious poetry found in Martz's *Poetry of Meditation* (for the *Holy Sonnets*, see pp. 43–56), has been corrected by a counteremphasis on Augustinian Protestantism: see especially William Halewood, *The Poetry of Grace: Reformation Themes and Structures in Seventeenth-Century English Poetry* (New Haven, Conn., and London: Yale Univ. Press, 1970) and Lewalski's *Protestant Poetics*.

33.   I include Donne's service to Dean Morton in the years preceding the composition of his own polemical works.

34.   In the introduction to her edition, Evelyn Simpson calls the *Essays* "essentially private

meditations" (p.x), while Joan Webber says they are "closet sermons" (*Contrary Music: The Prose Style of John Donne* [Madison: Univ. of Wisconsin Press, 1963], p. 16). Bald cites an undated letter to Goodyer in which Donne refers to his preparation for Communion by solitary "arraignment of my self" in which practice he "digested some meditations of mine, and apparelled them (as I use) in the form of a Sermon" confessing "I have not yet utterly delivered my self from this intemperance of scribbling" (*Letters*, p. 228, quoted in Bald, *Life*, p. 299).

35.   Donne writes of the biblical Israelites that all their sufferings "were . . . as Physick, and had only a medicinall bitternesse in them" (p. 90).

36.   Bald (*Life*, pp. 298–99) believes the reference to *"desart retiredness"* points to Donne's Mitcham years, but it is as likely that the *Essays* were written on a visit to a place like Sir Edward Herbert's Montgomery Castle or while Donne was in France.

37.   Peter Beal ([comp.] *Index of English Literary Manuscripts* [London and New York: Mansell, 1980–], 1:247) points out a manuscript copy of the poem in Goodyer's hand. British Library MS Add. 25707 entitles the piece "Mr J. Dun*ne* goeinge from S^r H G: on good fryday sent him back this Meditac*ion* on the waye" while British Library MS Harl. 4955 has "Riding to Sr Edward Herbert in wales" (See Gardner, *Divine Poems*, p. 98). See Bald, *Life*, pp. 269–71. Some four days after Donne arrived at Montgomery Castle he wrote the following socially complimentary letter to an ill Sir Robert Harley:

> I could almost be content to be desperate of seeinge you while I am in thys contry if I might hope well of your health. The conversation of thys noble gentleman, who refuses me not in hys house, recompences the want of any company; but my sensiblenes of any frind's sicknes ys encreased by the healthfullnes of thys place; for I thinke if Bellarmine knew what immortality dwells here, he would looke that hys Enoch and Elias should come out of thys castle to fight against hys Antichrist. But, Sir, as I was willinge to make thys paper a little bigger than a physician's receit lest that representation should take your stomach from yt, so I wyll avoyd to make it very longe or busy, least your patient would have done. It shall, therefore, onely say that which if I were goinge to my grace should be the honorablest peice of my epitaph, that I am your humble and affectionate servant.
>
> —*HMC Portland*, 3:6

38.   On the symbolism of movement in the poem, see A. B. Chambers, "Goodfriday, 1613. Riding Westward: The Poem and the Tradition," *ELH* 28 (1961): 31–53.

39.   Donald Friedman, "Memory and the Art of Salvation in Donne's Good Friday Poem," *English Literary Renaissance* 3 (1973): 421. Cf. Sicherman, "Donne's Discoveries," pp. 68–74.

40.   Friedman, "Memory and Salvation," p. 430.

41.   Friedman, "Memory and Salvation," p. 424.

42.   Friedman, "Memory and Salvation," p. 441.

"Darke texts need notes": Versions of Self in Donne's Verse Epistles

DAVID AERS AND GUNTHER KRESS*

Donne's verse epistles have not received much notice from the awesome critical industry centred on his work. Any explanation of this surprising fact would include reference to factors such as an assumed lack of poetic richness in these poems, the assumption that patronage poetry is too conventional to merit serious critical attention, and perhaps even some embarrassment at a deification of living patronesses.[1] But we believe that the most significant factor is an unrecognized one: namely the lack of a descriptive and theoretical framework within which the real interest of these poems can be perceived and analysed. In this essay we attempt to establish such a framework and carry out an analysis which will locate, describe, and account for versions of the self emerging within these verse letters. In the course of this critical inquiry we will build on John Danby's hints about the explicitly social basis of so much seemingly purely metaphysical speculation.[2] We hope to develop an approach which through its very attention to the minute movements of a particular text reveals how these only become intelligible when inserted in a wider context which includes the writer's precise social situation. We hope that the critical method being evolved here will ultimately be explored in connection with the whole corpus of Donne's work.

I

In 1608 Donne wrote a poem beginning, "You have refin'd mee," a verse epistle to his new patroness Lucy, Countess of Bedford, in what seems to have been the most personally testing period of his life.[3] Although Donne himself includes the comment that "darke texts need notes," his editors and critics do not seem to have found this a particularly interesting poem. However, we think it both demands and rewards scrutiny. These are the first two stanzas:

*_Literature and History_ No. 8 (1978): 138–58. Reprinted with the permission of the Editorial Board, _Literature and History_.

MADAME,
You have refin'd mee, and to worthyest things
   (Vertue, Art, Beauty, Fortune,) now I see
Rarenesse, or use, not nature value brings;
And such, as they are circumstanc'd, they bee.
    Two ills can ne're perplexe us, sinne to'excuse;
    But of two good things, we may leave and chuse.

Therefore at Court, which is not vertues clime,
   (Where a transcendent height, (as, lownesse mee)
Makes her not be, or not show) all my rime
Your vertues challenge, which there rarest bee;
    For, as darke texts need notes: there some must bee
    To usher vertue, and say, *This is shee.*[4]

In the editorial glosses on these stanzas they come across as being fairly unproblematic. Grierson finds Donne's introduction of himself in "as, lownesse mee" (stanza two), "quite irrelevant" (and is more unsettled than Milgate), yet he assumes that he has solved any minor enigmas, and the lines seem not to need extended commentary.[5] However, on closer inspection there are important and unresolved tensions in these lines. The countess is alchemist, a near creator (as lines 21–22 of the poem make explicit) through whose agency the poet can now perceive things as they *really* are. This sets up a dichotomy between things as he perceives them now and things as he perceived them before. *Now* he sees that value is the product of contingent social relationships. Already there may be hints, clarified later in the poem, that value, being generated by rareness or use, is an aspect of market transactions. Even seemingly transcendent, platonic forms, Vertue, Art, Beauty, "worthyest things" indeed, get their worth in this way and so have to be placed in the same category as the thoroughly contingent sub-lunar abstraction, Fortune. But before his "refinement" he had assumed, in good idealist (platonic or stoic) fashion that value transcended the contingent placings of social practice; he had assumed that value was a reflection of the object or person's intrinsic nature, that, in his own words, "nature value brings."

Such relativistic talk, appropriate to a market, may not surprise readers today. But when we recall that the poem is addressed to Lucy, and that Donne is overtly talking about her, the worthiest thing whom he is both worshipping and elegantly asking for patronage, it is, at the very least, a strange and rather risky compliment. After all, the poem implies that she is not inherently valuable, that her worthiness is a product of contingent social circumstances, and that her refining has given him perceptions of this kind. (The second stanza is connected to the first by the logical connector "Therefore," thus removing any lingering doubts that the first stanza is also about Lucy.) The countess's value as one of the "worthyest things" paradoxically *depends* on her being "circumstanc'd" in a social situation where her attributes (virtues, it so happens) are most valuable precisely because they are rare, the court rather conspicuously not being the "clime" of virtue.

This does have a rationale and can be resolved once we see the structure of Donne's basic model here. He is actually working with a model which assumes the existence of two worlds or "climes." One is a platonic clime in which Lucy exists with platonic forms, and which her usher-exegete has knowledge of. (This world of essences transcends all contingency and relativity, and so supersedes all notions of value deployed by social man.) A second clime is the present historical world, the world of the court, Mitcham, and Donne's frustrated daily existence, one where value is a function of contingent market relations, supply and demand, mere "circumstance." It is in this second world that the countess is "worthyest," most valuable, and it is here that Donne so desperately wishes to find employment as the official usher of the valued one. His role is to introduce the myopic courtiers to the rare (and useful?) worthy one. In this he himself gains value as the indispensable spectacles through which courtiers can perceive the rare and hidden riches of that dark text, Lucy. The "alienated intellectual" overcomes his alienation, finds community, wins employment and use as an essential mediator between the two climes.[6] However, Donne fails to show us why the lower clime should value virtue, why this particular rare commodity should be desired by courtiers at all. The unexamined gap in his argument here is simply leapt over as he assumes, optimistically, that the second clime must find use and market value for representatives of the higher world.

Donne does not resolve the paradox in the way we have been doing, but wisely leaves it in its highly compressed form, with only hints that the very absence of virtue at the court makes the countess "worthyest" and endows both her and her usher-exegete with value. It is understandable enough that Donne should not have wanted to express the views we have described in this plain form, and so we already have sound reasons for a wish to darken the text. Of course, the double-edged nature of the paradoxical compliment to the countess could have been simply handled by leaving it out, thus obviating the danger of relativising the countess's virtue. Nevertheless, this would not have permitted Donne to introduce the important self-reference so well worked into a complex image of the relations between poet, patroness, society and ethical idealism. Here we have a non-trivial explanation for his desire to keep the text dark, one which offers an account of verbal processes and relevant social and psychological motivations.

We mentioned the significant degree of self-reference in the poem and this facet invites some further consideration, especially in the light of Donne's "egocentricity," widely commented on by critics.[7] The statement of this egocentricity is inevitably more complex here than in many of the *Songs and Sonnets*, where the poet-lover focuses on himself and his relations with a lover. This poem, however, is focused on the patroness, and since he delicately seeks patronage the relationship is one which needs most careful handling; not the time, one would think, for an overt display of egocentricity. In this connection it is interesting to note how the poem begins with a reference to himself. It does certainly bestow credit on the countess—she, as alchemist, has succeeded in refining him. Yet the image also turns Donne into the central object of attention, just as the alchemist's attention focuses on the materials he desires to transform. And as the success of the alchemist is defined by his success in refining the material, so the countess's success is defined in terms of her effectiveness in working on the present material, the poet. Thus at the very opening of the poem the overt focus on the patroness has been inverted and become part of a rather complicated self-referring process. Lines two and eight (the self-mentioning, which Grierson found "irrelevant") again refer to him; so do lines nine, eleven and twelve. Without doubt there is a large enough amount of self-reference in the opening stanzas at least to attract one's curiosity.

In addition there are some peculiarities of reference, predominantly in the pronouns. Line one contains the two pronouns, *you* and *mee*: in the same line there is the "pronoun" *worthyest things*. Its reference is ambiguous: Donne has just been refined, so that one possible reference is *mee*. If he is included in the category of *worthyest things*, then he belongs to the same class as Lucy (*you*), another possible referent of this phrase. *Worthyest things* is plural in number, and so it can indeed refer to both Lucy and the poet. Presumably Donne intended the reference to be multiply ambiguous; at any rate it is not immediately clear, and in searching for an appropriate and permitted referent, the reference to the poet will arise, have to be assessed, and decided on. The fact that in the next line Donne glosses *worthyest things* as "Vertue, Art, Beauty, Fortune" shows that he acknowledged the need to provide a gloss. As we pointed out above, this list collapses platonic categories into the social and contingent clime of "Fortune," relativizing and undercutting the platonic model. By the time we reach the end of the second line *worthyest things* has accumulated a wide range of possible references: "you," "mee," "you" and "mee," "Vertue, Art, Beauty, Fortune." All of these lead into "Fortune," and are placed in the same category as Fortune, so that the relativizing tendency has become thoroughly pervasive.

The fourth line of the poem continues to draw on the multiple ambiguity under discussion: "And such, as they are circumstanc'd, they bee." Here *they* may refer to all the referents mentioned. Another pronoun, *such*, is introduced. It in turn may refer to all three and to *they*; or it may pick out just one of these. If the latter, then we get at least the following readings: (1) Lucy (such → worthiest things → You), the countess, such as she is circumstanced so she is—as she is placed in the contingent social market of fortune, so she is valued, worthiest. (2) Donne (such → worthiest thing → me → refined), the poet, such as he is circumstanced so he is—as he is placed in Lucy's platonic world, as a new creature, so he is valued, worthiest. As he is placed in the contingent social market, so he is valued, as nothing. His appeal to Lucy is therefore that she should "translate" his worth in her platonic world, into a recognised use and hence value in the market, in the appropriate place: as an indispensable usher. The countess is well able to do this. So the reading as it stands is: I, as I am circumstanced so I am, as I am *now* placed in the social market of fortune so I am currently valued—as nothing.[8] At this point the paradox, deploying the model of two climes, functions to give line four another, Donne's real, though covert, reading: I am (not as I *am*, but) as I am *circumstanced*. The paradox enables Donne to present simultaneously two versions of the self here: one, the platonic one covertly (I am as I am regardless of social valuation and placing); the other, the one constructed according to market values overtly (I am as I am circumstanced). He puts one against the other in a most complex and rather disturbing form, and asks Lucy to realize his worth in one "clime," the platonic, as "value through use" in the other "clime," that of contingent social situation and of fortune.

On the surface the statement is of course less complicated: the countess has refined him and now he sees that either rareness or use (being used by or of use to someone) brings value. It is precisely the patronage relationship which makes the poet useful to someone who can use him, and therefore valuable. Until he is used his identity is bestowed by his circumstances and, through no fault of his, or of nature, he is circumstanced such that he has no value.

Stanza two now becomes clearer. It refers to the countess but it also refers to Donne. At court he does not appear (either he is physically absent through having no position, or if there is not noticed) because he currently has no value. He places himself in a revealing structural relationship with the countess: her value does not appear at court owing to transcendent height, while his does not appear owing to an opposite *lownesse*. So the structural opposition links him firmly with her, in a link which comes close to an equation. This provides a perfect explanation for the difficulty Grierson recorded, and indeed it would be most odd if such a phrase appeared in one of Donne's patronage poems without precise significance and motivation. The concluding couplet gives us a final confirmation: this is about her and about him. She is the "darke text" (as is the poem, as is his motivation) and "darke texts need notes."

We should ask what or whose need this is. As we noticed earlier, it is most obviously the potential audience of the text, the benighted courtiers. It is also the countess's need, she who is the "darke text" needs to be explicated if she is to be truly valued in the lower "clime." She needs an exegete, like Donne. Lastly, it is Donne's need: exegetes *need* "darke texts," and above all Donne needs to be an exegete, he needs to be of specific use to the countess and the community. Just as the "need" has to be explained, so too with the "must" in the same line. "Some must bee" refers to the exegete, implicitly Donne himself, so that this *must bee* seemingly has the force of an existential imperative, and it echoes the *not be* of line nine. That "not be" takes in both Lucy and Donne; how does the non-existent poet of line nine come into existence as the necessary exegete-usher of line eleven? By being employed: and this employment not only brings him into existence, creates him indeed (as lines 21–2 make explicit[9]), but also brings the countess's virtue into the social world, thus indirectly giving her existence and, as we saw earlier, value. This is an astonishingly delicate combination of begging and self-assertion, and the relations hinted at are very complex.[10] Donne is the created creature, she the creator; he low, she high; he patronized, she patron; he exegete, she dark text; he usher, she virtue, he excluded, she included. Yet she too is excluded until he realises her social potential and value for her. Structurally Lucy and Donne are opposed and yet equated, transforms of each other creating each other from shared invisibility into apparent existence and social value.

II

We have by now accounted for the text's darkness. It lies in the double-layered model Donne uses to understand his complex relationship with his patroness and their mutual relations to the social world and value. But we need to go further. On this level the explanation has entailed an account of the supplicant's perception of himself, and we now wish to explore this perception in more depth. We have made clear the way the first two stanzas offer distinct and contrasting versions of the self. To recapitulate, one version of self thus refers an autonomous self to inherent values which would doubtless be recognized in a platonic utopia or by stoic and platonic individuals who have detached themselves from existing societies and are strong enough to pursue a Crusoe-like existence (without dog or man Friday of course). The other version of self sees it as socially constructed and dependent, either through equal relationships (as those between friends) or the social relations of the market based on rareness, use and contingency. It is not difficult to believe that Donne could see these two versions of the self as competing and contradictory. But then, it is also plausible to see them as complementary, so that only those who do have inherent worth, participating in the platonic forms, *ought* to be usable, find employment and value. Such, however, is obviously not the case in the world which Donne strove so hard to convince about his marketable potential and use. For Donne these competing versions of self-identity became highly problematic and a constant, often agonized, preoccupation, in the period before his ordination.

The two stanzas with which we opened our discussion are thus legitimately seen as explorations of the self. The question of the poet's consciousness of this exploration is one which we have not treated here. Nor do we exclude a range of other possible readings of these stanzas, or for the rest of the patronage poems. But we are suggesting that this reading goes to the heart of these poems and points to their place in Donne's central preoccupations and problems. We believe these neglected poems have much to teach us about these preoccupations and the poetic and intellectual strategies with which Donne confronted them.[11]

The double version of self we have been exploring certainly connects most of the verse epistles, for they are attempts to work out self-identity, polarizing or clustering around one or other of these two basic stances. Above all, it invites us to link abstract metaphysical problems with the concrete reality and pressures of the poet's existence.

One important feature we have touched on in our depiction of the versions of the self in "You have refin'd mee" can now be brought into prominence. We noted that in presenting contrary versions of self-identity and evaluation Donne envisaged his own level of being in a necessarily equivocal way. He does exist in some mode, but he needs refining, and even creation, by a patroness-alchemist; he does not exist or is not visible (lines 7–12) at court, yet he, or some, "must bee To usher vertue." Later in the poem he defines himself as one of Lucy's "new creatures," part of a "new world" created by her (lines 21–22). In other poems to patronesses this tendency becomes an overt assertion by Donne: that he is nothing. In "T'Have written then" he says (again to the Countess of Bedford), "*nothings, as I am, may / Pay all they have, and yet have all to pay*" (lines 7–8). Of course, line seven is paradoxical: the *am* asserts existence, *I am*; and syntactically the verb *to be* functions to relate entities to other entities or to qualities. That second function is prominent here: the classification of an individual, though he exists, as *a nothing*. Classifications are culturally and socially given, conventional and subject to historical change. Nevertheless they tend to assume the force of eternal, changeless forms. This is particularly so as the syntactic form X is Y is used to make classifications established by changing cultures and conventions (e.g. "I am a ratepayer") as well as those relating to the impersonal, natural order (e.g. "The sun is a star"). In this way language blurs the distinction between the two kinds of statements and their reality-status. But over and above that any member of a society is socialized into sets of value systems which become "reality." In other words, if we look at Donne's "actual" situation, even at this, his worst time, we cannot by any stretch of the imagination see him as nothing: a reasonably comfortable house in Mitcham, one or two servants, frequent trips to London, to influential friends who remain loyal and help in a host of ways, access to books, writing poetry which has an appreciative audience, no hunger. . . . To the landless labourer in Mitcham Donne would have seemed the opposite of "nothing." But this only confirms the strength of the conventionally given quality of perception, which meant in Donne's case that not being of the court group was not being at all. For Donne therefore these lines do not have the force of paradox: *being* is defined in terms of membership of the group to which he aspires: creation is therefore a social act, the act of admitting, drawing in the individual to the group.

Nevertheless, no sooner has Donne offered a negative version of self reflecting his present social situation than he proposes a contrary version of the self as having a transcendental and valuable identity: "Yet since rich mines in barren grounds are showne, / May not I yeeld (not gold) but coale or stone?" (lines 11–12). Donne is certainly at the moment barren ground, in so far as he is anything at all. Yet in the same breath he *assumes* that he is also a rich mine. This draws, precisely in the ways we have shown before, on the versions of the self as having intrinsic value, whatever the social market value. But the image is mostly subtly chosen for it also informs the patron of the self's potential market value, however hidden that may be. The intrinsically valuable platonic, private and independent self turns out to be as much the property of the patron as the public social self. In specifying the kind of rich mine (line 12) it may be that Donne loses confidence, moving from coal to stone. But whatever the exact market value, this hidden self is certainly cashable. Indeed, he suggests the most valuable kind of mine: a gold mine (negation being the permissible way of articulating the nearly forbidden). Still, however high the self-estimation, however much he feels he has a self beyond the *nothing* which he is socially, the clash between secret hidden core and apparent social identity forces him to invoke an external agent to strip away this surface (where before it was to burn away impurities), to dig up the riches, so that he may "yeeld" the riches to someone else. Syntactically *yield* always occurs in forms such as "*yielded* something for/to someone," where the *someone* is never *I*. Thus the image and the syntax are tied absolutely into *use*, commerce and markets. The social creator is here revealed as a potential and willing social user and exploiter, while creation turns out to be the discovery of market value in the human being. Conversely, the sense of nothingness, negation, has a social origin— namely, the absence of such exploitive use. Again, the metaphysics of annihilation, of being and of nothingness, the fundamental questions of identity raised in these poems find very tangible social explanation.

"Creation" becomes a specific term here, meaning admission to the desired social group. Some present members of such groups had membership from the beginning and did not need creation. But the process is a general one and may apply to any individual at any social level in relation to any coveted group. The only exception to this is the king, hardly surprising in the time of James I, Donne's ultimate patron, who proclaimed that kings "are not onely Gods Lieutenants vpon earth, and sit vpon Gods throne, but even by God himselfe they are called Gods."[12] In the poem "To Sir H. W. at his going Ambassador to *Venice*," the king fulfils the role of creator for Wotton: "And (how he may) makes you almost the same, / A Taper of his Torch, a copie writ / From his originall . . ." (lines 4–6). This view of the individual and society encourages one to ask whether it was a common mode of perception at that time or especially found in any specific group; or whether, for example, Donne's origins from an institutionally excluded group—the community of Roman Catholics—disposed him to view self in this way. Much more work on the lines we are suggesting will be necessary before satisfactory answers can be given.

The source of the creator's credentials could become problematic for anyone who is not totally content to accept the social order and the processes maintaining it. This is, in fact a constant concern in the epistles, and is the obverse of his anxiety about his own lack of being, his own lack of credentials. In the light of this consideration, lines such as these from the opening of "You have refin'd mee" take on a peculiarly bitter and ironic tone: "now I see / Rareness, or use, not nature value brings; / And such, as they are circumstanc'd, they bee." It is the removal of his blindness which makes him see this unpalatable truth; the countess is indeed creator, though not because of her inherent virtues or nature but because this is how she happens to be circumstanced. The removal of his own blindness makes him see the more massive blindness of the social system to which he seeks admission. Donne's reiteration of the theme that the countess's virtue might go unrecognised (and so her value diminish) except for his good offices takes on a somewhat darker note in this context; here Donne covertly assumes for himself the role of creator. The situation is complex enough for Donne to see himself as nothing, as inherently valuable, and possibly as creator, all simultaneously. All these involved shifts are firmly related to a highly specific set of social relationships. Discussions which perpetually divorce the literary language, the psychological, and the social, will inevitably introduce grave distortions and prove limiting in disabling ways.

We have space to glance at only one more patroness poem, "To the Countesse of Salisbury" in 1614. The first half of this poem ("Faire, great, and good") uses material from "A nocturnall upon S. Lucies day" and the two Anniversaries for Elizabeth Drury. Donne argues that "all is withered, shrunke, and dri'd / All Vertues ebb'd out to a dead low tyde," with all striving for universal annihilation, "to draw to lesse, / even that nothing, which at first we were" (lines 1–21). In this state she, the patroness, like the Countess of Bedford or Elizabeth Drury is the female creative deity: "you come to repaire / Gods booke of creatures" (lines 7–8).[13] And as we saw in "You have refin'd mee," however much Donne may negate his being in response to the social situation he simultaneously puts an intrinsically valuable self as her seer and exegete (lines 31–6, 65–74). Yet, once more, this stage is superseded as he acknowledges that it is the countess herself who (like God here too) illuminates the dark text he is able to study. The poem concludes with a similar movement worked out in terms of a socially given blindness (lines 75–84). This is contrasted with an intuitive angel-like vision which transcends the lack of "social eyes" through inner illumination. Characteristically, Donne does not leave the matter here. Just as the angelic intuition is actually dependent on a higher power, so Donne's illumination depends on a higher power within the profane, social world—the Countess of Salisbury (lines 71–4, 79–82).[14] Again metaphysical language and imagery actually mediates and transforms specific social relationships. To understand and describe this process is not reductive of Donne's art or his metaphysical stratagems: quite the reverse, we follow the full implications and subtlety of the art and metaphysics Donne is using to manage, under grave difficulties, the social situation which was absolutely central to his psychic, intellectual and poetic development.[15]

III

One way of grasping Donne's situation is in the terms proposed by Mark Curtis and Michael Walzer in their studies of intellectuals and their employment in Donne's England. Both historians point out that during the early Stuart period there was a group of intellectually trained people unable to find a "place," either in the church (on which both concentrate) or in the state. Walzer and Curtis see them as "alienated" from the society's leading groups, to which they felt they had a right to belong. The origins of the exclusion were complex, due in part to an overproduction of graduates, in part to continued pluralism and non-residency which decreased the number of livings for those leaving university, and in part to disadvantageous changes in the patterns of patronage. Though this subject needs detailed study, it seems clear that this group was large in terms of the total number of intellectuals in the community. Curtis sees them as "an insoluble group of alienated intellectuals who individually and collectively became troublemakers in a period of growing discontent with the Stuart regime."[16] Puritan lectureships offered one important oppositional institution for at least some members of this group, but Curtis presents them as essentially isolated in their alienation, though they did "exhibit an *esprit de corps* that both originated in their peculiar specialized function and marked their self-conscious alienation from the rest of the clergy."[17] Here Walzer's study differs seriously from Curtis's. He agrees that this group bred "trouble-makers" who were absolutely central in the development of radical politics in Stuart England, but he sees these "advanced intellectuals," these "free men," as specifically *Puritan* intellectuals, men "capable of organizing themselves voluntarily on the basis of ideological commitment," men committed to "enthusiastic and purposive activity" in new associations *outside* the traditional patterns, ties and institutions of Elizabethan England.[18] In his *The Revolution of the Saints* he offers an acute and nuanced account of the wider group of "alienated intellectuals," providing essential ideological and psychological discriminations which allow deeper insight into the varied processes and causes of this alienation and radicalization. Walzer's richer model allows us to understand the position of Roman Catholic clerics and intellectuals—a very necessary factor when one is concerned with Donne, a member of a Romanist family which included martyrs. Catholics were estranged from the established institutions, just as the saints were, and Walzer notes "significant parallels" between the two groups of alienated clerics: "the priests had taken the lead in the Catholic struggle and their new power—somewhat like that of the

Puritan clergy—was related to the collapse of the traditional lay leadership. Among the Catholic clerics the Jesuits especially resembled the Puritan ministers both in their impatience with episcopal control and their willingness to experiment politically." But, and in Walzer's view this is vital, the Catholic experience was not formed by a radical ideology, for they were "closely bound to the traditional social order and were most often willing to work within the limits of the feudal connection of lord and chaplain. The ultimate effect of their labour was to create a pariah culture, an enclave of secure traditionalism." This formed a strong contrast to Calvinist intellectuals who depersonalized and objectified social and ideological conflicts and tended towards organization "outside the traditional structure of authority, placing less emphasis upon great personalities."[19]

If we look at Donne in this light, certain of the complex, contradictory features which we have been highlighting become more intelligible. As Walzer's work illustrates so well, the processes which lead to the formation of such specific groupings inevitably mark the individuals involved psychologically and ideologically.[20] Donne, in this period, provides a classic example of an excluded intellectual. Structurally, he *started* from an excluded position as a Roman Catholic, a member of a group exiled from the political nation. This initial exclusion was not based on the kind of self-consciously acquired and held ideological commitment which Walzer described in Calvinist intellectuals. Quite the contrary, he was born into this situation, so that his struggle from the very beginning was to overcome an exclusion forced on him by an inherited ideological position for which he seems to have shown very little conviction.[21] His aim was *incorporation*, not opposition to established church, court and state. In gaining employment with Egerton he seemed to have succeeded in this and could look forward to a secure career within traditional institutions. However, his secret marriage to a social superior led to a new exile. Again the exile was not based on ideological commitment, so that even that sustaining force was not available to him.

Thrown back into the position of the alienated intellectual, Donne's feelings and ideas were complex, as we have seen in our discussion of the patroness poems. There he explored the new position in which he found himself; indeed, he constructed a complicated metaphysics in which a platonic model of eternal value was set off against a market model of use. Donne's critical attitude to the world which excluded him, and his self-estimation were bound up with the former model; yet he clearly wanted a place in the market and so had to assert his use as a secular servant, as usher/ideologue. Hence in his version of self the subtle sycophant[22] was always accompanied by the critical "troublemaker" who deployed the platonic model subversively against the values of the leading social groups into which he longed to be incorporated. Whereas the Puritan alienated intellectuals developed an ideology exalting their alienation, which they saw as a kind of freedom, and which enabled them to organize against the powerful established groups excluding them, Donne had no such sustaining ideological support, and hence could not see his exclusion as "freedom." All his efforts were directed towards inclusion in the traditional established group. While his use of the platonic model helped him to cope with the despair of his exile, and thus worked analogously to the Puritan intellectual's view of "freedom," it was never intended as a programme for social change: Donne wanted inclusion in the securely established traditional order, and in this he was therefore not all that far from the political tendencies of the Roman priests.

We now have a dual model of alienation: on the one hand the radical "free man," with an ideologically buttressed programme for social change, on the other hand the sycophantic seeker for admission to a securely established traditional order. We have shown some of the forces which lead to either position. We now need to ask whether those who belong to either group show any traces of the other position. In terms of our methodology and hypothesis we need to look at the poetry of those who had gained admission to see if there are signs of alienation. Of course some of Donne's earlier poems will do here, and in fact some of his "stoic" poems which we discuss below, are an excellent case in point, as some of these were written while he was with Egerton. We intend to show that they offer a social critique, but an unconvincing one, with the ring of a rote performance to them, as though it was the fashionable "thing to say" among a group of people. If this is so, then we have an example of people who are included, but who nevertheless deplore what Curtis described as "galloping venality and creeping monopoly [which] had combined to poison the sources of patronage. They were not only distasteful but frequently revolting to some well-intentioned, prospective servants of the State. Complaints about the Court and the indignities of waiting on patrons and winning influence . . . took on in these years overtones of disillusionment and even disgust that formerly had been less obvious."[23] Curtis places this in the reign of James I, and clearly this is too late; furthermore we should note that not just prospective but some actual servants of the state found these things unsavoury. So one question that arises from Curtis's remarks and which relates very closely to our analysis of Donne's position is whether the attainment of a place did in fact overcome and do away with the indignities of the situation at court or in patronage.

Donne's early stoic poems suggest that it did not. Other evidence is provided by such apparently untroubled work as Jonson's *To Penshurst*. We do not have the space here for a detailed analysis, but a brief look at the negations in the poem will quickly reveal disturbances beneath the seemingly untroubled classical surface. The negations permit Jonson to call up—in denied form—the positive forms of assertions which it would be difficult, prohibited or even dangerous for him to make. He uses two types of negation, overt negation—forms with *not, no, un-*; and covert negations—forms which have a semantically negative content: "these *grudg'd* at"; and forms which work by "replacing" a form which should or might have been more appropriate. The negations cluster around four topics: the history of the house, the present state of the house, the position of the patronized poet, and the place and function of this house in relation to others like it. We will give some illustrative quotations, and indicate in outline how the negations work. First then the history of the house. Line 1: "Thou art not, Penshurst, built to envious show"—where a past action is presented as a present state, and the present state is contrasted with that of all other houses; line 6: "these grudg'd at [thou] art reverenc'd the while"— the denial of the application of the general rule in this case; lines 45–47: "thy walls . . . are rear'd with no mans ruine, no mans grone, / There's none, that dwell about them, wish them downe,"—here again we find the overt negation of a state that applies to all other houses and, more tellingly, a straightforward rewriting of the history of the house, which, as Raymond Williams points out, was built on the ruins of an enclosed village.[24] Here we have a revealing insight into the use of negation: a troubling reality which the poet wishes, somehow, to control and to transcend, and which surfaces in the form of the negation of that reality. The negations surrounding the present state of the house concern, as Williams again has pointed out, the complete transformation of social and human processes into natural ones. This process is perhaps best described as negation by transformation; human agents, human labour, social relations, are negated and presented instead as thoroughly and unquestionably natural ones. The major examples of this are in those passages where nature of itself, unasked, provides its riches for the house; natural entities act as agents providing for the depersonalized house. Two examples will show the process— lines 19–20: "Thy copp's . . . never failes to serve thee season'd deere,"; line 24: "The middle ground thy mares, and horses breed." In fact this process extends to the production of exotic fruits: fig, grape, peach, apricot, without any human effort.

The position of the patronized poet is presented predominantly in terms of negatives: again this serves to call up what may be regarded as the normal situation, and in which a nervousness regarding his own situation also shows itself—

> Where the same beere, and bread, and self-same wine,
> That is his Lordships, shall be also mine.
> And I not faine to sit (as some, this day,
> At great mens tables) and yet dine away.
> Here no man tells my cups; nor, standing by,
> A waiter, doth my gluttony envy:
> But gives me what I call, and lets me eate. . . .
>
> (lines 63–69)

This passage calls up starkly and vividly the humiliation of situations which Jonson must have known and, judging by the immediacy of the language, felt himself. Last but not least there is the negation, implicit in this text, of all those poems that could and should have been written about the reality of the country house period. The prohibition on that however was so strong as to amount to total self-censorship by any poet who wanted patronage.

We are forced to ask about this intellectual, who in Curtis's terms is *not* alienated, is he undisturbed, untroubled? What is his motive for his production of a patronage poem, a poem which involves such a massive re-ordering and reclassification of the social world, and of known history? Is not this very act of producing a poem as a commodity to be exchanged for the "lord's owne meate . . ." the very sign of alienation? Not now of course alienation in the sense of Curtis and Walzer, but in one classic sense, where the producer sells his labour-power as a commodity to a master who unilaterally determines in what commodity this labour-power shall be manifested.[25] Of course, this is the situation, within the Marxist model, of all labour until the coming of the socialist millenium; however, it is the starkly apparent application and working of this model in the sphere of poetry which we find revealing here; and it may be both useful and necessary to add this notion of alienation to the dual model outlined above.

Donne, at least partly, sees the patronage situation in this way. In his quest for incorporation he reluctantly accepts the necessity of turning himself, his abilities, and certain of his poems which are absolutely overt tokens of exchange—witness the usher and mine images—into commodities. Alienated and critical intellectual that he was, he had no wish to be excluded from the traditional ruling circles, and no ideology to encourage an oppositional stance which would entail action with new associations, and he certainly had no wish to be a "troublemaker." Our approach to Donne from this perspective suggests to us that the whole issue of "the alienated intellectual" in this period not only casts light on his own situation but also needs considerably more research done on it. This research would include and develop the lines of inquiry and methods of analysis which we are applying to Donne's verse epistles in this article. Ideally it would be a collective enterprise bringing together historians, linguists, and literary critics. One important general question which would be focal in such an inquiry would be at what times certain intellectuals became alienated *and* sufficiently organized to form radical, highly critical groups, acting for change against the reigning hegemony.[26]

IV

We conclude this study by looking at three verse epistles which were *not* written to patronesses. The first two we consider, "Sir, more then kisses" (To Sir Henry Wotton) and "Like one who in her third widdowhood" (To Mr Rowland Woodward) were probably written around 1597–1598, a decade before the poems which we have just considered and, significantly, before

Donne was dismissed by Egerton and ejected into a social wilderness inhabited by these various "alienated" intellectuals.

It is striking that in these two poems Donne assumes a simple version of the self, one having a virtually autonomous existence, identity without social relationships, and certainly without "creators." The disturbing issues about alternative versions of the self and its value, central in the later patronage poems are, at least on the surface, conspicuous by their absence. Donne assumes that the individual can retreat into a safe, inherently and unproblematically valuable core. The world around may be obnoxious but the individual has his own mental and moral edifice into which he may retreat, like the snail (To Sir Henry Wotton, lines 49–52).

Given this stance, it is not surprising that Lawrence Stapleton, one of the few critics to attend to the verse epistles with seriousness, should claim, that in those letters, written before 1600, Donne reveals "the assumptions by men of his circle, of a stoical attitude of detachment . . . man must dwell in himself, to house his spirit, as the snail his body."[27] Nevertheless, the same critic registers something odd about these apparently stoic poems: "The reader feels indeed that in such verses as this Donne is but conning over, genuinely enough, the social lessons of self-mastery . . . Donne had not, of course retired to any of the uncongenial country residences that he later owed to the help of relatives or friends and resorted to through necessity. He was fashioning an attitude of detachment which might save him from corruption in the world of affairs."[28] Stapleton leaves the issue there; in the context of this study we wish to look more closely at the "stoical attitude" and the stoic self which Donne seems to be cultivating here.

Having roundly abused the whole social world, countries, courts and towns, Donne offers Henry Wotton the following advice:

> Be thou thine owne home, and in thy selfe dwell;
> Inne any where, continuance maketh hell.
> And seeing the snaile, which every where doth rome,
> Carrying his own house still, still is at home.
> Follow (for he is easie pac'd) this snaile,
> Bee thine owne Palace, or the world's thy gaile.
> And in the worlds sea, do not like corke sleepe
> Upon the waters face; nor in the deepe
> Sinke like a lead without a line: but as
> Fishes glide, leaving no print where they passe,
> Nor making sound; so closely thy course goe,
> Let men dispute, whether thou breathe, or no.
> (lines 47–58)

Stapleton's feeling that Donne is here "but conning over . . . social lessons of self-mastery" seems to be a response to the flaccid, simple-minded version of the self informing this passage. There is no recognition that the self may well have internalised unpleasant aspects of the social world which Donne attacks (but inhabits—and ambitiously so), no acknowledgement of the individual's complicity in the state of the society to which he owes his continuing work and existence, no sign that there is any tension between participation and retreat.[29] In Christian terms, one might add, such "stoical" stances are surprisingly blind to the effects of the fall—the corruption of the will and blindness of the intellect. There are one or two hints of these vital problems: "Let no man say there, Virtues flintie wall / shall locke vice in mee, I'll done but know all," (lines 35–6); and at line forty-eight: "Inne any where, continuance maketh hell." This suggests that retreat into the self will have to come to terms precisely with evil inside. But this hint is not developed and these earlier poems are innocent of the real difficulties involved in questions of identity discussed above.

Nevertheless, while the surface suggests no complexities, when we look at the poems more closely they reveal movements which make us doubt that the stoic stance was ever at all congenial to Donne, let alone seriously held as a conviction to live by.

The version of self in the poem to Sir Henry Wotton advocates retreat leading to stasis and peace. The external world's instability does provide a threat, and we noted the hinted threat from internal vice. But no change of self is envisaged or demanded: the snail remains a snail within the house, the fish glides along leaving no print and remains exactly the fish it has always been. In the poem to Mr. Rowland Woodward the beginnings of an analysis of self are evident. It has been spatialized so that "wee" may turn into "our selves":

> So wee, if wee into our selves will turne,
> Blowing our sparkes of vertue, may outburne
> The straw, which doth about our hearts sojourne.
>
> (lines 22–24)

That is, the self has become an inner and outer self, with the inner seen as the heart around which there is the straw of the outer self. The latter can be burned off. Here then is an advocacy of change.

However, if we consider the interactional structures of the poem to Sir Henry Wotton we find the stasis we described rather undercut. The whole poem is organised as a dialogue. Overtly it begins with an address to a friend, in a formal tone; it ends in a gently earnest plea for the friend's love. The overall frame of the poem is thus address and plea, an interaction, and the overt content of the poem needs to be read within this context: retreat, in tension with the interaction of the friend. Contained within this overall frame are the linguistic forms of interaction: commands, questions, statements, mirroring the alternating forms of conversation. Furthermore, they are conducted in the form of intimate address: thou, thine, thy.

In other words, in its formal structure the poem is the very antithesis of retreat: it is constructed around the core forms of the language of social interaction, and whatever version of self is depicted in the apparent stoic pose, there is a deeper version where the self is defined in interaction with others. The others are friends, intimate, and the poet seeks their love, which seems essential to him. With this in mind we can see how the disturbance at lines thirty-five, thirty-six and forty-eight reflects the way the retreat is a very limited one, with the continuing, and sought after support of friends. So the two versions of self in the poem to Wotton are straightforwardly contradictory.

Yet we are struck by the amazing confidence with which, despite this, Donne's poem exhorts his friend to behave and act in ways which seemingly follow from an uncomplicated stoic stance toward the world. This combination of confusion and confident advice, urges us to examine the underlying view of social processes that allows such contradictions and even makes them seem unproblematic. To do so we shall look at the syntactic forms, first pointing out the agents operating in the poem. A selection serves to indicate the kind of agents they are. Initially, some non-human ones: *They* (Rockes, Remoraes) break or stop ships (lines 7–9); *Virtue's flintie wall* shall lock vice in me (lines 35–36). Then some human ones: *men* play princes (lines 23–24); *men* retrieve and greet themselves (lines 43–5). Third some passives, with the agent deleted: two temperate regions *girded in* (line 13); you, *parch'd* in court, in the country *frozen* (line 15); shall cities *be chosen* (line 16); falsehood *is denizon'd* (line 34). In the first group, non-human agents act concretely on other entities, and the actions are physical ones, making, breaking, curing, locking. In the second list, human agents act, but significantly the actions are not direct, concrete, nor do they act on other entities. Instead they are reflexive (e.g., "retrieve and greet themselves") or non-physical actions, "see," "know," ("play-actions" literally, such as "playing princes"). In the last group, the passives, we have no way of recovering who the agents were—who "froze," "parch'd," "built," "denizon'd."

Without further analysis we think it sound to claim that *men* are perceived and presented as peculiarly inactive, passive, reflexive; the real agents are non-human, concrete or abstract. The imperatives from line forty-seven onwards ("Be thou thine owne home and in thy selfe dwell . . . Follow . . . this snaile . . . Bee thine owne Palace . . .") are no exception, for while they do advocate actions by human agents they are figurative actions which are difficult to understand precisely or to perform: they exhort the addressee to be in a certain kind of state, rather than indicating the processes which would lead someone to be in that state. The poem discloses a failure to grasp specific and relevant agents, an inability to specify the processes and agents by which or by whom the new state is to be implemented. In short, there is a marked lack of understanding of processes, agents, and causations in the world. Yet Donne has superimposed a seemingly confident stoic stance on this uncertainty. His shaky perception of agency and process explains the presence of the non-stoic formal frame and the plea for friendship, a call for support. The underlying content of this poem might then be described as being about interaction, but one which proceeds without clear grasp of the "ground rules" of processes in the social world.

The second of the pre-1600 poems we are considering is to Mr. Rowland Woodward, "Like one who'in her third widdowhood." This has many elements in common with the poem to Sir Henry Wotton just discussed and is open to very similar comment. As Donne advises, "Seeke wee then our selves in our selves" (line 19), we see that the active self is still envisaged as unproblematic in its autonomy, and the complicated perceptions of the patroness poems are again absent. Lines thirty-one onwards may appear to contradict our judgement: "Wee are but farmers of our selves, yet may, / If we can stocke our selves, and thrive, uplay / Much, much deare treasure for the great rent day." Here farming, thriving, stocking and uplaying treasure may seem to be the very stuff of known social practice and relationships. We believe not, for the field and its cultivation is figured as purely individualistic and autonomous while the market in which the produce can be cashed for payment of rents is a heavenly one, located outside society and beyond history, at the Last Judgement. Despite the apparent Christian dimension here, and despite the explicit mention of original sin and the doctrine of imputed merit (lines 13–18), the self is again envisaged in such a way that the problems about corruption of the will and intellect, or the need for grace in farming the self, let alone questions about the complex interactions between individual and society, cannot arise. Nevertheless, as in the poem to Sir Henry Wotton, the poem has an interactional structure, e.g., "*You know*, Physitians, when they would infuse" [line 25, our italics] and ends not only with assurance of Donne's love for Woodward, but a strong statement of his need for Woodward's love in return: "But to know, that I love thee'and would be lov'd" (line 36). The intense need for love is expressed in a command to Woodward to love him, a most un-stoic conclusion.[30]

Clearly, there are continuities between the poem to Wotton and this one; the version of the self is a little more elaborate here and the "stoicism" a little more openly uncertain. If we look at agency, as we did in the other poem, interestingly enough we find a large number of the human agents involved in real, physical processes (though "metaphorically" used to indicate psychological processes): gathering the sun's beams, blowing sparks, outburning straw (lines 20–24). There are far fewer passives, and the deleted agent is in all cases Donne himself (or one of his attributes): *tyed* to retiredness (line 2); seeds *were sown* (line 6); *betroth'd* (line 8). The imperatives are commands to perform actions: manure thyself; with vain outward things be no more moved; to thyself be approved (lines 34–5). Compared with the poem to Wotton there is an increase of agentiveness, awareness of agency, and the realization of what are possible processes which men may carry out to reach a desired state. This increase in the poet's awareness of what social interaction and change could be about is accompanied by signs of a decrease in emphasis on the linguistic forms of interaction, as though a progress in understanding the causes of action leads to a progress from talk to action.

Of course, the stoic stance is classically one which the alienated intellectual may assume. We are interested to note—beyond the versions of self revealed—the uncertainty with which Donne holds this stance, an uncertainty which, as our analysis reveals is based on his wish for incorporation (the plea for friend-ship, the interactional forms) and an insufficient understanding of social processes. The latter may be a direct consequence of the fact that he was not, as we have pointed out, committed to an ideologically based critique of his society.

In conclusion we turn briefly to a poem written in the period of the patroness poems discussed above. In 1610 Donne addressed "Man is a lumpe" to Sir Edward Herbert, the son of one of his patronesses. The shifts in Donne's approach to the self which had taken place over the preceding ten years in his drastically changed circumstances of renewed "exile" are clear. They link up with the attitudes to self we discussed in relation to his patronage poems. This poem, written to a friend, fellow poet, and fellow philosopher, shows much of the obsession with negativity and annihilation (social and metaphysical) so marked in the patroness poems. The possibility of a virtuous and unequivocally valuable inner core, held out to Wotton and Woodward earlier, is now much further removed as he offers a traditional, compound platonic-Christian image of man composed of destructive and warring beasts which can only be con-trolled by equally destructive energies directed against the self, and a vision of a Christian God viciously indifferent to the fate of his creatures. Despite some surface suggestions that man may act autonomously to transcend internal wars and external social relations, in fact we get a version of the self and of society which is extremely close to that we described in the contemporary poems. Man in general only acts reflexively—given that "the beasts" and "nature" are his *own* beasts and his *own* nature. And though his "businesse is, to rectifie / Nature, to what she was" (lines 33–4), we note that immediately Donne shows that this is not what man does, for "wee'are led awry." In all this Donne seemingly presents the friend as a means of overcoming the viciousness of man's existence. However, the last few lines of the poem undercut any such reading decisively:

> You have dwelt upon
> All worthy bookes, and now are such an one.
> Actions are authors, and of those in you
> Your friends finde every day a mart of new.
> (lines 47–50)

The friend produces, every day, actions, which are authors, which are books. And every day there is a market of these actions/authors/books. The principle of commodification is applied to the actions of the friend/patron; his friends, the real authors, may buy and may plagiarize. If the friends are poets in need of patronage they buy the already written texts; so the book or poem which Donne writes to the friend is not in fact written by Donne the poet, but by the friend/patron. Here the friend acts analogously to the patroness/creator, for while she creates the poet and with him his future actions and values, the friend in appropriating the very labour of the poet creates him as poet. The reality, as Donne presents it, is that the friend negates the actions of the poet and thereby the poet. The implications of this stance are if anything an even more savage comment by Donne on his society, where even those whom he calls his friends and lovers reduce him to powerlessness and inferiority. Here the friend is like the creator of the patroness poems; despite the negative view which Donne presents of this friendship, he needs it, either to be created, or written into the social world which he views so critically.

Notes

1. J. Danby, *Elizabethan and Jacobean Poets* (originally published as *Poets on Fortune's Hill*, 1962), ch. 1.

2. "Donne's assumption is the relationship of poet to patron as of nothing to everything, and out of this he spins his conceits direct. He makes metaphysics out of the poet and patron relations, and a poet-patron relation out of metaphysics," *Elizabethan and Jacobean Poets*, p. 39.

3. See R. C. Bald on this period in *John Donne: A Life* (1970), ch. 8; see too Donne himself in letters reprinted by E. Gosse, *Life and Letters of Donne* (reprint 1959), especially vol. I, pp. 114–15, 166, 181, 185–187, 191.

4. All quotations are from *Donne's Poetical Works*, ed. H. J. C. Grierson (1912, reprint 1966), vol.I; referred to hereafter as Grierson. We have also used W. Milgate's edition of *The Satires, Epigrams and Verse Letters* (1967).

5. Grierson, vol.II, pp. 156–7; cf. Milgate, pp. 256–7.

6. See M. H. Curtis, "The Alienated Intellectuals of Early Stuart England," *Past and Present*, 23 (1962), reprinted in *Crisis in Europe*, ed. T. Aston (1965). On Donne's desperate wish for "incorporation" see the letter to Goodyer in Gosse, vol.I, pp. 191–2.

7. One of the best studies of this issue is by R. Ellrodt, *L'inspiration personnelle et l'esprit du temps chez les poètes métaphysiques anglais*, 3 vols. (Paris, 1960), vol.I, especially chs. 3–4.

8. As Danby suggested, Donne is obsessed with his nothingness (note 2, above). For examples of the explicit social causes for his sense of being *nothing*, and its remedies, see especially prose letters in Gosse, vol.I, pp. 181, 167, 191–2, and on loss of employment as death, for example, p.291; also vol.II, pp. 28, 42; and the verse epistles to the Countess of Bedford and the Countess of Salisbury.

9. See previous note.

10. In contrasting Donne with Jonson, very much at Donne's expense, Danby, like other commentators, misses these rich complexities in Donne's stance.

11. Nor is the manner in which the concept of self is being explored in these poems confined to Donne. That questions about value in just the way we are discussing were current in the milieu from which Donne received his training, is suggested by Shakespeare's *Troilus and Cressida* which includes, among its central preoccupations, a study of conflicting versions of value and their relation to social fabric and metaphysical frameworks.

12. James I, 1609 speech to Parliament, in *The Political Works of James I*, ed. C. H. McIlwain, (reprint 1966), p. 307.

13. There remain important connections to be examined with the political Petrarchanism cultivated under Queen Elizabeth and discussed in L. Forster, *The Icy Fire* (1969). The theological vocabulary in patron poems has also been studied by B. K. Lewalski in *Donne's Anniversaries* (1973); relevant here are chapters 1 and 2: her approach (well illustrated in comments on p.46) tends to isolate the metaphysical and the social in a way, we think, which distorts both areas.

14. It is worth noting how Donne is contemptuous of the market contingencies which donate those very same social eyes he actually covets so strongly!

15. Indeed, we believe the kind of analysis here advocated can be fruitfully applied to many of Donne's poems, secular and religious, and in due course we hope to do just this.

16. M. H. Curtis, *op.cit.*, pp.299, 312, where he also refers to G. E. Aylmer's study, *The King's Servants* (1961), chs. 3–4. For Walzer see *The Revolution of the Saints*, (1965), chs. 1–4.

17. Curtis, *op.cit.*, pp. 308–311.

18. Walzer, *op.cit.*

19. Walzer, *op.cit.*, pp. 130–132; see chs. 4–6 *passim*.

20. Probably it is worth drawing attention to the relevance of the work of the Frankfurt School to this area of study. See especially: M. Horkheimer, *Critical Theory*, (1972); T. Adorno, *Minima Moralia*, (1972), and "Society," *Salmagundi*, 10–11, (1969–70), pp. 144–153; H. Marcuse, *One-Dimensional Man* (1972).

21. On Donne's early life see especially R. C. Bald, *John Donne*, chs. 1–4.

22. Not always so subtle: see the letters to Rochester which Gosse sadly called "somewhat ignominious," published in the *Life and Letters of John Donne*, ed. Gosse (1959), vol.II, pp. 22–23, 28; on this episode see Bald (extremely sympathetic to Donne), *John Donne*, pp. 272–274, 313–14.

23. Curtis, *op.cit.*, p. 312.

24. R. Williams, *Country and City* (1973), pp. 27–34.

25. See especially, I. Meszaros, *Marx's Theory of Alienation* (1972), ch. 4; B. Ollman, *Alienation* (1971), part three. Also relevant here is C. B. Macpherson, *The Political Theory of Possessive Individualism. Hobbes to Locke* (1964).

26. Walzer has some suggestive speculations on this topic in his conclusion to *The Revolution of the Saints*.

27. L. Stapleton, "The Theme of Virtue in Donne's Epistles," *SP*, 55 (1958), pp. 187–200, reprinted in *Essential Articles for the Study of John Donne's Poetry*, ed. J. R. Roberts (1975), pp.451–2. On the date of "Sir, more then kisses," see Milgate, *op.cit.*, pp. 227–8, and Grierson, *op.cit.*, vol.II, pp. 140–1.

28. Stapleton, *article cit.*, p.452.

29. There is no space here to contrast the profound explorations of such issues in Marvell's *Upon Appleton House*.

30. The conclusion of a classic contemporary stoic poem, Ben Jonson's fine *To the World* ("False world, good night") provides the essential contrast here.

The Obscure Object of Desire: Donne's *Anniversaries* and the Cultural Production of Elizabeth Drury

RONALD CORTHELL*

READING INTO THE *ANNIVERSARIES*

In his recent book on Donne's *Anniversaries*, Edward Tayler complains that "[l]ike *Lycidas* and *Hamlet*, the *Anniversaries* have come to function as hermeneutical barometers in the sense that the commentary on them seems to betray rather more about the critics and their cultural climate than about the poems themselves."[1] This was so from the first readings of the poems. Ben Jonson damned them as blasphemies and Donne defended them as the expression of an "Idea of a Woman." Academic critics have always been drawn to the poems. In the work of Coffin and Nicolson, now neglected or dismissed but formerly influential in forming a generation's views of Donne and his period, the *Anniversaries* were central to their theses of a decentered century. Two of the most important theories of seventeenth-century English literature to emerge between the New Criticism and New Historicism, were generated by work on the *Anniversaries*. Louis Martz's "poetry of meditation" offered not only an explanation for the structure of the poems but also an historical analogue to New Critical claims about poetry as the fusion of thought and feeling; Barbara Lewalski's historical investigation of the particular symbolic mode of the poems is a prolegomenon to her theory of a "protestant poetics" in devotional literature of the period. More recently, the first full-blown poststructuralist account of Donne, Thomas Docherty's *John Donne, Undone*, finds in the poems a paradigm of Donne's writing as a transcendental masquerade.[2] Aiming "to set the record straight," Tayler himself draws upon intellectual history to discredit Lewalski's highly influential book and, apparently, to inoculate readers against new historicist and other poststructuralist interpretations still to come. Tayler's own critical preoccupations are inscribed in his reading. As Antony Easthope argues, "Literary value is a function of the reader/text relation, and cannot be defined outside the history in which texts—some more

*This essay was written specifically for this volume.

123

than others—demonstrably have functioned intertextually to give a plurality of different readings transhistorically: the greater the text, the more we are compelled to read it through a palimpsest of other interpretations."³ The *Anniversaries* are a strong case in point.

Most readings of the *Anniversaries* have been devoted to determining *what* is being represented in the poems. More recently, aspects of the how and why of representation—social and material conditions of production—have been emphasized.⁴ This essay aims to balance this recent new historicist critique of representation against a psychoanalytic notion of identification in order to argue for the importance of desire in the process of producing and interpreting the *Anniversaries*. I approach the two *Anniversaries* entitled "An Anatomy of the World" and "The Progres of the Soule," the poem entitled "A Funerall Elegie," the prefatory poems by Joseph Hall, and the critical tradition—the *Anniversaries* palimpsest—as the construction of a subject of Donne. Under "a subject of Donne" I include the following interrelated positions: the speaking subject who produces (and is produced by) Elizabeth Drury as the Idea of a Woman for Sir Robert Drury in the two *Anniversaries*; the academic subject "John Donne" produced by readings of the *Anniversaries*; and the reading subject who produces (and is produced by) that "John Donne" and who thereby also instantiates a relationship between the Renaissance and the present.⁵ In all three processes of subjectification I mean to emphasize the psychological investment in the work of producing Elizabeth Drury as the centering "shee" of the poem and to explore the role of desire, particularly in the form of identification, in this production of the enigmatic "shee."⁶

The *Anniversaries* construct, and are constructed by, "the *Idea* of a Woman." In *The First Anniversary* the Idea is mostly felt as absence and loss ("shee's dead"). This loss is represented through images of weakness and disintegration "wherein," as the subtitle tells us, "the frailty and decay of this whole world is represented." *The Second Anniversary* gradually pulls away from the imagery of the world's decline, recuperating speaker and reader through a positive identification with Elizabeth as a religious master signifier of power.⁷ This recuperation, I will suggest, is also implicated in an aesthetic ideology. In Hall's prefatory poems the processes of idealizing Elizabeth and of anatomizing the dead world are presented as the work of art; according to Hall, the *Anniversaries* enact what Stephen Greenblatt would call "aesthetic empowerment," by which ideological work is transformed into the work of art.⁸

But Drummond reported that Donne claimed to have described the Idea of a *Woman*. In the many readings of the *Anniversaries* surprisingly little is made of Donne's gendering of his idea, except in a broadly typological or symbolic register.⁹ I think it is significant that the poems are occasioned by the death of the daughter of a would-be patron. A reading such as mine, which places pressure on the work of ideology, must consider the relationship between representation, identification, and the idea of a woman in the production of

the subject of the *Anniversaries*. In the patronage relationship within which
the poems originated, but which by no means contains them (witness the
"misreadings" of Jonson, a poet of patronage, and of some of Donne's female
patrons), the *Idea* of a *Woman* is produced by a transaction between a lost
daughter, a father, and her male celebrant ("let thy makers praise / Honor thy
Laura," writes Joseph Hall in "The Harbinger to the Progres"). Lynda Boose's
arresting thesis is pertinent here: "Inscribed within patriarchal narrative is
something more specific than just a general erasure of woman. What is
specifically absent is the *daughter*."[10] One might say that the daughter "is
specifically absent" both in Donne's poems—since they focus on the absent
daughter of Sir Robert Drury—and in commentary on the poems, which is
chiefly concerned with discovering a symbolic value for the missing "shee"
(i.e., which sustains the absence of the daughter). This is another way of
saying that the signifying economy of loss and recuperation that produces the
empowered reading subject of the *Anniversaries* is also a male economy of
desire.

"MOTION IN CORRUPTION"

As their individual titles—"An Anatomy of the World" and "Of the Progres
of the Soule"—suggest, the *Anniversaries* are poems of process or movement.
"An Anatomy of the World" locates the subject of the poem (that is, Donne,
Elizabeth Drury, and readers) somewhere between death and life. Early in the
"Anatomy" Donne seems to back down from the claims of the master conceit
of the poem—that the world is dead, its soul having departed:

> For there's a kind of world remaining still,
> Though shee which did inanimate and fill
> The world, be gone, yet in this last long night,
> Her Ghost doth walke. . . .
>
> (67–70)

This curious condition of being both dead and alive is repeated in one of
Donne's most spectacular passages, at the opening of *The Second Anniversary*:

> Or as sometimes in a beheaded man,
> Though at two Red seas, which freely ran,
> One from the Trunke, another from the Head,
> His soule be saild, to her eternall bed,
> His eies will twinckle, and his tongue will roll,
> As though he beckned, and cal'd back his Soul,
> He graspes his hands, and he puls up his feet,

> And seemes to reach, and to step forth to meet
> His soule. . . .
> . . . .
> So strugles this dead world, now shee is gone;
> For there is motion in corruption.
>
> (10–21)

Donne pronounces the world dead, but then refuses to allow it to stay dead, breeding "new creatures" "from the carcasse of the old world." We might expect these creatures bred by twilight's influence to be revolting and fleshly (Manley cites Hamlet's sun, breeding maggots in a dead dog); instead we get something more like Eliot's "Lilacs out of the dead land, mixing / Memory and desire"—"So many weedlesse Paradises" (82).

This scene of Donne's ideological work is the twilit place of abjection, the world as a wasting corpse, the limiting body that we wish to cast off ("abjacere"). This condition has been related to the signifying process by Julia Kristeva in *Powers of Horror*.[11] For Kristeva the abject is that which must be expelled in order to take up a stable position in the symbolic order. As Elizabeth Grosz summarizes, "Abjection is a reaction to the recognition of the impossible but necessary transcendence of the subject's corporeality, and the impure, defiling elements of its uncontrollable materiality"; thus, "Abjection is the underside of the symbolic. . . . It is an insistence on the subject's necessary relation to death, to animality, and to materiality, being the subject's recognition and refusal of its corporeality."[12] I will later discuss how Donne, like Kristeva, locates the abject on the side of the feminine, but for now I want merely to use Kristeva's analysis to highlight the interdependence of Donne's projects of constructing an Idea of a Woman and anatomizing the corpse of the world. The production of Elizabeth as a an "Idea of a Woman" is dependent upon both the "recognition and refusal" of the body.

In addition to its manifestations in the breeding cadaver, the ghost, and the animate beheaded man, this abjection is most apparent in the First Anniversary's discourse of the body; it is a discourse of the abject—of rottenness, decay, sickness, disease, maiming, infection, disproportion, disfigurement, ugliness, monstrosity, and atomization, to use Donne's vocabulary in "An Anatomy." The poem famously comments on the disruption of "identity, system, order."[13] More subtle is the abjection underlying Donne's equally famous glorification of Elizabeth's body in "The Progres of the Soule." In sharp contrast to the limitations of the flesh and the impurities of the ordinary body, ". . . her pure and eloquent blood / Spoke in her cheekes, and so distinctly wrought, / That one might almost say, her body thought" (244–46). This purified body stands opposed to the abject bodies of the beheaded man, the ghost of Elizabeth, and most of all the putrifying yet paradoxically generative corpse of the dead world.[14]

The subject of the *Anniversaries* is constructed in the intermediate space opened up by Donne's anatomy of the dead world and his projection of a world to come—the world haunted by Elizabeth's ghost, the horror show of the beheaded man at the opening of *The Second Anniversary*: "motion in corruption." Both poems oscillate between languages of loss and recuperation, or rather they generate a language of plenitude from a language of loss and desire. This paradox is what Hall identifies as the curious experience of reading the poem: one feels empowered by Donne's account of powerlessness. Or I should say, someone feels empowered, but not everyone. The *Anniversaries* work to the degree that the reader can enjoy their recuperative display of desire, and this display, I want to argue, is gendered masculine.

TEEN ANGEL

To my knowledge, Arthur Marotti is the only critic who has suggested, even in passing, a psychoanalytic approach to the *Anniversaries*. Viewing the poems in light of Donne's political failure, he argues that they are "about loss and the need for recovery" and that their satiric scorn and idealization are "stances suitable to one responding strongly to narcissistic injury."[15] Marotti's biographical interpretation understandably leads him to consider Donne's personal narcissism, but I believe he has also touched upon an important feature of the culture of patronage to which the *Anniversaries* contribute.

In his paper "On Narcissism: An Introduction" Freud distinguishes between "object-libido" and "ego-libido" or narcissism, and tracks the survival of the latter in such adult forms as parental overvaluation of children and the lover's overvaluation of the beloved.[16] In the case of the *Anniversaries* parental overvaluation seems joined to another revival of narcissism which Freud treats at length in the paper, the formation of an ego ideal: "This ideal ego is now the target of the self-love which was enjoyed in childhood by the actual ego. The subject's narcissism makes its appearance displaced on to this new ideal ego, which, like the infantile ego, finds itself possessed of every perfection that is of value" (SE 14: 94).[17] Paradoxically, satisfaction of this revived ego-libido is bound up with surveillance and harsh judgment of the ego; Freud suggests that "what we call our conscience [later to be named the super-ego] has the required characteristics" of "a special psychical agency which performs the task of seeing that narcissistic satisfaction from the ego ideal is ensured and which, with this end in view, constantly watches the actual ego and measures it by that ideal" (SE 14: 95). This aspect of the operation of the ego ideal leads Freud, in a concluding paragraph, to suggest a link between psychological and social processes: "In addition to its individual side, this ideal has a social side; it is also the common ideal of a family, a class or a nation" (SE 14: 101). In the *Anniversaries* Donne's combination of satire and praise could in many ways be seen as narcissistic. The harsh judgment of the world and corresponding construction of "the Idea of a Woman and not as she was" recuperates a lost self-regard for Donne; for Donne's patron, the father of Elizabeth Drury; and for a society that appears to be in decline.

I have mentioned Robert Drury, Elizabeth's father and Donne's patron, but I have failed to mention Lady Drury. It remains for me to explain my interpretation of the *Anniversaries*, poems that commemorate the loss of a daughter and celebrate the Idea of a Woman, as poems that call the reader to a masculine subject-position. Narcissism and "what we call our conscience" play key roles in this argument. Freud discusses both of them as distinguishing features of melancholia, a type of response to loss privileged in the Renaissance (and, according to Giorgio Agamben, exemplified in Donne). Freud's analysis of this condition helps explain several features of the *Anniversaries*. I do not wish to claim that melancholy is the key to the mythology of the poems, but rather to suggest how Donne's work of recuperation and our own efforts at interpreting the poems are bound up with what Juliana Schiesari has discussed as a gendered "symbolics of loss."[18] The search for the symbolic identity of Donne's "shee" mimics Donne's own quest for a lost and transcendent object of desire. Scholar and poet are united in their melancholy, the mark of great *men*.

Freud's "Mourning and Melancholia" reads in places like a commentary on the critical history of the *Anniversaries*. He notes that both mourning and melancholy may be reactions "to the loss of a loved object." But, "in yet other cases [the cases that interest Freud] one feels justified in maintaining the belief that a loss of this kind has occurred, but one cannot see clearly what it is that has been lost." That is, we might know "*whom* he has lost but not *what* he has lost in him."[19] As Schiesari points out, this distinction "refocuses attention not on the lost *object* but on the loss, on the 'what' of the lost object, whose thingness points back to the *subject* of the loss (not the 'who' that is lost in mourning but the 'who' that presents himself as losing in melancholia)."[20] In interpreting the *Anniversaries*, this translates into the work of discovering *what* is lost (Wisdom, the regenerate soul, etc.), rather than who is lost (the Elizabeth Drury never seen by Donne). More important still, this shift of focus from the lost figure to the one who presents himself as losing is related to the fundamental distinction Freud draws between melancholia and mourning on the basis of narcissism. The "work of mourning" consists of the gradual detachment of the libido from the lost object, leaving the ego "free and uninhibited again"; melancholia, on the other hand, involves the importation of the lost object along with "the shadow of the object" (the mysterious "what" that the melancholic lost) into the ego by means of "an *identification* of the ego with the abandoned object" (SE 14: 249). Such narcissistic identification explains the melancholic's harsh self-criticism, the "impoverishment of his ego on a grand scale" (SE 14: 246). As Schiesari explains, "this shadow thus draws apart a portion of the ego into an identification with the lost object, over and against which the remaining portion of the ego can rage to assuage the narcissistic wound of its abandonment."[21] By means of this economy, the melancholic recuperates his loss in the form of moral superiority (SE 14: 257). Finally, the ostentatious display of loss functions, as Schiesari points out, like a fetish in both affirming and denying loss; "the melancholic display of loss paradoxically increases the value (hence accumulating to the gain) of the subject of loss. . . . In other words, the greater the loss, the greater the wisdom or 'truth' claimed by the loser, who then profits from this turn of psychic events by gaining from the loss."[22]

As indicated earlier, I do not so much wish to press this psychoanalytic interpretation on John Donne as to suggest a narcissistic dynamics at work in the *Anniversaries'* cultural production of Elizabeth Drury. Such an understanding thickens the description of Donne's writings as a product of a culture of patronage, a description that always threatens to reduce writing to a bid for support or an embittered reaction to failure to receive support. What interests me is the mutually-sustaining relationship between client and patron—a relationship not entirely explained by economics, on the one hand, and the important cultural work of recuperation performed by the poems, on the other.[23]

As both R. C. Bald's *Donne and the Drurys* and his biography of Donne make clear, Donne and Robert Drury shared the experience of "unsuccessfully seeking public employment overseas."[24] The Drurys had also lost both their children, the first-born Dorothy having died at age four in 1597 and Elizabeth, of course, just before turning fifteen in 1610. (Donne, on the other hand had six children by this time, the seventh arriving 31 January 1611.) Even allowing for changes in attitudes towards children (particularly female children), these losses were considerable.[25] As Lynda E. Boose notes, "because a daughter was the least economically useful member of a patrilineal and primogenitural institution, social historians tracing evidence such as this have perhaps been overhasty to infer that she was likewise the least-cherished."[26] Cherish is probably not the word to use here, but Shakespeare's plays and Donne's *Anniversaries* are two massive pieces of evidence for the importance placed on keeping daughters. Some of the investments in daughters can be felt now that feminist historians and cultural critics have begun to recover the daughter, heretofore a nearly invisible figure in anthropological studies of the family. Boose's discussion of the father-daughter relationship in terms of exogamous exchange and the incest taboo focusses on the father's loss and returns us to the theme of narcissism: "although the daughter was clearly regarded as legal property inside the family, she has never been a commodity to be bartered in the same way as an ox or an ass. She is explicitly a *sexual* property acquired not by economic transaction but from the father's sexual expenditure and his own family bloodline—which makes the father's loss of her a distinctively personal loss of himself."[27] Boose is concerned with the loss of the daughter to another man in marriage or to "the world of paternal institution" outside the father's house, but her main point—the "distinctively personal loss of himself" that is bound up with the loss of a daughter—would seem to hold for the loss of a daughter in death (and, ultimately, to the definitive world of paternal institutions) as well.

It is, so far as I know, an unchallenged assumption among commentators that the *Anniversaries* have virtually nothing to do with the "real" Elizabeth Drury.[28] I believe the ease with which Elizabeth has been dismissed needs to be examined. What I have been suggesting is 1) that the extravagance of the *Anniversaries* might in fact resonate to the felt loss of Robert Drury; 2) that the loss of a daughter can be seen as a defining instance of the narcissistic loss described by Freud;[29] and 3) that the *display* of such loss participates in a tradition of melancholy writing devoted to recuperating male loss.

As I implied earlier, nearly every major reading of the *Anniversaries* could be cited in support of the theory of narcissistic loss in two respects: the readings explicate the poems in literary terms that correspond with Freud's analysis of melancholia; and the readings themselves, like Freud's essay, declare their solidarity with the tradition of melancholy genius by recovering the hitherto lost moral truth of the poems and by adopting their rhetoric of superlatives— e. g., Tayler's claim that they are "the two greatest poems written between *The Fairie Queene* and *Paradise Lost*."[30] Nearly everyone agrees that Donne is not mourning the loss of Elizabeth Drury. Rather, she is is "a kind of counterpart image for the self, a symbol" (Earl Miner), "a *symbol* of virtue that may fitly represent the Image and Likeness of God in man" (Louis Martz), "a poetic symbol" of the "Image and Likeness of God in Man" (Barbara Lewalski)—all corresponding to Freud's mysterious "*what* he has lost in him" (in this case, her; SE 14: 245).[31] Recent studies that forgo a symbolic approach tend to be more explicit, if inadvertent, in advancing the thesis of narcissistic loss; in addition to Marotti, there is Docherty, who admits to coming "very close to arguing that the poet is in fact none other than Elizabeth Drury," and Tayler, who purports to "set the record straight" by exposing the fallacies and anachronisms of all previous interpretations and who concludes his study with a chain of equations—"Poet is poem is subject is reader."[32]

These scholar critics follow the logic of the writing of the *Anniversaries*. The melancholy equation of loss and gain, "wherein a kind of satisfaction is gleaned in the idealization of loss *as* loss, in the perpetuation and even capitalization of that sense of loss,"[33] is announced in the first lines (if not in the title) of Hall's "To the Praise of the Dead, and the Anatomy" and is carried through both prefatory poems: "Wel dy'de the world, that we might live to see / This world of wit, in his Anatomee." In "The Harbinger to the Progres" Hall quite explicitly presents the capitalization of loss as literary "immortalitie":

> So while thou mak'st her soules Hy progresse knowne
> Thou mak'st a noble progresse of thine owne,

> From this worlds carcasse having mounted hie
> To that pure life of Immortalitie.
>
> (27–30)

Less obvious, perhaps, is the degree to which the project of recuperation depends upon an emptying of Elizabeth's corporeal womanhood. This theme is sounded in "A Funerall Elegie," published with the first edition of the "Anatomy" but probably written before it,[34] where a remarkable description of Elizabeth's ethereal body—elaborated in famous lines in *The Second Anniversary* already cited (241–46)—prepares for the remarks to follow, upon Elizabeth's fortunate escape from marriage. Donne compares her newly-assigned place to newly-discovered stars:

> So the world studied whose this peece should be,
>   Till she can be no bodies else, nor shee:
> But like a Lampe of Balsamum, desir'd
>   Rather t'adorne, then last, shee soon expir'd;
> Cloth'd in her Virgin white integrity;
>   For mariage, though it doe not staine, doth dye.
> To scape th'infirmities which waite upone
>   Woman, shee went away, before sh'was one.
>
> (71–78)

As Docherty also notes, it is important for Donne that the deceased was a girl of 14, before, as Donne remarked of another woman in his "Epithalamion Made at Lincoln's Inn," she had the chance to marry and "put on perfection, and a womans name." In psychoanalytic terms, Donne seems here to capture something of what Freud treated in his essay "On Narcissism" as an aspect of woman's difference. Freud observes that some women display a self-contentment and inaccessibility which resemble the child's charming narcissism. Sarah Kofman, in her close critical reading of Freud's writings on women, summarizes the argument. "What is attractive, what accounts for all the charm of this narcissistic woman, is not so much her beauty. . . . [W]hat is attractive in woman is that she has managed to preserve what man has lost, that original narcissism for which he is eternally nostalgic. It may thus be said that man envies and seeks that narcissistic woman as the lost paradise of childhood (or what he fantasizes as such). . . ."[35]

If this idea of a woman stands in for Donne's own loss, the corporeal, sexual, married woman, on the other hand, is identified with original loss in Donne's misogynistic account of the Fall, which occurs in the section of the "Anatomy" on the "dangers and diseases of the old" world. "We are borne ruinous" (95): the sickness of the world is immediately linked to women through a joke on the birthing process that makes mothers appear partly to blame for it. This leads easily enough to the epigram, the "first mariage was our funerall" (105), and the further elaboration that "singly, one by one, they kill us now" (107). Rather than opposing regenerate souls and the old world of sin, Donne here presents original sin and death, its consequence, as caused by woman's frustration of even "Gods purpose." The speaker is thus aligning himself and the reader with a subject position gendered as masculine. The loss or lack represented by Elizabeth Drury's death is traced back to the "One woman" who, "at one blow, then kill'd us all" (106). As Manley notes in his commentary, this is usually said of Adam; Donne's substitution of Eve allows him to generate two paradoxes that bear upon the "Anatomy" as a whole. Although the woman is made the agent of man's original sin, man now happily gives himself over to dying: "We do delightfully our selves allow / To that consumption" (108–109). The phrasing is very subtle here: the word "allow" preserves some male pride; women are still the active party in sex—"they kill us now" (107). From here it is a short step to the commonplace that orgasm shortens life: "We kill our selves, to propagate our kinde" (110).

Marotti describes these passsages as "comic antifeminism" and refers to the claim about orgasm "a flimsy folk belief."[36] I find nothing in the texts or contexts of the *Anniveraries* to support a "comic" interpretation of these lines. On the question of orgasm, the research of Thomas Laqueur would suggest that this view had a currency that extended beyond folk culture.[37] The paradox of reproduction that underlies the belief has, in fact, proven to be remarkably durable, turning up in Freud as the victory of species over individual and in Lacan as the statement "that the living being, by being subject to sex, has fallen under the blow of individual death."[38] In the "Anatomy" itself, Donne devotes the next two subsections to wittily expatiating on the "flimsy" commonplace in terms of reduced life spans and "smaleness of stature."

Of course, the overriding reason for replacing Adam with Eve is the symmetry achieved by balancing Eve's sin against Elizabeth Drury's innocence. Donne empties Eve of her sin, or her womanhood, which amounts to the same thing, to produce Elizabeth as the Other Woman, or the Woman as Other (soul of the world), the knowledge of which becomes the guarantee that he exists (i.e., that he has a soul):

> When that rich soule which to her Heaven is gone,
> Whom all they celebrate, who know they have one,
> (For who is sure he hath a soule, unlesse
> It see, and Iudge, and follow worthinesse,
> And by Deedes praise it? He who doth not this,
> May lodge an In-mate soule, but tis not his.) . . .
> —"Anatomy," 1–6

This sense of self entails membership in an elite—those who "see, and Iudge, and follow worthinesse." As Schiesari points out, such a "difference from the common *vulgus* is the sign of the melancholic's virtue and intellect," particularly as the melancholy man was revised by Ficino into "one whose quest for knowledge is inspired by an eros that fuels his desire for a relationship with the transcendent."[39] But more important here is the interpellation of the reader as an elite soul mate through a process of mirroring, also narcissistic in structure, whereby the reader sees himself in the poem, which itself mirrors the rich soul: as Hall puts it, "Admired match! where strives in mutuall grace / The cunning Pencill, and the comely face" ("To the Praise of the Dead, and the Anatomy," 17–18).[40]

In his brilliant essay on "The Articulation of the Ego in the English Renaissance" William Kerrigan proposes "that there is a form of narcissism, as well as a form of the imaginary anatomy, peculiar to Renaissance literature."[41] In terms obviously relevant to Donne's *Anniversaries,* he remarks that "the anatomy of the [Renaissance] ego might coincide, through language, with the structures and textures of the cosmos—a (relatively) benevolent narcissism that helps to explain the pronounced integrity of Renaissance literature, its disaffinity with fragmentation" (303). But this cosmic ego risked dispersion: "the Donne of the *Anniversaries* . . . dilated the snug human world outward into the potential diffusions of the cosmos," and ultimately, with the coming of the new cosmology, "anthropomorphism was exposed as a solely interior phenomenon" (300, 301). If this is the historical moment of the *Anniversaries,* its turn toward interiority is also supported by narcissistic identifications, the mutual admiration society of Elizabeth Drury, Donne, Hall, and all "who know they have one" ("Anatomy," 2).

In that phrase, I hear all "who know they have the phallus." By "one," of course, Donne means a soul, but this soul is carefully separated from female qualities in Donne's construction of the Idea of a Woman.[42] The knowledge that one has a soul, emphasized at the outset, is dependent on the denigration of the corporeal woman. The *Anniversaries* can then recover narcissistic loss by constructing the woman as a powerful Other capable of securing for the speaker and reader a position of wholeness and self-knowledge.[43] Janel Mueller, with considerable understatement, has recently noted that this project "often take[s] us a great distance from any recognizable female presence."[44] As "Aire and Angels" demonstrates, this elevation of woman to the place of the Other entails a countermovement to restore a position of male dominance. Elizabeth Drury is mirrored by Donne and the reader. "Poet is poem is subject is reader."

This position entails an escape from Eve, both as lover and mother. Thus in *The Second Anniversary,* Donne, apparently in imitation of Christ,[45] celebrates the Virgin "more for being good, / Then for her interest, of mother-hood" (343–44). More interesting still is his inversion at the opening of the "Progres":

> Immortal Mayd, who though thou wouldst refuse
> The name of Mother, be vnto my Muse,
> A Father since her chast Ambition is,

Yearely to bring forth such a child as this.
These Hymnes may worke on future wits, and so
May great Grand-children of thy praises grow.

(33–38)

This fascinating sequence encapsulates the process of male loss and recuperation that fuels the *Anniversaries*. Donne at once wills the maid into fatherhood
and becomes himself a kind of mother of "hymnes" that will inseminate
"future wits."[46] The restoration of loss that is the work of "The Progres of the
Soule" is represented here as a patriarchal transmission, a tradition, of "hims"
of praise.

Donne's "shee" covers an absence at the center of the poem. Donne fills it in
with a variety of impossibilities—regenerate soul, Wisdom, and Queen Elizabeth are a few that have been suggested. It seems that none can stick, because
the loss that Donne keeps gesturing toward cannot be represented; as Donne
writes in *The First Anniversary*, "ruine," in the form of woman, "labour'd to
frustrate / Euen Gods purpose" (99–101), and "The world did in her Cradle
take a fall" (196). There was and is, it appears, no paradise other than the
paradise within. It is always tempting to present Donne as a titanic subjectivity
at work, capable of eclipsing the sun with a wink. But the argument I have
tried to advance here is the inverse: not a subject at work, but work towards
producing a subject.

At the outset of *The Second Anniversary* Donne remarks upon this aspect
of process in the poems: "Yet in this Deluge, grosse and generall, / Thou seest
mee striue for life" (30–31). In this respect I find the *Anniversaries* to resemble
what Julia Kristeva terms "works in progress": "Art is the possibility of
fashioning narcissism and of subtilizing the ideal. . . . A life, a work of art: are
these not 'works in progress' only in as much as capable of self-depreciation
and of resubmitting themselves to the flames which are, without distinction,
the flames of language and of love?"[47] The striving of the *Anniversaries* is away
from corporeality, women, and especially mothers toward an object of desire
nominally female—"shee"—but actually, as Mueller has noted, "a great
distance from any recognizable female presence." In Kristeva's terms, it is a
rewriting into a religious symbolic (the Lacanian symbolic order, that is) of
the "semiotic *chora*"—"the place where the subject is both generated and
negated, the place where his unity succumbs before the process of charges and
stases that produce him."[48] Kristeva cites the virgin birth as a foundational
example of this process in the Christian symbolic: "In asserting that 'in
the beginning was the Word,' Christians must have found such a postulate
sufficiently hard to believe and, for whatever it was worth, they added its
compensation, its permanent lining: the maternal receptacle, purified as it
might be by the virginal fantasy."[49] In this context Jonson's oft-quoted criticism, "that he told Mr Donne, if it had been written of ye Virgin Marie it had

been something,"[50] is sharpened to disclose the severity of Donne's patriarchal bias; Elizabeth Drury died a pubescent virgin, and that, Donne says, is all to the good.

Such a denial of the material origins of the subject, the cost of a successful entrance into the symbolic order, can leave the subject, as John Lechte writes, "at the level of a static, fetishized version of language."[51] Donne's repetitive, ritualized use of the signifier "shee" works like the fetish both to display and deny loss. He even seems to acknowledge this aspect of his work as a type of "mis-devotion" at the close of *The Second Anniversary*, where he alludes to the fact that he wrote the poem while attending Sir Robert Drury in France:

> Here in a place, where mis-devotion frames
> A thousand praiers to saints, whose very names
> The ancient Church knew not, Heaven knowes not yet,
> And where, what lawes of poetry admit,
> Lawes of religion, have at least the same,
> Immortal Maid, I might invoque thy name.
> Could any Saint provoke that appetite,
> Thou here shouldst make mee a french convertite.
>   (511–18)

Donne immediately corrects himself; there is finally only one, paternal Word:

> But thou wouldst not; nor wouldst thou be content,
> To take this, for my second yeeres true Rent,
> Did this Coine beare any other stampe, then his,
> That gave thee power to doe, me, to say this.
>   (119–22)

This move pulls the cover off Donne's object of desire, his "shee," to disclose it as a stand-in for male loss.[52] "Shee" is the site of men's discourse on loss and recuperation. These and the following lines create a homology between secular and divine "power," "will," and "Autority"—between Sir Robert Drury and God:

> his [Sir Robert's, God's] will is, that to posteritee,
> Thou shouldest for life, and death, a patterne bee
> And that the world should notice have of this,
> The purpose and th'Autority is his.
>   (523–26)

In this unexpected allusion to the client-patron relationship that informs the *Anniversaries* ("my second yeeres true Rent") Donne both acknowledges and restores Sir Robert's loss and his own lack: "I ame / The Trumpet, at whose voice the people came" (527–28).

Donne's progress of the soul and Julia Kristeva's "work in progress" move toward opposed ends—his to a point of stability, a transcendental signifier, hers toward motility, openness, heterogeneity. But what characterizes both is motion, a foregrounding of the signifying process. In *Revolution in Poetic Language* Kristeva asks: "In short, isn't art the fetish *par excellence*, one that badly camouflages its archaeology? At its base, isn't there a belief, ultimately maintained, that the mother is phallic, that the ego—never precisely identified—will never separate from her, and that no symbol is strong enough to sever this dependence?" Kristeva goes on to complicate what at first sounds like a rhetorical question. Although "the poetic function . . . converges with fetishism," she writes, "it is not . . . identical to it. What distinguishes the poetic function from the fetishist mechanism is that it maintains a *signification*." That is, the text "is not a *substitute* but a sign."[53] The kinaesthetics of the *Anniversaries*, whether "motion in corruption" or stringing of beads and stars and "little bones of necke, and backe" ("Progress," 212), "maintains a signification" despite efforts to use them as a substitute for a lost Renaissance, to restore their lost meaning, their lost Renaissance context, once and for all.[54] But such scholarly labors of restoration are only complicitous with Donne's working toward a final, religious "Proclamation," a man's Idea of a Woman, one that depends on not knowing her "as she was."[55]

Notes

1. Tayler, *Donne's Idea of a Woman: Structure and Meaning in* The Anniversaries (New York: Columbia University Press, 1991), 2. Tayler's complaint is a grumpy version of T. S. Eliot's 1931 disclaimer of his earlier views on Donne: "It is impossible for us or for anyone else ever to disentangle how much was genuine affinity, genuine appreciation, and how much was just a *reading into* Donne our own sensibilities . . ." (quoted in John R. Roberts, "John Donne's Poetry: An Assessment of Modern Criticism," *John Donne Journal* 1 [1982]: 56.). Unlike Eliot, Tayler is quite certain of his ability to disentangle Donne's from "our own sensibilities."

2. Charles M. Coffin, *John Donne and the New Philosophy* (New York: Columbia University Press, 1937); Marjorie H. Nicolson, *The Breaking of the Circle: Studies in the Effect of the "New Science" upon Seventeenth-Century Poetry* (1950; rev. ed., New York: Columbia University Press, 1960); Louis L. Martz, *The Poetry of Meditation: A Study in English Religious Literature of the Seventeenth Century* (1954; rev. ed., New Haven: Yale University Press, 1962); Barbara K. Lewalski, *Protestant Poetics and the Seventeenth-Century Religious Lyric* (Princeton: Princeton University Press, 1979); Thomas Docherty, *John Donne, Undone* (London: Methuen, 1986). Jonson's criticism of the poems, and Donne's reply "that he described the Idea of a Woman and not as she was," are recorded in *Conversations with William Drummond of Hawthornden* in Jonson, *Works*, ed. C. H. Herford and Percy Simpson (Oxford: Clarendon Press, 1925), 1:133.

3. A. Easthope, *Literary into Cultural Studies* (London and New York: Routledge, 1991), 59. Easthope's argument, I wish to emphasize, is on the side of a historical understanding of the "reader/text relation": "a text of literary value can be distinguished from one with merely historical interest by the degree to which its signifiers have actively engaged with new contexts, contexts different ideologically but also different in the protocols of literary reading in which the text is construed. An historical observation, this is a description of how literary value works, not a definition of what it *is*" (58).

4. See, especially, Arthur F. Marotti, *John Donne: Coterie Poet* (Madison: University of Wisconsin Press, 1986). Tayler argues that the poems are about "a specifically *human* process of intellectual abstraction" (18, my italics). Although my argument turns on a crucial qualification of Tayler's "human process," I share his concern with process and with the relationship between speaker, reader, Elizabeth Drury, and the Idea of a Woman.

5. For a different approach to *The First Anniversary* through the reader, see Kathleen Kelly, "Conversion of the Reader in Donne's 'Anatomy of the World,'" in *The Eagle and the Dove: Reassessing John Donne,* ed. Claude J. Summers and Ted-Larry Pebworth (Columbia: University of Missouri Press, 1986), 147–56.

6. On the importance of desire in ideology, see Mark Bracher, *Lacan, Discourse, and Social Change: A Psychoanalytic Cultural Criticism* (Ithaca: Cornell University Press, 1993), 19–52, and Slavoj Žižek, *The Sublime Object of Ideology* (New York: Verso, 1989). The text I cite for the poems is *John Donne: The Anniversaries,* ed. Frank Manley (Baltimore: Johns Hopkins University Press, 1963).

7. My characterization of the poems is influenced by Lacan's idea of the Imaginary and Symbolic orders, with "The Anatomy" corresponding to a disintegration of imaginary wholeness in the world's body and "The Progress" corresponding to the identification with a master signifier—the idea of a woman—that fills in for the lack touched upon in "The Anatomy." On the concepts of the imaginary and the symbolic orders I have drawn on *Écrits: A Selection,* trans. Alan Sheridan (New York: Norton, 1977), chaps. 1, 3; *The Seminar of Jacques Lacan, Book I: Freud's Papers on Technique 1953–54,* ed. Jacques-Alain Miller (New York: Norton, 1988), esp. chap. 11; and such lucid expositions of Lacan's thought as Kaja Silverman, *The Subject of Semiotics* (New York: Oxford University Press, 1983) and Bracher, *Lacan, Discourse, and Social Change: A Psychoanalytic Cultural Criticism.*

8. S. Greenblatt, *Shakespearean Negotiations: The Circulation of Social Energy in Renaissance England* (Berkeley: University of California Press, 1988), 5.

9. Exceptions, abbreviated though they are, would include Lindsay A. Mann, "The Typology of Woman in Donne's *Anniversaries,*" *Renaissance and Reformation* 11 (1987): 337–50; Ira Clark, "'How Witty's ruine': The Difficulties of Donne's 'Idea of a Woman' in the First of His *Anniversaries,*" *South Atlantic Review* 53 (1988): 19–26; Janel Mueller's paragraph in "Women among the Metaphysicals: A Case, Mostly, of Being Donne For," *MP* 87 (1989):150–51 [reprinted in this volume]; and Docherty's discussion in *John Donne Undone,* 227–31, where the *donna* quickly becomes Donne. Of course, Marjorie Hope Nicolson notoriously gendered Donne's idea as the "she" and "double shee" in *The Breaking of the Circle* (Evanston: Northwestern University Press, 1950), 65–104.

10. Lynda E. Boose, "The Father's House and the Daughter in It: The Structures of Western Culture's Daughter-Father Relationship," in *Daughters and Fathers,* ed. Boose and Betty S. Flowers (Baltimore: Johns Hopkins University Press, 1989), 20.

11. Julia Kristeva, *Powers of Horror: An Essay on Abjection,* trans. Leon S. Roudiez (New York: Columbia University Press, 1982). Kristeva characterizes the abject as neither object nor subject, but something "in-between, the ambiguous, the composite" (4): "The abject has only one quality of the object—that of being opposed to *I.* If the object, however, through its opposition, settles me within the fragile texture of a desire for meaning, which, as a matter of fact, makes me ceaselessly and infinitely homologous to it, what is *abject,* on the contrary, the jettisoned object, is radically excluded and draws me toward the place where meaning collapses" (1–2). See also Chapter 5, ". . . Qui Tollis Peccata Mundi," which relates abjection to Christian relocation of sin in subjectivity.

12. Elizabeth Grosz, "The Body of Signification," in *Abjection, Melancholia, and Love,* ed. John Fletcher and Andrew Benjamin (London and New York: Routledge, 1990), 87–8, 89.

13. Kristeva, *Powers of Horror,* 4.

14. As Elizabeth Grosz remarks, "The corpse signifies the supervalence of the body, the body's recalcitrance to consciousness, reason or will. It poses a danger to the ego in so far as

it questions its stability and its tangible grasp on and control over itself" ("The Body of Signification," 92).

15.   Marotti, 236.

16.   Sigmund Freud, "On Narcissism: An Introduction," in *The Standard Edition of the Complete Psychological Works of Sigmund Freud*, trans. James Strachey (London: Hogarth Press, 1953–74): "If we look at the attitude of affectionate parents towards their children, we have to recognize that it is a revival and reproduction of their own narcissism, which they have long since abandoned" (14: 91). References to this edition will appear in my text.

17.   Freud uses the terms "ego ideal" and "ideal ego" interchangeably. In Lacan's reworking of this passage in Freud, the two terms are distinguished according to Lacan's theory of the imaginary (ideal ego) and the symbolic (ego ideal) orders. See *The Seminar of Jacques Lacan, Book 1*, 118–42.

18.   Juliana Schiesari, *The Gendering of Melancholia: Feminism, Psychoanalysis, and the Symbolics of Loss in Renaissance Literature* (Ithaca and London: Cornell University Press, 1992). Although she does not discuss Donne in her book, Schiesari (110) quotes Giorgio Agamben's study of melancholy, *Stanze: La parola e il fantasma nella cultura occidentale*: "A second epidemic is in Elizabethan England: the exemplary case is that of John Donne" (*Stanze*, 16). My discussion of Freud's "Mourning and Melancholia" is dependent on Schiesari's brilliant chapter, "The Gendering of Freud's 'Mourning and Melancholia.'"

19.   Freud, "Mourning and Melancholia," SE 14: 244–45.

20.   Schiesari, 43.

21.   Schiesari, 47.

22.   Schiesari, 47, 52–53.

23.   For an analysis of the discursive interdependence of suitors and patrons, see Frank Whigham, "The Rhetoric of Elizabethan Suitors' Letters," *PMLA* 96 (October 1981): 864–82.

24.   R. C. Bald, *John Donne: A Life* (Oxford: Clarendon Press, 1970), 240. For fuller account of Donne's relations with Drury see *Donne and the Drurys* (Cambridge: Cambridge University Press, 1959).

25.   The argument for the absence of affective familial relations during this period is most famously set out by Philippe Aries, *Centuries of Childhood: A Social History of Family Life*, trans. Robert Baldick (New York: Vintage, 1962). For an interesting counterexample and a bibliography of debate on this issue, see Margaret L. King, "The Death of the Child Valerio Marcello: Paternal Mourning in Renaissance Venice," in *Renaissance Rereadings: Intertext and Context*, ed. Maryanne Cline Horowitz, Anne J. Cruz, and Wendy A. Furman (Urbana: University of Illinois Press, 1988), 205–24. For a summary of attitudes towards female offspring in the period, see Margaret L. King, *Women of the Renaissance* (Chicago: University of Chicago Press, 1991), 1–80.

26.   Boose, "The Father's House," 45.

27.   Boose, "The Father's House," 46. See also Boose's article, "The Father and the Bride in Shakespeare," *PMLA* 97 (1982): 325–47.

28.   In her suggestive feminist reading, Elizabeth Harvey comments on the ideological significance of Elizabeth Drury's absence from the poems: "That Donne never knew the person he was elegizing and that his depiction of her remains so idealized as to lack any human specificity at all enhances his ability to usurp her speechlessness, her absence, and to colonize her dead spirit, as it were" (*Ventriloquized Voices: Feminist Theory and Renaissance Texts* [New York: Routledge, 1992], 114). Harvey interestingly brings another Kristevan text—"Stabat Mater"—to the poems in order to elucidate Donne's treatment of virginity and motherhood. Her approach to the Donnean "voice" as "a construction that takes place within a cultural and historical matrix" (78) parallels in some respects my notion of a "subject of Donne." Although I emphasize masculinity rather than maternity in relation both to the originating culture of patronage and to the ongoing cultural effect of the poems, I believe our readings are compatible.

29.   In this instance the mysterious "what" that is lost in the object and that Freud says

is "withdrawn from consciousness" (SE 14: 245) would be that which is forbidden by the incest taboo.

30. Tayler, ix.

31. As quoted in Tayler's convenient gathering of "symbolic readings" in *Donne's Idea of a Woman*, 12–13. The statements are taken from Earl Miner, *The Metaphysical Mode from Donne to Cowley* (Princeton: Princeton University Press, 1969); Martz, *The Poetry of Meditation*; and Lewalski, *Donne's* Anniversaries *and the Poetry of Praise*.

32. Docherty, 229; Tayler, ix, 135. Docherty's argument is more complex than Tayler makes it out to be, but it is still ironic that Tayler debunks Docherty for claiming much the same thing that he ends up asserting at the close of his book.

33. Schiesari, 52.

34. See Bald, *A Life*, 240, and Tayler's reconstruction of the cynic's "worst-case" composition history, 5–7.

35. Sarah Kofman, *The Enigma of Woman: Woman in Freud's Writings*, trans. Catherine Porter (Ithaca: Cornell University Press, 1985), 52. Also pertinent to Donne's poetic argument here is Freud's suggestion that the man's overvaluation of the love object is in some cases occasioned by an attempt to regain a plenitude that, again following Freud's characterization of feminine sexuality, would make the man lovable (Freud repeatedly stresses the difference between masculine love, which is active in its aim to love, and feminine love, which is passive in its aim to be loved). In the instance of the *Anniversaries* Donne's attempt to "follow worthinesse" as represented in the soul of Elizabeth Drury will make Donne lovable in the eyes of both Robert Drury and the Eternal Father.

36. Marotti, 239. For two serious yet quite different treatments of Donne's misogyny see Christopher Ricks, "Donne after Love," in *Literature and the Body: Essays on Populations and Persons*, ed. Elaine Scarry (Baltimore: Johns Hopkins University Press, 1988), 33–69; and Achsah Guibbory, " 'Oh, Let Mee Not Serve So': The Politics of Love in Donne's *Elegies*," *ELH* 57 (1990): 811–32 [reprinted in this volume].

37. Thomas Laqueur, *Making Sex: Body and Gender from the Greeks to Freud* (Cambridge, Mass.: Harvard University Press, 1990).

38. On Freud and Lacan see *Feminine Sexuality: Jacques Lacan and the* École Freudienne, ed. Juliet Mitchell and Jacqueline Rose (New York: Norton, 1982), 35; and Jacques Lacan, *The Four Fundamental Concepts of Psycho-Analysis*, trans. Alan Sheridan (1977; reprint, New York: Norton, 1981), 205.

39. Schiesari, 115. The apparently paradoxical combination of this enhanced sense of self and self-loathing is also explained by Freud's analysis of narcissistic loss. The identification of part of the ego with the lost object produces a split in the ego "in which hate and love contend with each other; the one seeks to detach the libido from the object, the other to maintain this position of the libido against the assault"; this ambivalence "is represented to consciousness as a conflict between one part of the ego and the critical agency," and "the ego may enjoy in this the satisfaction of knowing itself as the better of the two, as superior to the object" (SE 14: 256, 257).

40. As Elizabeth Grosz points out, Lacan's famous theory of the mirror stage "can be interpreted as his attempt to fill in the genesis of the narcissistic ego"; "the mirror stage initiates the child into the two-person structure of imaginary identifications, orienting it forever towards identification with and dependence on (human) images and representations for its own forms or outline" (In Grosz, *Jacques Lacan: A Feminist Introduction* [London and New York: Routledge, 1990], 31, 48).

41. In *The Literary Freud: Mechanisms of Defense and the Poetic Will*, ed. Joseph H. Smith, M. D., Psychiatry and the Humanities Vol. 4 (New Haven: Yale University Press, 1980), 289. Other references to this article appear in my text.

42. Schiesari writes of the Renaissance melancholic: "The sense of loss privileges a male subject as historically sensitive or lyrically sentient. *He* is the one privileged to understand and

to speak the loss of God in a philosophical register that reinstates God's omnipotence, the loss of textual authority through a proliferation of citations that seeks to reclaim that authority, the loss of a phallus refound by the very discourse that mourns that loss *insofar as that mourning is marked by a masculine prerogative*" (256). There is also a *class* dimension to this tradition: "melancholy is equivalent to spiritual grandeur and characteristic of certain men in whom is displayed a nobility of line and a nobility of spirit" (258–59).

43. Lacan's formulation in *Encore* seems apropos: "For the soul to come into being, she, the woman, is differentiated from it . . . called woman and defamed." For this passage and for a discussion of the elevation of woman to the place of the Other I am here again drawing on Jacqueline Rose, "Introduction II," in *Feminine Sexuality*, 48–9, 50.

44. Mueller, 149.

45. See Manley's note, which cites Luke 11: 27–28.

46. Manley points out the pun ("hims") in line 37. Ira Clark (23) also comments on these lines and relates them to Donne's larger misogynistic argument. For a rich discussion of maternity and the *Anniversaries*, see Harvey, chap. 3.

47. Quoted from a discussion paper by Kristeva on *"Histoires d'amour—Love Stories"* for the Institute of Contemporary Arts, in John Lechte, "Art, Love, and Melancholy in the Work of Julia Kristeva," *Abjection, Melancholia, and Love: The Work of Julia Kristeva*, ed. John Fletcher and Andrew Benjamin (London and New York: Routledge, 1990), 25.

48. *The Kristeva Reader*, ed. Toril Moi (New York: Columbia University Press, 1986), 95. This passage and Kristeva's extended discussion of "the signifying process" as constituted by the two "modalities" of the semiotic and the symbolic is found in *Revolution in Poetic Language*, trans. Margaret Waller (New York: Columbia University Press, 1984). I am following also Elizabeth Grosz's discussion of religious discourse as a "recoding" of the semiotic in symbolic terms in her critique of Kristeva, "The Body of Signification," in *Abjection, Melancholia, and Love*, 99.

49. Quoted by Grosz, 99, from *Tales of Love*, trans. Leon S. Roudiez (New York: Columbia University Press, 1987), 251.

50. In the *Conversations with Drummond*, Herford and Simpson, 1: 133.

51. Lechte, 27.

52. See Rose, 49: "In relation to the man, woman comes to stand for both difference and loss." See also Schiesari, 111–12. It is curious that Donne uses the image of the coin impressed with the King's seal, which recollects the Aristotelian account of procreation as male form impressed on female matter and also oddly foregrounds the financial client-patron relationship out of which the *Anniversaries* arose. Both nuances make it possible to read the paternal "stampe" as referring to God and to Sir Robert.

53. *The Kristeva Reader*, 115–16.

54. In Lacanian terms, the *objet petit à*, the lost object of desire that would restore the feeling of plenitude, always eludes symbolization. On the *object à*, see Bracher, 40–45.

55. I wish to thank Kent State University's Research Council for a summer grant that enabled me to complete this article.

Quod oportet *versus* quod convenit: *John Donne, Kingsman?*

ANNABEL PATTERSON*

> The much of privileg'd kingsmen, and the store
> Of fresh protections make the rest all poore.
> —Elegy 14

> All the great eulogists—Spenser, Donne, Jonson, Dryden—were profoundly conservative in their politics.
> —Lauro Martines, *Society and History in English Renaissance Verse*

Encapsulated here in the quotation from Lauro Martines is the myth I continue to wrestle with—that most "canonical" writers from the early modern period were "profoundly conservative in their politics," by which Martines means, specifically, monarchical in terms of constitutional theory and elitist in terms of class. In the case of Donne, this legend was given its strong form at the end of the nineteenth century. In 1899 Edmund Gosse delivered his own assessment of Donne as a preacher, which locked him into a class attitude:

> He belonged to an age in which the aristocratic element exercised a domination which was apparently unquestioned. Although of middle-class birth, the temperament, manners, and society of Donne were of the most distinguished order. The religious power of democracy had been discovered. . . . The Rebellion, and still more the success of the Rebellion, driving men and women of incongruous classes close to one another in the instinct of self-protection against the results of a common catastrophe, began the democratization of the pulpit. But of Donne we must think as untouched by a least warning of such a political upheaval. He belonged, through and through, to the old order; was, indeed, in some ways, its most magnificent and minatory clerical embodiment. . . . This unity of purpose, this exaltation of a sovereign individuality, made to command

*From *Reading between the Lines* (Madison: University of Wisconsin Press, 1993), pp. 160–209. Reprinted by permission of the publisher, except for those parts appearing in the following earlier publications, which are reprinted with the publishers' permissions: "All Donne," in *Soliciting Interpretation: Literary Theory and Seventeenth-Century English Poetry* (Chicago and London: University of Chicago Press, 1990), pp. 37–67 and "John Donne, Kingsman," in *The Mental World of the Jacobean Court*, ed. Linda Levy Peck (Cambridge and New York: Cambridge University Press, 1991), pp. 251–72, 347–53.

in any sphere, gave to the sermons of Donne their extraordinary vital power; and if this particular charm has evaporated. . . . it is that the elements in ourselves are lacking, that we no longer breathe the aristocratic Jacobean atmosphere.[1]

We know now, of course, that as a member on his mother's side of a recusant family that included Sir Thomas More, his grandfather William Rastell, who fled to Louvain, two maternal uncles who became Jesuits, one of whom was captured in 1583 and sentenced to death, though not executed, Donne would have had, at the very least, some complicated feelings about what "the old order" was. Gosse's relocation of Donne in terms of class calmly substitutes "belonging" (which can here be only a matter of sensibility or style) for the recalcitrant fact of middle-class birth. But even in psychological terms, Gosse's construction of his subject as a pillar of the establishment can be accomplished only by ignoring everything that makes Donne interesting, paradigmatic of a culture marked by social mobility and contested religious affiliations. Nevertheless, ex cathedra statements like these tend to retain their subliminal effect, even after their bias has been noted.

In the wake of Gosse's portrait (behind which lay the hagiographical *Life* by Isaac Walton, published in 1640 as a sign of the "old order" in a time of political upheaval), the picture of Donne has changed considerably—and yet, in crucial respects, not changed at all. First came Donne's recuperation by Grierson in 1921, and then, more influentially, by T. S. Eliot.[2] It was no coincidence that Eliot chose to elevate Gosse's Donne while demoting Milton, the literary hero of the Whigs. Then came the modern biography by R. C. Bald, which revealed all too clearly Donne's absorption by the Jacobean patronage system.[3] And this was followed by John Carey's iconoclastic study,[4] which boldly converted to a post-Freudian analysis materials that for Bald were simply the occasion for moral evaluation. This more subtle phase of the legend of Donne's "conservatism," though the terms Carey used were "ambition" and "apostasy," requires a more complex refutation. Looking at the middle period of Donne's life, the period immediately before his decision to take orders, Bald was forced to admit that it did not present "a particularly edifying spectacle"; from his letters, especially, Donne appeared to Bald "as one who had mastered the arts of the courtier, and it is clear, even when he finally turned to the Church, that he did not intend to abandon those arts, but to rise by them" (301). Here lies the origin of John Carey's thesis, complete with the term—arts—that he would make structural. Bald struggled with the evidence, and wished to give Donne the benefit of the doubt—"the truth seems to be," he wrote, "that these qualities in him were not essential and permanent traits of his character; rather, they were symptoms of his despair" (301); but he (and Gosse behind him) nevertheless created the premises on which Carey (and after him Jonathan Goldberg)[5] erected their more sinister portraits.

Hagiography's converse, then, was the spectacle of John Donne the careerist, marked by a devouring ego, acting always from expediency, and obsessed with a desire to replicate his sovereign's status and style in his own life and writings. We were told of the "thwarted, grasping parasitic life that Donne was forced to lead"; that after Donne's ecclesiastical promotion "he grew repressive, as people generally do with age and success"; and that "the egotism manifest throughout his career is what impels the poetry."[6] This form of psychobiography sought to account for everything Donne wrote as the fallout of two fatal decisions, which in Carey's chronology are melded into one: the decision to abandon his family religion, shortly after the death of his brother Henry while in prison for consorting with a Jesuit priest in 1593; and the decision to seek advancement at all costs. Not only did the bad conscience Donne suffered while practicing the arts of apostasy and ambition produce its symptoms in the imagistic texture of his poems, but, it was argued, Donne embraced the very powers that had driven his family into martyrdom and outlawry. Carey noted (correctly) that James's presence and doings are insinuated into private poems that appear to deny their importance; but he also believed that this denial was always effected, as it is in *The Sunne Rising* or *The Anniversarie*, in terms of the speaker's claim himself to royal status, to monarchical absolutism: "What the real court and the real king may be doing stays at the back of his mind, and as if to counteract this the poem evolves its announcement of personal kingship. . . . Royalty glowed in the depth of his consciousness. . . . In giving his unqualified allegiance to James, Donne answered the need of his imagination";[7] and Goldberg repeated this observation with the statement that "Donne's self constitution is absolutist."[8]

I do not wish to deny this psychological insight. Carey's approach has considerable explanatory force with respect to Donne's fascination by the terms (martyrdom, recusancy, idolatry, canonization) suggestive of his abandoned and outlawed religion; and Carey was particularly acute on the way intelligence is shaped by early repression, on the "sense of perilous trespass" that made Donne an outsider who both despised those whose rules rejected him and longed for incorporation.[9] But about Donne's politics in the stricter sense Carey was both reticent and mistaken, while Goldberg leaped on the mistake and accentuated it. From the records that Donne left us to consider (and from some that he never intended for the scrutiny of anyone except his closest friends), it is impossible to produce a single-minded person, let alone a coherent pattern of behaviors. The story of Donne's politics is one of self-division and self-contradiction; and we will learn more about both Donne and his culture by noticing the contradictions than by trying to smooth them away.

Before proceeding, however, I must first acknowledge two rather different accounts of Donne's thought and situation. In a study subtitled "Religion, Politics, and the Dominant Culture," Debora Shuger has attempted to replace the over-simple opposition between orthodoxy and its legitimation on the one hand, and opposition and subversive ideas on the other, by a more complex model.[10] Shuger, whose primary topic, despite her subtitle, is theology and ecclesiology (in Lancelot Andrewes, Richard Hooker, and Donne himself), found the *established* religious culture more protean, "probing, and self-critical than has often been assumed" (14–15). Nevertheless, she too sees Donne's sermons as exemplifying his "absolutist theology." In any case, by addressing only an audience that is itself extremely sophisticated in literary theory, the larger political implications of the argument are rendered, by their exclusiveness, innocuous.

The second (though chronologically prior) is Arthur Marotti's account of Donne as a "coterie poet," which begins with the important reminder that Donne's poetry belonged to the world of manuscript circulation and therefore spoke to a self-selected audience in a culturally encoded language.[11] This recontextualization of Donne's work was an important first step in complicating his image and rendering him less amenable to Gosse's confident description. Marotti's able deployment of Inns of Court attitudes and conventions, for instance, led him to pay more attention to the iconoclastic satires and elegies; while his serious investigation of the poetry of compliment, especially as addressed to female patrons, led him to a more subtle account of Donne's relation to the patronage system than Carey's or Goldberg's. In a summary statement poised on the threshold between Donne's youthful and aborted career under Elizabeth and his amazing success under James, Marotti remarked: "Donne was simply neither the social and intellectual rebel nor the flattering importunate courtier: he contradictorily assumed both roles and his complex behavior changed according to circumstances. To characterize him accurately, one need not accept either the hagiographical pattern laid down by Walton . . . or the model of Donne as the intellectual skeptic-hero who refused to compromise himself for crass worldly ends. The fact is that he was both jauntily, if not self-destructively, *subversive of* as well as contritely *deferential toward* the Establishment" (182). Yet the fact is also that Marotti's study, like Shuger's, is directed at what is in effect a contemporary coterie audience; if not the relatively small number of intellectual historians who are up-to-date on literary theory, then the equally small world of Donne specialists.

My own argument is both more straightforwardly polemical and addressed, *deo volente*, to a wider audience. It is what Donne has represented in the institutionalization of literature and literary criticism in general that justifies making him a cause, if not a cause célèbre. I too wish to promote a more nuanced account of his work, or, putting it in human terms, to achieve better justice for Donne by demonstrating that he was never so simply the king's man, never so simply careerist or absorptive of absolutist monarchism as twentieth-century literary critics (with the exception of Marotti) have been led or chosen to believe. To this end, I make central the peculiar products of Donne's transitional period, from 1606 to 1615, when he was clearly engaged in an intellectual agon with his environment—works that Marotti passes over in a few suggestive pages. This message is addressed to any reader of literature who has too easily accepted the paradigm for which I unfairly make Lauro Martines responsible. But because the effect of this focus is to highlight political events (including Donne's own brief experiment with active politics as a member of parliament) and to tackle in some detail what Donne actually thought about absolutist monarchy, the argument may be of some interest also to historians of the early modern period. In particular, this view of Donne's career could shed light on current debates about motivation. If the two major competing models of motivation are principle and self-interest,[12] it may be useful to show how difficult it is, in certain complex political careers, to tell which of these is, from moment to moment, speaking to us from the past through the textual record; which, for this topic, must certainly include literature.

Perhaps more than any other Renaissance poet Donne challenges us to conceive of subjectivity in environmental terms, to see how socio-economic and political circumstances interact with a particular temperament to produce the historical person, who is both partly conscious of the rules by which he must play and partly the director of all his roles.[13] But once we enter the territory where psychobiography and cultural history merge, another Donne legend complicates our task: the myth of maturation and renunciation to which Donne himself contributed. In 1619, putting his life in order before departing for Germany as a member of the embassy James was sending to Bohemia, Donne wrote to Sir Robert Carr, the cousin of the king's favorite and one of Donne's closest friends, and sent him the manuscript of *Biathanatos*, his essay on suicide, along with a letter that, perhaps better than any poem, tells the story of Donne's ambivalences:

> It was written by me many years since; and because it is upon a misinterpretable subject, I have always gone so near suppressing it, as that it is onely not burnt: no hand hath passed upon it to copy it, nor many eyes to read it: onely to some particular friends in both Universities, then when I writ it, I did communicate it: . . . Keep it, I pray, with the same jealousie; let any that your discretion admits to the sight of it, know the date of it; and that it is a Book written by *Jack Donne*, and not by *Dr. Donne*: Reserve it for me, if I live, and if I die, I only forbid it the Presse, and the Fire: publish it not, but yet burn it not: and between those, do what you will with it.[14]

This letter attempts to negotiate a space "between": between "the Presse" and "the Fire," open publication and absolute self-censorship. By the same token, we can imagine a self-characterization somewhere between Jack and the Doctor, in the sense that neither of the two can exist without drawing on the other's resources; and as Jack's book has been kept by the Doctor in a marginal category strangely described as "onely not burnt," so Donne himself exists in an autobiographical limbo between past and present. Unfortunately, this dramatic act of self-division has also inhibited the project of resituating

Donne in the cultural environment that made him, with his own collaboration, what he was. For whatever their motives (polishing or darkening the image), critics and scholars have tended to count on the divide between Jack and the Doctor, in order to save the Donne they prefer from his other self. In addition, the problem of dating posthumously published poems has been bedeviled by Ben Jonson's statement that Donne had written "all his best pieces ere he was 25 years old,"[15] a generalization that begs the question of value. In contrast, I shall argue here that Jack and the Doctor inhabited the same psychic and cultural space—the space between full publication and full suppression—from the time Donne entered Lincoln's Inn in 1592 until his death in 1631; and that reading between the lines of *all* his work (or at least some of the lines of all of the *kinds* of that work) will give us a fairer picture.

Spied Spies and Dark Doubles: The Satires

Nothing he wrote more evidently belonged in that "onely not burnt" category than Donne's satires, which can be roughly assigned to the time when Donne was a law student in London and during his appointment as secretary to Sir Thomas Egerton, the Lord Keeper, in 1598.[16] In another letter, perhaps to Sir Henry Wotton, perhaps in 1600, Donne insisted that "no coppy shall bee taken" of any of the "compositions" he has been and will be sending his friend. "Call not this," he wrote, "a distrustfull but a free spirit": "to my satyrs there belongs some fear and to some elegies and these perhaps, shame. Against both which dispositions although I be tough enough, yet I have a ridling disposition to bee ashamed of feare and afrayd of shame. Therefore am I desirous to hyde them without any over reconing of them or there maker."[17] For reasons that will become obvious, none of the five satires was published during Donne's lifetime (though they evidently circulated fairly widely in manuscript). When the posthumous edition of Donne's poems was being prepared in 1633, the satires (and five of the elegies) were excluded from the license to publish, although at the last minute permission was granted for the satires, perhaps because the object of their critique is so evidently Elizabeth's regime that the licenser thought them safely archaic. But for us they can do more to explain the political Donne than any of the more famous "Songs and Sonets," or any of the Jacobean sermons.

The last of the five is the most clearly Elizabethan. Addressed both to the queen herself, "Greatest and fairest Empress," and to an unnamed justicer who is surely Egerton, the poem bears a certain awkward likeness to Spenser's Legend of Justice. Here the satire is pitched at authorized bribery, that aspect of the patronage system which requires all access to the Law to be mediated by state officials, so that the legal world is divided into two populations, officers and their suitors. Officers adulterate the law; suitors are complicit in its adulteration by paying the fees demanded of them. "Th'Iron Age *that* was, when justice was sold," wrote Donne, implicitly aligning Elizabeth with Astraea and Egerton with Spenser's Artegall, but going one better (or worse): "now / Injustice is sold dearer farre" (lines 37–38).[18] For tactical reasons, Donne briefly offers to separate his two addressees from the abuses of the system for which they are responsible, assuming ignorance in the queen and a desire for reform in the minister:

> Greatest and fairest Empresse, know you this?
> Alas, no more than Thames calme head doth know
> Whose meades her armes drowne, or whose corn o'rflow:
> You Sir, whose righteousness she loves, whom I
> By having leave to serve, am most richly
> For service paid, authoriz'd, now beginne
> To know and weed out this enormous sinne.
>
> (Lines 28–34)

But no sooner has he observed the conventional distinction between monarch and government than he drops the pretense of advising his superiors and returns to his real purpose: advising the have-nots to despair of the system:

> If Law be in the Judges heart, and hee
> Have no heart to resist letter, or fee,
> Where wilt thou'appeale? Powre of the Courts below
> Flow from the first maine head, and these can throw
> Thee, if they sucke thee in, to misery,
> To fetters, halters. . . .
>
> (Lines 43–48)

Like Spenser, Donne alludes to the dubious extension of the doctrine of equity, which when viewed negatively could be seen as extending the power of the judiciary, so that law may be seen as residing not in the words of parliamentary statutes, but in "the Judges heart."[19] The topic was particularly germane in a poem partly addressed to Egerton where, more daringly, Donne extends the reign of injustice to the measures taken against Roman Catholics, who (under Kafka's sign of the Goddess of the Hunt) were tracked down by special officers called pursuivants, and sometimes indicted merely for having in their possession ritual objects of the old religion. Donne invites anger from those who never show it (stoic, coward, martyr) at a scene worthy of Kafka:

> To see a Pursivant come in, and call
> All his cloathes, Copes; Bookes, Primers; and all
> His Plate, Challices; and mistake them away,
> And aske a fee for comming. . . .
>
> (Lines 65–68)

And though he momentarily permits the alternative vision of an absolute, allegorical justice ("Oh, ne'er may / Faire lawes white reverend name be strumpeted"), that possibility is never given narrative space. Rather, it is Law as a personification who dictates economic injustice, who "tells us who must be / Rich, who poore, who in chaires, who in jayles" (lines 72–74). Finally the satirist, it seems, is addressing himself; and the dream of law reform is dissolved in an Aesopian fable about illusion, *The Dog and the Shadow*: "Thou'art the swimming dog whom shadows cosened, / And div'st, neare drowning, for what vanished."[20]

The theme of Law as the heart of an oppressive society had been anticipated in Satire 2, directed against a bad poet who becomes a worse lawyer. This epitome is, however, inadequate to the spreading stain Donne envisages in Elizabethan legal practice and beyond. Far from specifying a particular, isolated charlatan, the poem is packed with wide-reaching charges, some deviously inserted as if they were merely metaphors. For instance, the introductory and secondary theme of bad literature includes a playwright who

> (like a wretch, which at Barre judg'd as dead,
> Yet prompts him which stands next, and cannot reade,
> And saves his life) gives ideot actors meanes
> (Starving himselfe) to live by'his labor'd sceanes.
>
> (Lines 111–14)

So the primary theme of bad Law enters surreptitiously, in parenthesis. It also enters ambiguously; for though the comparison between poverty-stricken playwright and condemned criminal sounds contemptuous at the level of epithet ("wretch," "idiot"), at the narrative level it points to a natural generosity among the underprivileged, along with the ingenuity that allows them to exploit the absurd and the obsolete in the juridical system (the benefit of clergy and the use of a rudimentary literacy—the "neck-verse"—to claim it).[21]

The body of the satire also entangles legal corruption and the art of writing in a difficult argument, one that spreads across society and subsumes, again through metaphor, most of the supposedly intellectual practices of church and state in a single indictment. The corrupt lawyer, Coscus, is described as accumulating land by sharp practice, deliberately producing flawed legal documents so that he may later profit from his own errors:

> Peecemeale he gets lands, and spends as much time
> Wringing each Acre, as men pulling prime.
> In parchments then, large as his fields, hee drawes
> Assurances, bigge, as gloss'd civill laws,
> So huge, that men (in our time's forwardnesse)
> Are Fathers of the Church for writing lesse.
> These hee writes not; nor for these written payes,

Therefore spares no length; as in those first dayes
When Luther was profest, he did desire
Short *Pater nosters*, saying as a Fryer
Each day his beads, but having left those lawes,
Addes to Christs prayer, the Power and glory clause.
But when he sells or changes land, he'impaires
His writings, and (unwatch'd) leaves out, *ses heires*,
As slily'as any Commenter goes by
Hard words, or sense; or in Divinity
As controverters, in vouch'd texts, leave out
Shrewd words, which might against them cleare the doubt.

(Lines 85–102)

Who would be better placed than a lawyer-in-training to recognize the more disreputable aspects of the profession? Assurances, or title deeds to property, have grown so complicated that they can be deployed to cheat those whom they should protect. As Milgate pointed out, the tendency of an over-complex law to defraud the uneducated was already a commonplace of social criticism. In Philip Stubbes's *Anatomy of Abuses* there is a lament for "times past when men dealt uprightly" and "sixe or seven lines was sufficient for the assurance of any peece of land whatsoever," whereas now (in the 1580s) two or three skins of parchment will hardly serve: "Wherein shalbe so many provisoes, particles, and clauses . . . that it is hard for a poore ignorant man to keep halfe of them: and if he fail in one of the lest, you knowe what followeth" (Part II, sig. E7v).[22]

John Lauritsen has rightly observed that the real subject of this satire is not merely the law but the "rather broader matter of the perversion of the word, whether this be in law, theology, or poetry."[23] Donne equates fraudulent legal writing to textual scholarship which avoids precisely the "hard words" that most need glossing, or the dishonest theological controversy which, when citing the text of Scripture, leaves out those intractable passages which cannot be brought into line with the position being argued. But what makes this broader conception possible is the huge territory that "law" covered, virtually synonymous with "society," or "the system," but a system without coherence. Common law, civil law, canon law; all three were competing for jurisdiction in Elizabethan England, a situation creative at least of relativism, at worst of cynicism. The satire concludes by naming a fourth category, statute law, which, though produced by Parliament and including such venerable protections for the citizen as Magna Carta, might well have become the most dangerous of the four, at least for a satirist. Yet in naming the danger Donne defies it: "my words none drawes / Within the vast reach of th'huge statute lawes." The first two treason acts of Elizabeth's reign (1 Eliz. c. 5 [1559]; 13 Eliz. c. 1 [1571]) specifically included words along with overt acts in the definition of treason; four other parliamentary statutes in the sessions of 1571 and 1572 were intended to deal with the new threat posed by the Jesuits and by Elizabeth's excommunication and to further extend the definition of treason. In 1585 a new act (27 Eliz. c. 2) covered the mere presence in the realm of a Jesuit or newly trained seminary priest or the act of receiving a traitor into one's house. As John Bellamy has argued, the piling of statute upon statute led to a confusion fortuitous for the government, dangerous for the subject:

> The policy, which was quite apparent later in the sixteenth century, of framing indictments so that they might be said to be founded on several statutes was a deceitful subterfuge to gain procedural benefits, like avoiding the need to produce witnesses. . . . Many of these weaknesses and difficulties might have been resolved if the scope of the treason laws had been open to criticism. Unfortunately, the heightened political and religious tensions tended to make men curb their tongues for fear of being regarded as betrayers of their prince, church and realm. Very noticeably, there was no opposition by the nobility as the fourteenth- and early fifteenth-century kings had met with when they sought to change the scope of the treason laws. The magnates of those times had been great experts on illegal accusations and precedents in general, but in the sixteenth all those with a good knowledge of the law seem to have been in thrall to the crown. With no accepted and organized opposition for much of the period, there was not the same need to observe the letter of the law so strictly.[24]

Satire 2 stands, in effect, as Donne's manifesto for the satiric program, as a writerly exposé of a crisis in Law in the most comprehensive sense; and in its focus on the *textual* nature of malfeasance, the complicity in systemic corruption of writing and the intelligence that drives it, it helps to explain not only the other satires, but also Donne's political poetics.

As Lauritsen noted (117–30), the satires also develop prophylactically the self-division Donne defined in the letter to Carr about *Biathanatos*, and that became, I shall argue, the strongest symptom in his middle years of an inability to decide securely between principle and self-interest, between a dangerous integrity and a prudent clientage. In Satire 1 the division is between the "fondling motley humorist" whose passions are clothes and women, and the scholar who, though wishing to remain "coffin'd" in his study surrounded by his books, is cajoled out into the streets, without which expedition the satire, it needs hardly be said, would be empty of material. In Satire 4 this scenario is repeated, as the speaker, having unwisely gone to court, finds himself trapped, his back against a wall, by a version of himself: that is to say, one who pretends a commitment to the Elizabethan court ("If of court life you knew the good, / You would leave lonenesse"), but who in reality wishes only to exchange scandalous gossip:

>   he nigardly
> As loth t'enrich me, so tells many'a lie,
> More then ten Hollensheads, or Halls, or Stowes,

> Of triviall household trash he knowes; He knowes
> When the Queene frown'd, or smil'd, and he knows what
> A subtle States-man may gather of that;
> He knowes who loves; whom; and who by poyson
> Hasts to an Offices reversion;
>
> . . . .
>
> He like a priviledg'd spie, whom nothing can
> Discredit, Libells now 'gainst each great man.
> He names a price for every office paid.
>
> (Lines 95–102, 119–21)

This passage functions as insidiously as the court gossip moves from the trivial (which, as signified by the Tudor chroniclers, may not be so trivial after all) to the deeply corrupt; for the focus of Donne's satire, evidently, is not the gossip but what gives rise to it. Repeating it, he credits it; while at the same time, by mentioning Burghley's and Walsingham's well-known spy systems, he warns those like himself who may be tempted to discuss scandalous events and practices that those with whom they share their outrage may actually be engaged in entrapment.

And, more profoundly, Donne then proceeds to bring to full analytical consciousness, and into structural relation, three complex ideas: the problem of complicity inherent in satire as a genre; the fact that scandal, as an interpretive posture, is actually created by censorship, which transforms social criticism into a dangerous, outlaw activity; and the psychic experience of guilt, which religion explains as the effect of original sin, but which may, in this larger analysis, have sociopolitical origins:

> I more amas'd then Circes prisoners, when
> They felt themselves turne beasts, felt my selfe then
> Becomming Traytor, and mee thought I saw
> One of our Giant Statutes ope his jaw
> To sucke me in; for hearing him, I found
> That as burnt venom'd lechers doe grow sound
> By giving others their soares, I might growe
> Guilty, and he free: Therefore I did show
> All signes of loathing; But since I am in,
> I must pay mine and my forefathers sinne.
>
> (Lines 129–38)

Indeed, having escaped the physical presence of this alter ego (who is dressed, significantly, in the same black velvet, though shabbier, that Donne wears in his youngest portrait) the speaker of Satire 4 finds that he has caught, as an infection, the scandalous *mentalité*. "At home in wholesome solitarinesse," he finds himself not returned to scholarly serenity, but on the contrary overtaken by a Dantesque vision:

> a trance
> Like his, who dreamt he saw hell, did advance
> It selfe on me; Such men as he saw there,
> I saw at Court, and worse, and more.

In the last lines of the poem, the speaker returns, awake and voluntarily, to court, where, feeling inexplicably threatened by the sight of the queen's guards, he "shook like a spyed Spie" (line 135). The merger of innocent and guilty, self and libellous other is complete, but completely ambiguous. And if the writer has become the spy, is it now the reader who should fear entrapment?

Despite Ben Jonson's own gossip about chronology, it seems clear that much of Donne's lyric poetry was staged as a response to Jacobean, not Elizabethan, culture. *The Canonization* distinguishes between the "Kings recall, or his stamped face,"[25] that is to say, his image on coinage, as Elegy 10 speaks of love impressing his heart "As Kings do coynes, to which their stamps impart / The value" (84). More significantly, *The Sunne Rising* and the lesser known *Loves Exchange* refer to the king's hunting, an unmistakable code (shared with *King Lear*) that specifies James as the royal referent.[26] Likewise the speaker in Elegy 15 includes in his maledictions against the man who betrayed the lovers into quarreling the hope that "his carrion coarse be a longer feast / To the Kings dogges, then any other beast" (98). This theme connects erotics to a more sinister account of the Jacobean Hunt (as Kafka allegorically conceived the state's pursuit of offenders). *Pseudo-Martyr* (1610) refers to "any such hunting as [the Jesuits] will call intemperate,"[27] an allusion that on the surface appears to defend the king against his Roman critics, but which could also relate to the activities of the pursuivants. *The Courtier's Library*, a parodic bibliography based on Rabelais, written in Latin, and never published in Donne's lifetime, contains in its preface the following address to the courtly aspirant: "The engagements natural to your life at court leave you no leisure for literature [sleep, dress, meals, and amusements]. . . . But still you condescend to keep up an appearance of learning, to enable you occasionally to praise with grace and point your fellowmenials, the royal hounds."[28] In this context the specifically Jacobean clue, "the royal hounds," is unmistakably presented in a contemptuous light, implying the conventional relationship between fawning dogs and flatterers.

This alone might counter the claim that Donne in the reign of James was totally dominated by the personal style and utterances of his sovereign. But the refutation must go deeper. Intricately connected to the workings of James's court Donne certainly was, and he had more direct dealings with James than most of his "literary" contemporaries. Like James, Donne was a learned controversialist, whose intelligence was bent to the king's agenda; but he was *equally* connected to the opposition group in the troublesome Jacobean parliaments. His writing is therefore marked by a deep ambivalence about the world of influence in which he both desperately wanted and deeply disdained to participate.

One of the earliest of Donne's verse letters was sent to Sir Henry Wotton as he left for his embassy to Venice on July 13, 1604, and its language reflects, as well as the complimentary function of the poem, the optimism that generally accompanied the opening of the new reign, the political honeymoon. Donne referred there to "those reverend papers" that gave Wotton his commission, "whose soule is / Our good and great Kings lov'd hand and fear'd name,"[29] the symbolic combination of text, person, and office in the royal signature. But by no means all of the Jacobean writings retain this idealistic stance. The *Essays in Divinity*, for example, show Donne in transition between what his son, who published them, called "Civill business" and his later career in the church. They contain (like the fourth satire) gibes at royal favorites and financial mismanagement, which helps to explain why John Donne, Jr., dedicated them to Sir Henry Vane in 1651, suggesting that "the manner of their birth may seem to have some analogie with the course you now seem to steer . . . being so highly interested in the publick Affairs of the State."[30] Donne's anti-Catholic polemic, and even more the products of his deanship of St. Paul's, the majestic sermons that account for Gosse's construction of Donne as a pillar of the "old order," would seem to make him the king's man; between 1623 and 1626 there appeared first *Three Sermons upon Speciall Occasions*, then *Foure*, and then *Five*, their publication and republication indicating the importance Donne took them to have in public affairs, and the title of the volumes indicating the extent to which he had accepted the role of a high priest of public events, if not of public policy. But even in his 1622 sermon to the Virginia Company Donne recorded the ethical dangers of tying the pulpit to secular purpose: "Birds that are kept in cages may learne some Notes, which they should never have sung in the Woods or Fields; but yet they may forget their Naturall Notes too. Preachers that bind themselves alwaies to Cities and Courts, and great Auditories, may learne new Notes, they may become occasionall Preachers, and make the emergent affaires of the time, their Text, and the humors of the hearers their Bible."[31]

A JACOBEAN SATIRE?

Donne's transitional years, especially, were marked by contradiction and its writerly symptoms: on the one hand a continuation into the new reign of satirical, even subversive and unpublishable writings; on the other, the use of his extraordinary intellect and eloquence for official purposes. For a closer look at the bird not yet in the cage, we might do well to begin with Elegy 14, *A Tale of a Citizen and His Wife*, not least because efforts have been made to excise it from the record. Although it appeared in the 1635 and 1669 editions of Donne's poems and was accepted by Grierson with mild hesitation, John Shawcross defined it as "having generally been rejected" and omitted it from his own edition "in conviction of [its] spuriousness and in hope of helping rid Donne of [its] inferiority."[32] Helen Gardner had earlier discarded it from hers, with a revealing justification: "Although some students of Donne would not regard it as impossible that he should write an improper poem in 1609, at the time that he was writing *Pseudo-Martyr* and the "Holy Sonnets," it is surely in the highest degree unlikely that he would produce a weak *pastiche* of his earlier style, echoing phrases and lines from his own fourth Satire and Elegies at a time when he had developed a new style."[33] Gardner's exclusion of Elegy 14 begs precisely those questions the poem demands we answer, and was motivated by a moral and evolutionary theory of Donne's development not so very different, finally, from that of Walton, Gosse, or Bald.

As Gardner was well aware, *A Tale of a Citizen and His Wife* reiterates the strategy of Donne's fourth satire, of sedition-by-proxy. By now placing his satire in the mouth of a discontented Londoner, pretending all the while to be shocked at what is said, and flirting, while it is said, with the citizen's wife behind his back, Donne once again divided himself into two voices, the one asserting its loyalty but demonstrating its frivolity, the other supposedly rejected as treasonous, yet carrying a certain obvious conviction.

The poem is, moreover, saturated with issues contemporary to the first decade of James's reign. As the speaker attempts to make contact with the citizen whose wife is making eyes at him behind her husband's back, he tries to find topics likely to engage a London merchant—to establish (and Donne uses a word fashionable in our own literary practice) the local "discourse":

> To get acquaintance with him I began
> To sort *discourse* fit for so fine a man:
> I ask'd the number of the Plaguy Bill,
> Ask'd if the Custome Farmers held out still,
> Of the Virginian Plot, and whether Ward
> The traffique of the Inland seas had marr'd,
> Whether the Brittaine Burse did fill apace,
> And likely were to give th'Exchange disgrace;
> Of new-built Algate, and the More-field crosses,
> Of store of Bankerouts, and poore Merchants losses.

And the citizen, his tongue finally loosened by the theme of "Tradesmens gaines," launches into a heated critique of the Jacobean economy in its relation to the power structure:

> He rail'd, as fray'd me; for he gave no praise,
> To any but my Lord of Essex dayes;
> Call'd those the age of action; true (quoth Hee)
> There's now as great an itch of bravery,

> And heat of taking up, but cold lay downe,
> For, put to push of pay, away they runne;
> Our onely City trades of hope now are
> Bawd, Tavern-keeper, Whore and Scrivener;
> The much of Privileg'd kingsmen, and the store
> Of fresh protections make the rest all poore.[34]

As Grierson worked through the series of topical references,[35] the poem appeared to situate itself in late 1609 or early 1610. Aldgate was rebuilt by 1609, and on April 11, 1609, "Britain's Bourse," constructed by Salisbury to draw financial business away from the City, was formally opened and so named by the king. The reference to Custom Farmers refers to a transaction initiated by Salisbury in 1604, with Arthur Ingram as his agent, by which the so-called Great Farm of the Customs was leased out to merchant syndicates, who from their profits, so the justification went, would lend money to the crown; but by 1609/10 they were becoming increasingly reluctant to do so. There were two expeditions sent to Virginia in 1609, one in May and one at the end of the year. The reference to Ward, a notorious pirate, though less chronologically specific, also relates to this period. There were numerous complaints from the Venetian ambassador, and the issue of pirate control was raised in the 1610 Parliament. As for the "Plaguy Bill," 1609 was a particularly bad year for plague. There were no theatrical performances at court during the winter 1609–10, and, more to the point, on September 29, 1609, James issued a proclamation further proroguing Parliament until February 9, citing plague as the primary reason.[36] Another proclamation on September 22, this time affecting the legal profession, adjourned part of Michaelmas term, also on account of plague.[37] The fact, therefore, that "the Plaguy Bill" of this poem echoes that of *The Canonization* ("When did the heats which my veines fill / Adde one more to the plaguie Bill?") may rather destabilize the presumed earliness of the lyric than the lateness of the satire; it surely cautions us that the sharp break between "early" and "mature" work posited by Gardner was a wishful critical construction.

Perhaps most tellingly, Grierson discerned in the citizen's complaint echoes of yet another royal proclamation, this time on March 25, 1610. If he was right, Elegy 14 belongs to the late spring of 1610, when many of Donne's friends were convened at Whitehall, protesting, among other things, the publication of John Cowell's *The Interpreter*, a book dedicated to Archbishop Bancroft and devoted to the praise and mystification of the royal prerogative. Phrases from the proclamation seem to have been lifted, not only out of context, but into an opposing "discourse," one might even say, a discourse of opposition. James's strategy in publishing the proclamation had been to preempt the parliamentary attack on Cowell, which had probably been led by Richard Martin,[38] by claiming that he himself was outraged by this unwarranted intervention by an amateur into constitutional theory. Yet the method

James chose to discredit Cowell in public was to deliver a broad attack on *all* public discussion of these issues, and to combine this prohibition with a lament for the good old days:

> The later age and times of the world wherein we are fallen, is so much given to verball profession, as well of Religion, as of all commendable Morall vertues, but wanting the action and deedes agreeable to so specious a profession, as it hath bred such an insatiable curiosity in many mens spirits, and such an itching the tongues and pennes of most men, as nothing is left unsearched to the bottome, both in talking and writing. . . . And therefore it is no wonder, that men in these our dayes do not spare to wade in all the deepest mysteries that belong to the persons or State of Kings or Princes, that are gods upon Earth: since we see . . . that they spare not God himselfe. And this license that every talker or writer now assumeth to himselfe, is come to this abuse, that . . . many men that never went out of the compasse of Cloister or Colledges, will freely wade by their writings in the deepest mysteries of Monarchie and politique government.[39]

To counter this "license" of talk and writing, James ended by proclaiming a new campaign for "better oversight of Books of all sorts before they come to the Presse"; in other words, an increase in censorship.

The phrases that Grierson discerned as carried over into the citizen's protest were the lament for "action and deedes," and a complaint against the "itching" of tongues and pens. Yet during the transfer, if such it were, the nostalgia for an "age of action" has become the clearly seditious claim that the only age of action was "my lord of Essex dayes." Donne himself had volunteered for the two expeditions against Spain in 1596 and 1597. Among Donne's friends, Sir Henry Goodyer, Sir Henry Wotton, and Sir Henry Neville all had had connections with Essex. Goodyer was knighted by Essex in Ireland in 1599. Wotton, who had been Essex's secretary and may well have introduced to him his good friend Donne, hastily detached himself when the breach with the queen seemed irreparable, and awaited in Venice James's accession. Which Henry Neville attended with Donne at the Mitre Tavern we cannot be sure. If it was Sir Henry Neville of Abergavenny, he was knighted by Essex at Cadiz; if it was Sir Henry Neville of Billingbear, Berkshire, he was later implicated in Essex's conspiracy, stripped of his offices, and imprisoned in the Tower from July 1601 until James's accession.[40] Sir Thomas Roe, another of Donne's close friends and correspondents, wrote a flaming satire about the Jacobean court that partly corroborates the citizen's complaint in Elegy 14. Roe's speaker, like Donne's in the fourth satire, went to court (but after 1603) and found there "Kings were but men":

> What Treason is, and what did Essex kill,
> Not true Treason, but Treason handled ill;
> And which of them stood for their Countries good,

Or what might be the cause of so much Blood.
He said she stunck, and men might not have said
That she was old before that she was dead.
His Case was hard, to do or suffer; loth
To do, he made it harder, and did both.
Too much preparing lost them all their Lives,
Like some in Plagues kill'd with preservatives.
Friends, like land-souldiers in a storm at Sea,
Not knowing what to do, for him did pray.[41]

Whoever attributed this poem to Donne, adding it to his satires in the 1669 edition, obviously believed that its tone and opinions were compatible with the five that preceded it;[42] and Roe's Jacobean satire also tells us much about the confusion and guilt, what one might call the survivor complex, that affected those who had looked to Essex as a focus for their own alienation and who, when the mortal danger of their allegiance dawned on them, "not knowing what to do," chose to be ineffectual. Carey berated Donne for apparently abandoning Essex as soon as his fall from favor was apparent, citing a letter of Christmas 1599: "My lorde of Essex and his trayne are no more mist here then the Aungells which were cast downe from heaven nor (for anything I see) likelyer to retourne" (71).[43] I, however, find it impossible to tell from this statement whether or not Donne was of the Devil's party, with or without knowing it. Neither Bald nor Carey mentions Elegy 14, the latter being therefore able to conclude that although "James's court was far more obviously corrupt and degenerate than Elizabeth's, Donne never ventured any criticism of it at all" (64).[44] "I am no Libeller, nor will be any," says the narrator, in introducing his citizen decoy, and dismisses his "harsh talke" as "void of reason." But as he listens, the narrator once again begins to "sweat for feare of treason." From this perspective, Elegy 14 becomes a significant exhibit in the cultural afterlife of the Essex rebellion, a tribute to the role played in that event (or in those that led up to it) by difficult intellectuals like Donne and his friends.

LAW VERSUS PREROGATIVE: CONSTITUTIONAL THEORY

The issue of the royal prerogative and what, if any, were its limitations was one of the central preoccupations of both James and his parliaments throughout the reign. Revisionist historians have denied that this *was* a preoccupation, at least of Parliament, and claimed that the issue did not become seriously contentious until the subsequent reign. I agree rather with those who perceive a steady development in the House of Commons of a *theory* of political opposition, one that was partly generated by James's own determination to theorize the prerogative, or an unlimited sovereignty, and partly a response to local issues of economics—taxes, monopolies, "the much of privileged kingsmen," and the responsibility of the Commons to monitor the nation's finances.

In *Biathanatos*, his essay on suicide, seemingly an unlikely location for the development of constitutional theory, Donne's thoughts on sovereign power were recorded in a way that is both supremely his own (that is to say, evasive) and specifically Jacobean. A religious case of conscience—the rightness or wrongness of taking one's own life—is to be settled by way of a political analogy, but one, it appears, of the same paradoxical structure as the treatise it supports. The personal liberty of conscience that permits a rational man to take his own life in defiance of the natural law of self-preservation is equated, not, as one might more easily imagine, to the liberty of the subject—that great and contentious topic of Jacobean parliamentary discourse—but to its equally contentious opposite, royal prerogative. The text insists perversely that "mans liberty" can be understood as an illimitable sovereign power of the individual to dispose of himself as he pleases: and (as Donne continues to upend the political analogy) the natural law of self-preservation operates only like those temporary stays on royal prerogative that parliamentary watchdogs attempt to provide: "as neither the watchfulnesse of Parliaments, nor the descents and indulgences of Princes, which have consented to lawes derogatory to themselves, have beene able to prejudice the Princes *non obstantes*, because prerogative is incomprehensible, and overflowes and transcends all law. . . . so, what law soever is cast upon the conscience or liberty of man, of which the reason is mutable, is naturally condition'd with this, that it binds so long as the reason lives."[45]

Now it might be possible to argue that Donne was here constituting himself in monarchist, absolutist terms in order to deflect his sense of power-lessness within the system; and/or that the statement that royal prerogative is unbounded is to be taken at face value, as proof of Donne's literal acceptance of the Stuart doctrine of the divine right of kingship. But neither of these meanings seems compatible with the genre of the paradox, whose substance is a profound alienation from commonly accepted belief, and which in Donne's practice elsewhere requires the reader at least to experience the temptation to read every statement in reverse, as a mirror image of itself. Nor, if we suppose that in this major paradox Donne was expressing a real, though controversial and indeed unpublishable, conviction of his own, is it likely that he would so toy with the concept of personal liberty as to *equate* it with precisely that power that was most inimical to freedom of religious practice in his own state. And indeed the language here is slippery. To call the prerogative "incomprehensi-ble" is potentially a subversive pun, combining what can not be understood with what can not be contained.[46] This implication is corroborated by the following statement that the prerogative "over-flowes and transcends all law."

This was a motif of political thought and discourse that was increasingly common from 1604 through 1610, especially among Donne's friends and associates. His reference to the "watchfulnesse of Parliaments" might appear to be evaluatively neutral, but the so-called "Mitre Tavern" ballad tells us that Donne, who himself would soon be returned as a member for Taunton in the truncated session of 1614, belonged to a group that included several members of the House of Commons: Christopher Brooke, Richard Martin, Arthur Ingram, Sir Henry Goodyer, Henry Holland, Sir Robert Phelips, and Sir John Hoskyns. More significantly, several of those were already well known, and some would later become notorious, as Parliamentarians who consistently opposed what they saw as unwarranted extension of the royal prerogative. On May 16, 1610, for instance, James had sent a message to the Commons forbidding them from debating any further his prerogative in the matter of impositions, or additional taxes levied on imports. John Hoskyns had thereupon challenged the newly mystified doctrine of the prerogative which Northampton and some of the higher clergy, in their separate ways, were attempting to place in the category of *arcana imperii*. "Methinks," said Hoskyns on May 18, "our answer should be that we may dispute [the prerogative]. And as to the phrases of infinite and inscrutable, they be things that belong to heaven and are not upon earth and he that looks for them here upon earth, may miss them in heaven." And Christopher Brooke, who had given away the bride at Donne's secret marriage and himself been thrown into prison in consequence, added with careful balance: "As I am always unwilling to argue the prerogative of my sovereign; so am I not willing to lose the liberty of a subject. The prerogative is great yet is it not endless nor boundless, but justice and equity are the bounds and limits of it."[47]

In his letter entrusting *Biathanatos* to Sir Robert Carr, Donne had defined suicide as the "misinterpretable subject." The same could be said both of the royal prerogative and of Donne's statements about it, which both resembled those of his friends and were yet not so easy to place in the ideological spectrum.[48] The fear of misinterpretation was one of Donne's most frequently expressed anxieties; and while it undoubtedly spoke to an age of official censorship, it also authorizes us to read his writings as *capable* of misinterpretation, deliberately so. This is no less true of *Pseudo-Martyr*, for all its status as an official text published with the king's encouragement and dedicated to him. We know that Donne had entered the controversy over the Oath of Allegiance at the urging of Thomas Morton, which may have been seconded by James himself. Apparently it was not without internal resistance. His dedication of *Pseudo-Martyr* to James begins, "As Temporall armies consist of Press'd men, and voluntaries, so doe they also in this warfare" (A2), leaving it open to inference which category he himself belonged to. There is certainly evidence here of sycophancy: Donne describes himself as turned into an exhalation drawn upward by the solar influence of the king's "Bookes," a metaphor for his "ambition, of ascending" to the king's presence in some permanent capacity (A2r). Yet prior to the dedication, Donne addressed the ordinary reader in a way that suggests the pressures upon him; for to prove his sincerity he inserted an admission of his Catholic upbringing, transforming a conventional rhetorical gambit into a gamble. "I have beene ever kept awake," he wrote, "in a meditation of Martyrdome, by being derived from such a stocke and race, as, I believe, no family, (which is not of farre larger extent, and greater branches,) hath endured and suffered more in their persons and fortunes, for obeying the Teachers of Romane Doctrine, than it hath done." Although the context is rejection, the language is that of family pride and solidarity.

That Donne refused to include his family in the massive attack he would mount against the Jesuit mission is confirmed by his treatment of Sir Thomas More. It was one of James's own concerns to shatter the More legend and disperse the aura of sanctity it emitted. In his *Triplici Nodo*, the royal reply to the pope's breves and to cardinal Bellarmine, James quoted More's defense before the House of Lords, and concluded that by "his owne confession it is plaine, that this great martyr himselfe took the cause of his owne death, to be onely for his being refractary to the King in this said matter of Marriage and Succession; which is but a very fleshly cause of Martyrdome, as I conceive."[49] To which Donne replied in *Pseudo-Martyr* by invoking "Sir Thomas Moore, of whose firmeness to the integrity of the Romane faith, that Church neede not be ashamed" (108). The comment is inserted parenthetically in an attack on the doctrine of Purgatory; yet what Donne destroys with one hand—integrity—he restores with the other as a property of both the Roman faith and the martyr who chose to die for it.

But *Pseudo-Martyr* contains a larger sign than family solidarity of Donne's resistance to his self-assumed role as the king's polemicist. His strategy throughout was to compare the claims made by James and Pope Paul V, respectively, and to assert that those of the pope were more excessive than those of the king; yet the inference remains that those of the king may be *somewhat* excessive. For instance, having stated that when princes assume "high stiles" they "do but draw men to a just reverence, and estimation of that power, which subjects naturally know to be in them," whereas popes "by these Titles seeke to build up, and establish a power, which was ever litigious and controverted," Donne continued: "And the farthest mischiefe, which by this excesse Princes could stray into, or subjects suffer, is a deviation into Tyranny, and an ordinary use of an extraordinary power and prerogative, of so making subjects slaves, and (as the Lawyers say) *Personas Res*" (43). It is hard to believe that he intended this to be reassuring!

It was, in fact, the ordinary use (to raise revenue) of an extraordinary power that the opposition group in the Commons perceived as particularly dangerous, not least because absolutist theorists of the law were currently arguing that taxation was *not* an ordinary function of royal power but a legitimate function of the prerogative.[50] If issues like impositions were governed not by *meum et tuum*, the principle at the heart of common law, but rather by *salus populi*, the principle of royal prerogative, the effect would indeed be, as men like Nicholas Fuller and Thomas Hedley argued, to make subjects slaves. In addition, however careful James had been in his early statements in England to present himself as a constitutional monarch, by early 1610 he had managed to give a contrary impression. On March 21 he addressed the new session of Parliament with a speech that referred to "doubts, which hath bene in the heads of some . . . whether I was resolved in the generall, to continue still my government according to the ancient forme of this State, and the Lawes of this Kingdome: Or if I had an intention not to limit my selfe within those bounds, but to alter the same when I thought it convenient, by the absolute power of a King."[51] Those doubts had been raised, in part, by an excessive reliance on proclamations during a long prorogation, and their publication in a single volume on February 3, 1610,[52] which gave the impression of *codification* just prior to Parliament's opening. At that opening, on February 15, Salisbury referred to those ill-affected persons who, "hearing of a course taken to bind up all the printed proclamations into a book to the intent that there may be better notice taken of those things which they commanded, have been content to raise a bruit that it was intended at this parliament to make the power of proclamations equal to the laws."[53] And especially in his speech of May 21 James exacerbated those doubts and bruits by his sharp and coercive tone. "If a king be resolute to be a tyrant," he said, "all you can do will not hinder him."[54] Although some modern historians have seen this speech as conciliatory, James himself said at the outset that his tone was negative: "I must complain of you to yourselves and begin with a grievance instead of a gratulation" (2:103). And its effect, John Chamberlain reported to Dudley Carleton, was "so litle to theyr satisfaction, that I heare yt bred generally much discomfort; to see our monarchical powre and regall prerogative strained so high and made so transcendant every way, that yf the practise shold follow the positions, we are not like to leave to our successors the freedome we received from our forefathers."[55] "Transcendant," we remember, was the term that Donne used of the "incomprehensible" concept of prerogative in *Biathanatos*, entrusted to Carr as unpublishable, and so, in his own mind, still potent nine years *after* he had published *Pseudo-Martyr*, his partly obedient defense of obedience to the crown.[56]

J. P. Sommerville, in providing us with the clearest account to date of the competing theories of government and sovereignty in the earlier seventeenth century, several times cites Donne, apparently in the belief that he belonged on the side of the theorists of absolutism: "Many writers—including Donne, Maynwaring, Willan, Rawlinson and Field—endorsed the view that Adam's power had been kingly. . . . If the power of the first fathers had been kingly, it followed that the doctrines of originall democracy and of the contractual origins of regal authority were false."[57] But in fact the statement in *Pseudo-Martyr* to which he alludes *combines* a theory of original democracy ("if a companie of Savages, should consent and concurre to a civill maner of living, Magistracie, & Superioritie, would necessarily, and naturally, and Divinely grow out of this consent") with the statement that "Adam was created a Magistrate" (83). And Donne's rejection of the transference theory ("Regall authority is not therefore derived from men, so, as that certaine men have lighted a King at their Candle" [169]) is part of a larger rejection, as "a cloudie and muddie search," of all arguments as to the human origins of sovereignty, "since it growes not in man." Certainly John Donne, Jr., did not think that the belief in Adam's magistracy was automatically a belief in kingship by divine and unlimited right; for when he dedicated the *Essays in Divinity* to Vane, he remarked (as one addressing a revolutionary general): "And although it bee objected, that the Sword be no good Key to open the Gates of Heaven, yet it was thought fit to protect and defend Paradise, and keep out even ADAM himself, who was the first and lawfull Heir, and who had for ever enjoyed his Prerogative, if he had not exceeded his Commission, in devouring that which he was forbidden to taste."[58] He evidently intended Donne's readers to apply this reproach to Charles I.

EQUIVOCATIONS

Despite these irruptions into the text of *Pseudo-Martyr* of what look like arguments *with* James I rather than for him, the treatise as a whole was obviously intended to be *taken* as a loyal exercise in Protestant nationalist propaganda. As such, it conflicts with *The Courtier's Library*, where Donne's butts include Protestant spokesmen Martin Luther and John Foxe, anti-Catholic polemicists Edward Hoby and Matthew Sutcliffe . . . , and Richard Topcliffe, one of the vilest agents of anti-Catholic persecution, whose name appears also in some of the manuscripts of Donne's fourth satire instead of the word "pursuivant." But the *Courtier's Library* also includes a strange item whose contents connect both to the fourth satire, to the troubled speaker "who dreamt he saw hell" at the Elizabethan court, and, more intensely, to the work that immediately followed *Pseudo-Martyr*, the *Conclave Ignatii*, entered in the Stationers' Register in January 1611. For the conclave is described by an anonymous speaker who fell into an "Extasie" and "saw all the roomes in Hell open to [his] sight," with Ignatius Loyola as *diabolus in cathedra*. And in the sardonic *Library* (like the *Conclave* written in Latin) the courtier is encouraged to read a book entitled *The Quintessence of Hell; or, The private apartment in Hell, in which is a discussion of the fifth region passed over by Homer, Virgil, Dante and the rest of the papists, where, over and above the penalties and sensations of the damned, Kings are tortured by a recollection of the past* (51–52). It looks, then, as if Donne continued to imagine a court in infernal terms, as much under James as Elizabeth, a fact that destabilizes the contrast drawn in the *Conclave* between a demonic Loyola down below, and the European monarchs, specifically James and Elizabeth, against whom (so the *Conclave* claims) the primary malice of the Jesuits is directed.

But the *Conclave* is in almost every way a radically unstable text. Published anonymously, first in Latin and then in a still anonymous translation by Donne himself, it was in both versions a tiny octavo, self-declared a satire, and mockingly dedicated not to James but to "the two Adversary Angels, which are Protectors of the Papall Consistory, and of the Colledge of Sorbon." Yet the book insists on establishing a mirror relationship with *Pseudo-Martyr*. Continuing the strategy Donne had developed for the fourth satire, where the authorial voice divides itself between the poem's "I" and the seditious courtier who corners him, the *Conclave* pretends in its address "To the Reader" to distinguish author from editor, while insisting that the author's identity is unknowable.

"Dost thou seeke after the Author?" asks the preface; "It is in vaine."[59] For the only thing known of him was conveyed to the fictional editor by a friend of the author's, in a letter, as follows:

> The Author was unwilling to have this book published, thinking it unfit both for the matter, which in it selfe is weighty and serious, and for that gravity which himselfe had proposed and observed in an *other* booke formerly published, to descend to this kind of writing. . . . At the last he yeelded, and made mee owner of his booke, which I send to you to be delivered over to forraine nations, (a) *farre from the father*: and (as his desire is) (b) his last in this kinde. Hee chooses and desires, that his *other* booke should testifie his ingenuity, and candor, and his disposition to labour for the reconciling of all parts. This Booke must teach what humane infirmity is.[60]

This extraordinary passage tells us more about the motives for returning to the Jesuits than Bald's hypothesis that the later work was a spillover, that Donne "had been unable to use a whole sheaf of the more extreme and ridiculous utterances of his opponents," and therefore published a second work from the cuttings (228). For the father from whose jurisdiction this squib escapes may be either its author or the patriarchal figure who commanded Donne's *other* book and dictated the gravity of its utterance. That second meaning admits the pressures on the self of the domains of law and authority, those territories entry into which Lacanian theory has identified with social and linguistic maturity and subsumed under the Name-of-the-Father. But if Donne intuits the point at which psychoanalysis will merge with sociology, he offers himself and his readers a strategy for self-management that Lacanian theory, with its stress on irreparable bondage, overlooks. Dividing himself between author and editor, reluctant utterer and eager promoter, dividing his utterance between this book, written in the alienated voice of satire, and the *other*, written from the "reconciling" perspective of the official propagandist,

Donne found a way to speak ambivalence. And though by this strategy Donne may not have been able to reconcile all parts of himself, his appeal to "humane infirmity" is both disingenuous and ingenuous at the same time, demanding for himself the toleration that his project denied to others.

The text of the *Conclave* is no less peculiar than its preface. As Dennis Flynn points out, Donne's marginal citations are almost exclusively from Catholic authors, indicating his access to a library "unusually strong and up-to-date in the areas of Catholic controversial theology, history, and hagiography."[61] In addition, the tone of the pamphlet makes it possible to feel that "Donne was not honestly or actively on the King's side," and that his trivialization of the royal arguments reflects adversely upon them. Indeed, as the preface reminds us of Donne's origins ("how hard a matter is it for a man ... so thoroughly to cast off the Jesuits, as that he contract nothing of their natural drosses, which are Petulancy, and Lightnesse" [5V]), the ironies of the text are so rebarbative that it looks suspiciously as if the author had reserved to himself the Jesuit strategy of "Mentall Reservation, and Mixt propositions," otherwise known, since the trial of Father Garnet, as the "art of equivocation" (55, 33). The *Conclave* consists in a demonic competition, presided over by Lucifer, between all the greatest innovators in contemporary thought, in theology, science, or the "Arts," "or in any thing which ... may so provoke to quarrelsom and brawling controversies: For so the truth be lost, it is no matter how" (13). Among the contestants, then, are Copernicus, Paracelsus, Machiavelli, Aretino, Columbus, and Ignatius Loyola, who will win; and in the course of putting his own case forward Machiavelli complains that the followers of Ignatius "have brought into the world a new art of Equivocation ... have raised to life againe the language of the Tower of Babel, so long concealed, and brought us againe from understanding one an other" (27). Conversely, Ignatius, who has argued against Copernicus' claims as insufficiently perverse ("those opinions of yours may very well be true" [17]),[62] attacks Machiavelli (his most formidable rival) on the grounds that his teachings have worked against the kingdom of Rome: "for what else doth hee endeavour or go about, but to change the forme of common-wealth, and so to deprive the people (who are a soft, a liquid and ductile mettall, and apter for our impressions) of all their liberty: & having so destroyed all civility and replublique, to reduce all states to Monarchies; a name which in secular states, wee doe so much abhor" (78–79). This statement establishes Loyola as a radical republican, discrediting Machiavelli's claims to the throne of Hell by making him an advocate of monarchical absolutism; but the description of monarchy, which comes into existence by depriving the people "of all their liberty" and "having ... destroyed all civility," carries its devious thrust. One cannot imagine James I being willing to endorse this description. The irony cannot, in other words, be intended to function by a simple discrediting or inversion of all that Loyola says, for that would nullify his malice and deprive the pamphlet of its point. If other texts of Donne's are slippery, this one is positively glacial; with the author absent and anonymous, there is no place for the reader to set her feet securely.

But equivocation is not restricted to Donne's Jacobean prose, and appears even in poems that would seem to have completely abandoned that territory of personal freedom to which Donne keeps alluding, in however peculiar a tone. We know, for instance, that Donne profited from the greatest scandal of James's reign, in which Frances Howard's divorce from the third earl of Essex and remarriage to the *other* and more famous Sir Robert Carr, now earl of Somerset, was made still more disreputable by the murder of someone who had resolutely opposed it. On September 14, 1613, Sir Thomas Overbury died in the Tower, poisoned, it was later charged, by the countess through her accomplices. Donne, in the meantime, had not only sought out Somerset as a new patron, but had accepted the position as his secretary that Overbury's imprisonment had vacated. By mid-December rumors were circulating that there had been foul play; so that Donne already knew how he had fulfilled one of the most horrible of the charges laid by the seditious speaker in his own fourth satire, where the first-person persona learns unwillingly "who by poyson / Hasts to an Offices reversion."

This may help to explain why Donne was late in contributing his own verse tribute to the Somerset-Howard marriage. He may have been very late indeed. Although the *Ecclogue* that prefaces the epithalamion is dated December 26, 1613, the date of the marriage, we know from his private correspondence that Donne did not begin it until several weeks later. The function of the *Ecclogue* is, in fact, to explain the delay in the poem's completion and delivery; and it provides the most sharply delineated version in Donne's work of that formally divided self to which he apparently had recourse when attempting to deal with ambivalence, here personified as Idios ("one's own," "pertaining to one's self") and Allophanes ("appearing otherwise," or, perhaps, "the face of the Other"). In their dialogue, Allophanes reproaches Idios for his absence from court on this great occasion of the marriage, only to be told that even in the country Idios so reveres the king and his style of government that he is not, in spirit, "from Court."[63] Yet the language in which Allophanes records the virtues of James and Somerset treads that slippery line whereby the claim for good can be rendered only rhetorically, as a denial of the converse imputation. It is a court "where it is no levity to trust, [?] / Where there is no ambition, but to'obey, / Where men need whisper nothing, and yet may"; and the question of Somerset's own role in that structure is addressed in the most oblique manner possible:

> the King's favours are so plac'd, that all
> Finde that the King therein is liberall
> To them, *in him*, because his favours bend
> To vertue, to *the which they all pretend.* [?]
> (Lines 81–84)

These lines "pretend" to unsay those lines in Donne's second satire which speak of lying "Like a Kings favourite, yea like a King" and which the editor of the 1633 volume of Donne's *Poems* thought too dangerous to print.[64] While the discreetly unnamed recipient of the king's favors supposedly is merely the conduit of those favors to "all" who desire them, and the king's liberality supposedly proven by the favorite's selfless virtue, the mobility of "all" as a qualifier may expand to include suitors, Somerset, king, all. All are then governed by the disabling and concluding verb "pretend," which obviously claimed its innocent meaning of "profess" while admitting the suspicious one, the one that, as the language evolved, drove out the neutral connotation. It is then not entirely surprising that the language Idios himself uses to explain his delayed eulogy is more elegiac than celebratory:

> I knew
> All this, and onely therefore I withdrew.
> To know and feele all this, and not to have
> Words to expresse it, makes a man a grave
> Of his owne thoughts; I would not therefore stay
> At a great feast, having no grace to say.
>
> (Lines 91–96)

If one reads these lines *without* a prior assumption that Donne when he wrote them was utterly cynical, they express rather clearly and painfully the particular version of the inexpressibility topos that actual and self-inflicted censorships had arranged. The crucial "whisper" ("where men need whisper nothing, and yet may"), political opposition or "sedition," is here introduced (through denial) in order to explain the mortal gap between knowing all and telling only part of it; while the powerful and indecorous image of the marriage celebrant becoming a "grave of his own thoughts" reintroduces the necrophilic imagination ("in this standing wooden chest . . . let me lye in prison, and here be coffin'd")[65] of Donne's first satire, and reveals, after all, what generic affiliates this pretended pastoral confesses to.

UNDERTAKING

This brings us to the meaning of Donne's participation in the ill-fated Parliament of 1614; for understanding which, however, we first need to glance back at 1610. As the 1610 Parliament ground its way toward stalemate, it was rumored that efforts were being made by the king's councillors to dismantle the opposition. On December 10, the Venetian ambassador, Marc Antonio Correr, wrote to his employers: "The business in Parliament has gone from bad to worse. Meantime they will try to win over some of those who have shown most opposition, and if they do not succeed Parliament will be dissolved altogether, so that the constituencies will elect new members. There are those who say that the King will never summon Parliament again, but his need of money is against that, and maybe this rumour is put about to frighten many of them."[66] In fact, as the dissolution approached, four of the most determined oppositionists, Lewknor, Fuller, Wentworth, and the redoubtable John Hoskyns, were sent for by Salisbury for a private conference.[67] On December 31, Correr continued his report: "Certain persons have been approached with a view to inducing them to bow to his Majesty's wishes and desires (I have information on this point from a good quarter, but it would only weary your Serenity)."[68] And on January 21 Correr reported the dissolution of the Parliament, which, after a series of adjournments, was dissolved by royal proclamation (in the middle of a prorogation) on December 31:

> This step, which is unusual, as Parliament is usually prorogued, and the rumour that the King intends to issue privy seals for the amount of one million six hundred thousand crowns, give rise to some talk. This loan once obtained his Majesty will summon a new Parliament; care being taken that those hostile to him shall not be re-elected. He will all the more readily obtain subsidies to pay back the loan, in that everyone will have an interest in voting it, and all the money will pass into the hands of the nobility. Some cry out that it is not well to exclude those who have forgotten their personal interest in the service of their country; others are unwilling that his Majesty should achieve by indirect ways what was refused him in Parliament. All the same . . . if he gains the Parliamentary leaders he will secure a return of a majority of members that suit his taste.[69]

Diplomatic reports are often, especially by revisionist historians, treated with a certain skepticism, dependent as they were, in Kevin Sharpe's words, "upon information, even rumour, from courtiers, M. P.'s, and newsmongers." Yet Sharpe also admits that "at times their reports may reflect the views of a courtier who spoke his mind but would not commit his opinion to the dangerous permanence of paper";[70] and Correr's report has precisely that quality of *talk*, of being part of a discursive formation, that connects it with Elegy 14.[71]

It also helps to explain the Addled Parliament, that *parlamentum inchoatum* (as John Chamberlain called it)[72] for which writs were finally called in the spring of 1614 (even, perhaps, while Donne was finishing his leaden tribute to Somerset). The grease that rendered the political territory unstable was, not surprisingly, self-interest. One of the questions that exercised the Commons in the few weeks between April 14 and June 7, when James dissolved them, was whether their proceedings had been destabilized by bribery.[73] Some modern historians have discounted the invidiousness of "undertaking" and defended the motives of Sir Henry Neville, who attempted to persuade James to call another Parliament on the grounds that the dissolution of the previous one was causing dissent and harming England's reputation abroad.[74] Neville had committed himself to negotiate with the "patriots" in the House of Commons on the basis of his friendship with them, and, in exchange for certain "graces," such as forgiven loans, "protections" against bankruptcy, and a commitment that no impositions should subsequently be levied except through Parliament, to neutralize their opposition. He claimed to speak "as one that lived and conversed inwardly with the chief of them that were noted to be the most backward and know their inwardest thoughts in that business"; and, in a phrase that subsequently entered the language as a new concept in political thought, he added: "So I dare undertake for most of them, that . . . [the king] shall find those gentlemen willing to do him service." But while it was probably true, as Roberts and Duncan argued, that the Commons was capable of distinguishing between such an undertaking and any attempt actually to pack the house by manipulating the election, and while Neville himself, whose "Advice" to the king[75] was subsequently circulated in the House, was cleared of any wrongdoing, there were certainly some who believed that undertaking, as the institutionalization of the deal, was inimical to genuine parliamentary process. As Sir John Holles complained to Lord Holles on April 28: "a schism is cast into the House by reason of some interlopers between the K. and the Parliament, whom they term undertakers, so named, because they have promised that the Parliament shall supply the King's want to his contentment . . . nor for that they envy these undertakers' reward but that they foresee a perilous consequence by this precedent to the State, when kings heartened by this success shall hereafter practise the like; and sprinkling some hires upon a few shall . . . so by little and little steal away the liberty and at the next opportunity overthrow Parliament itself."[76]

Even before the Privy Council had advised James to issue the writs for the election, Donne himself had written to a friend that "it is taken ill; though it be but mistaken that certain men (whom they call undertakers) should presume either to understand the house before it sit, or to incline it then, and this rumour beforehand, . . . must impeach, if it do not defeat their purposes at last."[77] Despite the cautious neutrality of this statement, its very occurrence shows that Donne was concerned on behalf of the Parliament's success. While we cannot tell from this letter *whose* purposes he supported, Donne, who received his seat through Sir Edward Phelips (no doubt through the request of his son, Sir Robert, who was one of Donne's personal friends), could well have shared the dilemma of Sir Robert and other opposition leaders,[78] that if they pursued the charge of undertaking too zealously, too many of their own group would be revealed to have benefited in some way from the court patronage system, and so be forced, defensively, into political defection. Sir John Holles himself, who had no patron since the death of Prince Henry, and who despised the Scottish favorites at court, had sometime in 1614 applied for assistance to Somerset.

There is no record of Donne's having spoken in the Commons, though he was named to important committees. One, in May, was to prepare a conference with the Lords so that both Houses could present a joint petition to the king against monopolies. The others were a series of select committees appointed to cope with a constitutional crisis in which Richard Neile, bishop of Lincoln, had declared that the Commons had no business meddling with impositions, that they were a *noli me tangere*. "Proud Prelate," said Sir William Strowde in the Commons; and Sir Edward Hoby, "Woe to that Time, wher an humble Petition of the grieved Gentry of England shall be called an entering upon the King's Prerogative."[79] But both Egerton (now Lord Ellesmere), Donne's former employer, and Sir George More, his father-in-law, defended Neile. The pressures on everyone were evident, and Donne more than others must have experienced those pressures as the pull of divided allegiances.

For Bald, the absence of evidence that Donne participated in the debates meant that he did not, although the official records are, to say the least, elliptical. "*No doubt*," wrote Bald, arguing from silence, "he judged it the part of discretion not to run the risk of expressing himself too openly or of giving offence. He seems to have been a good committee-man [and what a derogatory phrase that is] but he *probably* kept out of the debates *quite deliberately*, less he should spoil his chances with the King or the leading members of the Government" (289; italics added). By the time Carey retold the story, that "no doubt" and "probably" had hardened into statement: "Christopher Brooke and other *former* friends of Donne vehemently opposed these abuses of royal power. Donne discreetly held his tongue" (88).[80] But silence is notoriously hard to argue from. Is it merely by coincidence that one of Donne's love poems goes under the title of *The Undertaking* and begins (and ends) as follows:

> I have done one braver thing
> Then all the Worthies did,
> And yet a braver thence doth spring,
> Which is, to keepe that hid?
>
> (9–10)

BETWEEN THE LINES OF THE LYRICS

This brings us back, finally, to the poems that made Donne famous in our time, though not in his. When Carey performed his powerful analysis of the image patterns in Donne's love poetry, and noticed how frequently love relations are conducted from a position of monarchical power, he overlooked the fact that these poems are also riddled with a specifically political terminology, by no means all of which situates the speaker on the side of royal absolutism.

It is when one collects these terms into relation with each other, into what one might call a grammar of political consciousness, that the unstable tone of the canon as a whole becomes noticeable. To begin with the question of favorites, between the evidently hostile reference in Satire 2 and the ambiguous epithalamion for Somerset there are a series of references to this problem, more topical for a Jacobean audience than an Elizabethan one. *The Anniversarie* opens with the statement that "All Kings, and all their favorites . . . [are] elder by a yeare." *Elegy* 6 opens by denying in private relations the stance that Donne was willing to adopt in his public life:

> Oh, let mee not serve so, as those men serve
> Whom honours' smokes at once fatten and starve;
> . . . .
> As those Idolatrous flatterers, which still
> Their Princes stiles, with many Realmes fulfill
> Whence they no tribute have, and where no sway.
> . . . Oh then let mee
> Favorite in Ordinary, or no favorite bee.[81]

And the *Essays in Divinity*, certainly a Jacobean text, contain the following remarkable analogy for the doctrine of election:

> To enquire further the way and manner by which God makes a few do acceptable works; or, how out of a corrupt lumpe he selects and purifies a few, is but a stumbling block and a tentation: . . . will any favorite, whom his Prince only for his appliableness to him, or some half-vertue, or his own glory, burdens with Honours and Fortunes every day, and destines to future Offices and Dignities, dispute or expostulate with his Prince, why he rather chose not another, how he will restore his Coffers; how he will quench his peoples murmurings, by whom this liberality is fed; or his Nobility, with whom he equalls new men . . . ? (87)

This passage, with its clear reference to the problems in dispute between James and his parliaments from 1604 through 1614, is the *other* side of the untrue compliments in the 1614 *Ecclogue*, where Donne claimed that "the King's favours are so plac'd" in Somerset "that all / Finde that the King therein is liberall / To them."

As for the term *prerogative*, its recurrence in the lyrics is remarkable, and shows how preoccupations developed in Elizabeth's reign were deepened under James. In his fourth satire Donne had punned on "the prerogative of my Crowne," the coin he paid to get rid of his seditious companion, who "like a priviledg'd spie" he imagined to be drawing him into treasonous thoughts.[82] But in *A Valediction: of the booke*, using the metaphor of scholarship as a basis for writing the definitive history of his love affair, Donne gives it institutional or constitutional force:

> Here more then in their bookes may Lawyers find
> Both by what titles Mistresses are ours,

> And how prerogative these states devours,
> Transferr'd from Love himselfe, to womankinde,
> Who though from heart, and eyes,
> They exact great subsidies,[83]
> Forsake him who on them relies,
> And for the cause, honour, or conscience give,
> Chimeraes, vaine as they, or their prerogative.
>
> (28–29)

It scarcely needs pointing out that to speak of the prerogative as devouring the state, or as a vain chimaera, was not to align oneself with monarchical absolutism. In *Loves Deitie*, the poet complains that "every moderne god will now extend / His vast prerogative, as far as Jove," and calls it a "Tyrannie" against which his own posture is that of "Rebell and Atheist too" (49). And in *Love's Exchange* he agrees not to

> . . . sue from thee to draw,
> A *non obstante* on natures law,
> These are prerogatives, they inhere
> In thee and thine. . . .
>
> (32)

The *non obstante*, or "notwithstanding [any statute to the contrary]," was a term foregrounded in the debates of 1610, when Heneage Finch, insisting that "the prerogative of the king is not infinite," and that because it had been augmented in the past through Parliament it could also be diminished, used the phrase *non obstante* nine times. He concluded, focusing on the issue of protections, that "though a protection were granted in such a case with a *non obstante*, the judges will not allow such protection, for the king cannot protect him contrary to the law."[84] This casts a rather different light on the statement in *Essays in Divinity*, that "Nature is the Common law by which God governs us, and Miracle is his Prerogative. For Miracles are but so many Non-obstantes upon Nature. And Miracle is not like prerogative in any thing more then in this, that no body can tell what it is" (81).[85] If one suspects a certain irony here (remembering the "chimaeras" of the *Valediction*), one's suspicion is confirmed by the later statement that "multiplicity of laws . . . is not so burdenous as is thought, except it be in a captious, and entangling, and needy State; or under a Prince too indulgent to his own Prerogative" (94); a statement that John Donne, Jr., clearly remembered when he dedicated the book to Vane.

But perhaps the most surprising appearance of contemporary politics in Donne's consciousness is the *Second Anniversary*, a poem we know, along with its partner, *An Anatomy of the World*, to have been published in 1612 in honor of Elizabeth Drury, dead in her teens and not known personally to Donne; an occasion, therefore, for a meditation on what was wrong (everything) with the world that he knew. And in accordance with Donne's plan in these poems to balance his universal critique with extreme idealism, to make Elizabeth Drury, however inappropriately, the epitome of "the best that [he] could conceive," the *Second Anniversary* presents her soul as a perfect form of government:

> Shee, who being to her selfe a State, injoy'd
> All royalties which any State employ'd;
> For shee made warres, and triumph'd; reason still
> Did not o'rthrow, but rectified her will:
> And she made peace, for no peace is like this,
> That beauty, and chastity together kisse:
> She did high justice, for she crucified
> Every first motion of rebellious pride:
> And she gave pardons, and was liberall,
> For, onely her selfe except, she pardon'd all:
> She coy'nd, in this, that her impressions gave
> To all our actions all the worth they have:
> She gave protections; the thoughts of her brest
> Satans rude Officers could ne'r arrest.
> As these *prerogatives* being met in one,
> Made her a soveraigne State; religion
> Made her a Church; and these two made her all.
>   (237)

It would have been impossible for Donne's readers in 1612 not to notice, in this analysis, one by one, of the categories of the royal prerogative, what is missing: making war and peace, giving pardons, even protections; but not, significantly, impositions. Given this omission, one must also question Donne's *avoidance* of the easier metaphorical alignment between ideal woman and ideal monarch, and its replacement by the personification of a more ambiguous "soveraigne State."

Finally, however, we should consider a love poem in which Donne himself was not sovereign but very much subject to Eros, and in which that relationship was expressed in terms not of prerogative but its counterprinciple in English constitutional theory—personal liberty. In *Elegy 17* the speaker complains that while in the good old days of erotic conquest men were essentially polygamous, now, in an honor culture, "The golden laws of nature are repeald, / Which our first Fathers in such reverence held; / Our liberty's revers'd, our Charter's gone" (102). Nevertheless, in this newly restrictive context, "Onely some few strong in themselves and free / Retain the seeds of antient liberty" and continue the old tradition of libertinage. Donne's language here echoes that of the opposition in the 1610 Parliament, which frequently cited Magna Carta as the source of those ancient liberties which the new stress on prerogative looked in danger of abrogating. On June 28, 1610, Thomas Hedley drew his last and best argument against the impositions "from the ancient freedom and liberty of the subject of England, which appeareth and is confirmed by the great Charter of the liberties of England."[86] Yet the poem, as it speaks of "resisting hearts," itself resists solution. From a statement that such a return to the ancient liberty is only a different form of "subjection" to his "Soveraigne" Eros, Donne imagines a time when that liberty/subjection will be discarded also: "For our allegiance temporary is / When firmer age returnes our liberties" (103). And in the last redefinition liberty becomes a patient and contented monogamy. If the poem was a ruse by which to express a residual political independence, its behavior is as inchoate as the public forum in which such principles were debated; more likely it functioned in Donne's own mind as a therapeutic displacement into wit of contradictions that, in their real location, he was quite unable to resolve.

Perhaps the most telling statement was made after the 1614 session was over, when Sir John Holles was deciding whether his constituency should contribute to the forced loan. Holles' advice was yes, lest Nottingham stand out from its neighbor counties in isolated resistance; and, becoming philosophical, he added: "These foreseeings and cogitations decline me something from that *quod oportet* and draws me with the throng into the broad high way of *quod convenit*, which, though not so honest as the other, yet (as our nowadays wise will have it) more courtly and civil; so as I hold it expedient rather to *errare cum Aristotele*, to give as our fellows do, than to offer with one finger to stay a falling house."[87]

Such troubled testimony in others both has significant implications for parliamentary history[88] and permits in the "literary" arena a more generous view of John Donne than the ambitious apostate to whom we can feel superior. It allows us to recognize that *quod oportet* (principle) is seldom available in its pure form as a political option, and that *quod convenit* (interest), precisely because it can appear more courtly and civil, is that to which the majority of academics themselves aspire. Donne, however, seems to have struggled to permit the sense of what ought to be done and thought to appear between the lines of even his most conformist writing, and somehow, always, to put the merely conventional to shame.

It is beyond the scope of this chapter to tackle the enormous topic of Donne's career as a preacher, and to defend the compromise he chose by a close examination of the way he conducted himself, as (in Gosse's words) the pulpit's "most magnificent and minatory clerical embodiment." Yet it is only fair to Donne to end with one of his first sermons, preached "at Pauls Cross to the Lords of the Council" on March 24, 1617, the anniversary of James's accession to the crown, at a time when the king was in progress in Scotland. His audience included, as we know from John Chamberlain, "the archbishop of Canterburie [George Abbott], the Lord Keper [Sir Francis Bacon], Lord Privie-Seal [Edward Somerset, ninth earl of Worcester] the earle of Arundell, the earle of Southampton, the Lord Hayes, the controller, Secretarie Winwood, the Master of the Rolls [Sir Julius Caesar], with divers other great men"; and his sermon "was exceedingly well liked generally, the rather for that he did Quene Elizabeth great right, and held himself close to the text without flattering the time too much."[89] The sermon is, in fact, a defense of Jacobean policy with respect to international peacemaking, union with Scotland, and an aggressive anti-Catholic policy at home; but it is also a defense of Donne's own position. Preached on the text "He that loveth pureness of heart, for the grace of his lips, the king shall be his friend" (Proverbs 22.11), the sermon constitutes a claim that integrity ("pureness of heart") can be reconciled with patronage, that using his eloquence in the pulpit is more honorable than keeping it to himself. "Because thy wit, thy fashion, and some such nothing as that hath made thee a delightful and acceptable companion, wilt thou therefore pass in jest, and be nothing?" Donne asked himself as well as his auditors. "Thinkest thou to eat bread, and not sweat?" "Hast thou a prerogative above the common Law of Nature?" A man of talent who does not employ it in the service of the public is equivalent to a usurer who keeps his money out of circulation: "It is all as one as if he had no grace of lips, if he never have the grace to open his lips; to bury himself alive, is as much wrong to the State, as if he kill himself. Every man hath a Politick life, as well as a natural life; and he may no more take himself away from the world, then he may make himself away out of the world" (208–11). The sermons, then, mark not the end but the transformation of Donne's political poetics. The author of *Biathanatos* has redefined suicide as compliance in one's own silencing. And one could even say that Chamberlain's approval of this sermon for not "flattering the time too much" was insufficiently generous. For Donne, at this his first Paul's Cross appearance, came out in front of the privy councillors swinging his political principles. The opening lines of the sermon were as follows: "The Man that said it was possible to carve the faces of all good Kings that ever were, in a Cherry-stone, had a seditious, and a trayterous meaning in his words. And he that thought it a good description, a good Character of good subjects, that they were *Populus natus ad servitutem*, A people disposed to bear any slavish yoak, had a tyrannical meaning in his words" (183).

"Both in politics and theology," wrote Debora Shuger, completing her analysis of Donne's "absolutist theology," "modernity entails the rejection of the absolutist paradigm based on the polarities of power and subjection and therefore of the psychocultural formation which made this paradigm acceptable."[90] This remark comes as the climax of the claim that Donne saw his God as an absolute monarch who greatly resembled King James I, and to whom he related with a mixture of guilt and infantile dependency. In my own view, another thing that modernity entails is an immodesty with respect to the past and an underestimation of the capacity of people who anticipated us in time to anticipate us also in self-knowledge. The psychocultural formation that, in my view, Donne inhabited was not "the whole complex of archaic/ infantile emotions" that Shuger finds in his sermons, but a highly developed if unstable world of articulated choices, in which *quod oportet* negotiated with *quod convenit,* Jack with the Doctor, in which there was both a disposition and an equally strong indisposition to bear a slavish yoke.

Notes

1. Gosse, *The Life and Letters of John Donne,* 2 vols. (London, 1899), 2:236–37.

2. Eliot's interest in Donne was sparked by the appearance in 1921 of H. J. C. Grierson's anthology *Metaphysical Lyrics and Poems* (Oxford, 1921) which Eliot reviewed.

3. *John Donne: A Life* (Oxford, 1970).

4. *John Donne: Life, Mind and Art* (New York, 1981).

5. Goldberg, *James I and the Politics of Literature* (Baltimore, 1983). Goldberg makes Donne one of the chief exhibits of his thesis that James totally dominated early-seventeenth-century culture by the coercive force of his Word, hypostasized as *Works* in 1616.

6. Carey, *John Donne,* 19, 11.

7. Carey, *John Donne,* 109, 115.

8. *James I,* 219.

9. Carey, *John Donne,* 21.

10. *Habits of Thought in the English Renaissance: Religion, Politics, and the Dominant Culture* (Berkeley and Los Angeles, 1990).

11. *John Donne, Coterie Poet* (Madison, 1986).

12. See especially T. K. Rabb and D. M. Hirst, "Revisionism Revised," *Past and Present* 92 (1981):55–99.

13. Compare the argument of Ernest Gilman, in " 'To adore, or scorn an image': Donne and the Iconoclastic Controversy," *John Donne Journal* 5 (1986), that "the surviving portraits offer a series of shifting, carefully contrived poses that vividly reflect the several different selves Donne would fashion for himself—the resolute 'gentleman volunteer' at eighteen, the fastidious melancholiac at twenty-three, the sober courtier at thirty-four, the august divine at forty-nine" (68).

14. Donne, *Letters to Severall Persons of Honour* (1651), facsimile ed. M. Thomas Hester (New York, 1977), 21–22.

15. Jonson, *Works,* ed. C. H. Herford, P. Simpson, and E. Simpson, 11 vols. (Oxford, 1925–52), 1:135.

16. For a dispute about dating *within* this period, compare Bald, *John Donne: A Life,* 77, who spaces the five satires over a five-year period from 1593 to 1598, with John T. Shawcross, who locates them all in 1597–98, when Donne was first in Egerton's employ. See his " 'All Attest his Writs Canonical': The Texts, Meaning and Evaluation of Donne's Satires," in *Just So Much Honor,* ed. Peter A. Fiore (University Park, Pa., 1972), 245–72. For the only major study of Donne's satires, see M. Thomas Hester, *Kinde Pity and Brave Scorn: John Donne's Satyres* (Durham, 1982).

17. Donne, *Complete Poetry and Selected Prose,* ed. Charles M. Coffin (New York, 1952), 364; from the Burley MS.

18. Donne, *The Satires, Epigrams and Verse Letters,* ed. W. Milgate (Oxford, 1967), 23.

19. See J. H. Baker, *An Introduction to English Legal History* (London, 1979), 83–95; Baker, ed., *The Reports of Sir John Spelman,* 2 vols. (London, 1978), 2:37–56; *A Discourse upon the Exposicion & Understanding of Statutes With Sir Thomas Egerton's Additions,* ed. Samuel E. Thorne (San Marino, 1942), 54–67, 76–85.

20. Compare Spenser's use of this fable in *The Shepheardes Calender,* 50 above.

21. For an excellent summary of the legal history of benefit of clergy and its artibrary extension to laymen in the sixteenth century, see Baker, *Reports of Sir John Spelman* 2:327–33. Baker cites an intriguing comment by Sir Henry Hobart, to the effect that the protection of

the literate should continue as being "in favour of learning in generall, and in reverence of mankind, and man's blood (which in persons *of use* is not to be shed lightly")" (331; italics added), a comment capable of generating Donne's social cynicism.

22. See Milgate, *Satires, Epigrams and Verse Letters*, 127.

23. "Donne's *Satyres*: The Drama of Self-Discovery," *Studies in English Literature* 16 (1976): 123.

24. *The Tudor Law of Treason* (London and Toronto, 1979), 61–82, especially 82–83. And though not a treason statute, the "Act against seditious words and rumors" (23 Eliz. c. 2), sometimes referred to as the "statute of silence," introduced by the Lords in the 1581 Parliament, was another attempt to control discussion of the queen's marriage plans and the problem of the succession.

25. Donne, *Poetical Works*, ed. H. J. C. Grierson (Oxford, 1929), 14. I refer to this paperback version of the first volume of Grierson's edition on the grounds of its accessibility. The pagination differs from that of the original two-volume edition (Oxford, 1912) which contains annotation.

26. If there remains any doubt that the king's passion for hunting was a frontal issue early in the reign, James settled that doubt by issuing, on September 9, 1609, a proclamation against poaching that began: "We had hoped, seeing it is notorious to all our subjects how greatly we delight in the exercise of hunting. . . ."

27. *Pseudo-Martyr*, ed. F. J. Sypher (Delmar, N.Y., 1974), 187.

28. *The Courtier's Library, or Catalogus Librorum Aulicorum*, ed. E. M. Simpson (London, 1930), 40–41.

29. *Poetical Works*, 189.

30. Donne, *Essays in Divinity*, ed. E. M. Simpson (Oxford, 1952), 3.

31. Donne, *A Sermon Upon the VIII Verse of the 1 Chapter of the Acts of the Apostles. Preach'd To the Honourable Company of the Virginia Plantation. 13 Novemb. 1622* (London, 1622), 33. For an instance of Donne's resistance to the role of king's man in the pulpit, see my account, in *Censorship and Interpretation*, 97–101, of the sermon Donne was commanded to preach in September 1622 supporting James's *Directions to Preachers*, restraining the pulpit from discussing the affairs of the Palatinate.

32. Shawcross, ed., *Complete Poetry of John Donne* (Garden City, N.Y., 1967), xxiii.

33. Gardner, ed., *The Elegies and the Songs and Sonnets* (Oxford, 1965), xxxix.

34. *Poetical Works*, 95–96.

35. Grierson, *Poetical Works* (1929), 2:84.

36. See James Larkin and Paul Hughes, eds., *Stuart Royal Proclamations*, 3 vols. (Oxford, 1973), 1:232–33.

37. *Stuart Royal Proclamations* 1:230–31.

38. See Elizabeth Read Foster, ed., *Proceedings in Parliament 1610*, 2 vols. (New Haven, 1966), 1:25.

39. *Stuart Royal Proclamations* 1:243.

40. For a fuller account of the Neville identity problem, and of the "Mitre Tavern Ballad" as an important key to Donne's environment, see my "All Donne," an earlier version of this chapter, in *Soliciting Interpretation*, ed. Elizabeth Harvey and Katharine Maus (Chicago and London, 1990), 37–67.

41. Printed by Grierson in an appendix, *Poetical Works*, 375.

42. He may or may not have known that Donne's *Courtier's Library* (ca. 1609) contains two items indicating continued support for Essex after his indictment: "The Brazen Head of Francis Bacon: concerning Robert the First, King of England," an attack on Bacon for his betrayal of Essex; and "An Encomion on Doctor Shaw, Chaplain to Richard III, by Doctor Barlow," which equated Barlow's Sermon at Paul's Cross in 1601, as an attempt to manipulate public sympathy away from Essex, with Shaw's "sycophantic defence" of the murder of the Princes in the Tower (51–52).

43. For the letter, see Bald, *John Donne: A Life*, 117–18.

44. Carey did, however, note that "the thought of government spies and butchers like Topcliffe . . . never failed to turn his stomach. They are still among the targets in *The Courtier's Library*, which probably received its final form as late as 1611" (36).

45. Donne, *Biathanatos. A Declaration of that Paradoxe, or Thesis, that Selfe-homicide is not so Naturally Sinne, that it may never be otherwise* (London, 1646), 48–49.

46. Compare *The Courtier's Library*, 24: "Edward Hoby's Afternoon Belchings; or, A Treatise of Univocals, as of the King's Prerogative." This shows that Donne was certainly capable of irony on the subject.

47. See *Proceedings in Parliament 1610* 2:94.

48. Among the items in the *Courtier's Library* were "A few small Treatises supplementary to the Books of Pancirolli; to the Book of Things Lost is added A Treatise on Virtue and on Popular Liberty, begun by a chaplain of John Cade and finished by Buchanan." And in another, more economical joke Donne added, "Tarlton, *On the Privileges of Parliament*" (48, 53). The first item associates popular liberty both with outright and unsuccessful rebellion, in the form of Jack Cade's 1450 insurrection, and with James's formidable Scottish tutor George Buchanan, a name that stood for the theory of contractual monarchy, classical republicanism, and, if necessary, tyrannicide. The second item associates the privileges of Parliament, which from 1604 onward were consistently identified with freedom of speech, with a famous theatrical clown. It is impossible to determine, however, from which direction Donne's irony is coming.

49. James I, *Tripli Nodo, Triplex Cuneus. Or an Apologie for the Oath of Allegiance*, in *The Political Works of James I*, ed. C. H. McIlwain, 2 vols. (Cambridge, Mass, 1918), 1:106.

50. For a definition of the distinction between ordinary and absolute royal power, as it was articulated in 1606 by Sir Thomas Fleming, a common law judge, see Brian Levack, "Law and Ideology: The Civil Law and Theories of Absolutism in Elizabethan and Jacobean England," in *The Historical Renaissance*, ed. Heather Dubrow and Richard Strier (Chicago and London, 1988), 232. See also Francis Oakley, "Jacobean Political Theology: The Absolute and Ordinary Powers of the King," *Journal of the History of Ideas* 29 (1968): 323–46.

51. James I, "A Speech to the Lords and Commons of the Parliament at White-Hall, on Wednesday the XXI of March. Anno 1609," in *Political Works*, 306–7.

52. See *A Booke of Proclamations, published since the beginning of his Majesty's most happy reign over England, etc. until this present moneth of February 3. Anno Domini 1609* (London, 1610).

53. See *Proceedings in Parliament 1610* 2:22. And see also Larkin and Hughes, *Stuart Royal Proclamations* 1:v–vi: "The Jacobean proclamations are pointed expressions of attitudes and axioms of the Crown and of its wearer. . . . Constitutionally, these documents are perhaps most significant as a prime source of friction between Crown and Parliament, especially the Commons, which repeatedly advanced them as grievances against the common law."

54. *Proceedings in Parliament 1610* 2:103.

55. Chamberlain, *Letters*, ed. Norman McClure, 2 vols. (Philadelphia, 1939), 1:301. For an immediate response in the House, see James Whitelocke's statement that "he heard the speech yesterday and came ther with great desire and hope but went away exceeding sad and heavy and . . . saw nothing in that speech any way to restrain the power of imposing, even upon our lands and goods" (*Proceedings in Parliament 1610* 2:108).

56. See also the warning of Thomas Hedley in the 1610 debates that those who maintain "an unlimited and transcendent prerogative may peradventure be holden like the lovers of Alexander with Ephestion but never true lovers of the king with Craterus" (*Proceedings in Parliament 1610* 2:197).

57. *Politics and Ideology in England, 1603–1640* (London and New York, 1986), 30.

58. Donne, *Essays in Divinity*, 4.

59. The Latin is still more potent: "Autorem quaeris? Frustra." It is worth noting that when Kepler read the *Conclave* and noted its dependence on his own *Somnium*, he was unable to attach a name to it. See Marjorie Nicolson, *Science and Imagination* (Ithaca, 1956), 63, 67.

60. Donne, *Ignatius his Conclave* (London, 1611), A3r-5v; italics added. Succeeding references are to this edition, p. 228.

61. Dennis Flynn, "Donne's *Ignatius his Conclave*," *John Donne Journal* 6 (1987), 170, who surmises that Donne had access to the books of the earl of Northumberland, imprisoned in the Tower on suspicion of complicity in the Gunpowder Plot, and one of the first purchasers of the *Conclave Ignatii*.

62. T. S. Healey, ed. *Ignatius his Conclave* (Oxford, 1969), xxx, suggests that Donne did not wish to satirize Galileo and was uneasy with the attack on Copernicus.

63. Donne, *Poetical Works*, 118.

64. Donne, *Poetical Works*, 135. For the 1633 omission, see Milgate, *The Satires, Epigrams and Verse Letters*, 135.

65. Donne, *Poetical Works*, 129.

66. *Calendar of State Papers Venetian* 12:100, art. 151.

67. See Foster, *Proceedings in Parliament 1610* 2:344.

68. *Calendar of State Papers Venetian* 12:102, art. 153.

69. *Calendar of State Papers Venetian* 12:110, art. 164.

70. "Parliamentary History 1603–1629: In or out of Perspective?" in *Faction and Parliament*, ed. Kevin Sharpe (Oxford, 1978), 13. It is worth noting that Sharpe (12) cites the Venetian ambassador's report in 1607 that James had "reached such a pitch of formidable power that he can do what he likes," but not the subsequent reports which indicate oppositional behavior in the Commons.

71. Correr's information was, however, wrong as regards the loan. This did not occur until after the abortive session of 1614. In 1611 James and Salisbury instead fell back on a large-scale sale of baronetcies.

72. Chamberlain, *Letters* 1:539.

73. See Maija Jansson, ed., *Proceedings in Parliament 1614 (House of Commons)* (Philadelphia, 1988), xxiii–xxx.

74. This was Sir Henry Neville of Billingbear. See Clayton Roberts and Owen Duncan, "The Parliamentary Undertaking of 1614," *English Historical Review* 93 (1978), 481–98. Roberts subsequently published a second version of his argument (without his collaborator) in *Schemes and Undertakings: A Study of English Politics in the Seventeenth Century* (Columbus, Ohio, 1985). It is worth noting (with some historical irony) that this book, which makes Henry Neville the heroic pioneer of undertaking, seen as a valuable innovation in political practice, concludes with a praise of Margaret Thatcher as the heroic inheritor who brings the practice to perfection: "She, and only she, can undertake to manage the Queen's affairs in Parliament successfully" (251).

75. It was presented to James in July 1612. The full text is printed in S. R. Gardiner's *History of England from the Accession of James to the Outbreak of Civil War*, 10 vols. (London, 1883–84), 2:389–94.

76. Sir John Holles to Lord Norris, 28 April, 1614; H. M. C. Portland MSS 9:27.

77. Gosse, *Life and Letters of John Donne* 2:34. In the second version of his argument, Clayton Roberts mentioned Donne's letter (mistakenly referring to him as the dean of St. Paul's at this time) and claimed that it was the first recorded use of the term "undertaker" in this sense. See *Schemes and Undertakings* x. "Within three months," Roberts continued, "the word *undertaker* was on every man's lips."

78. After the session collapsed, the immediate provocation having been John Hoskyns' imprudent attack on the Scottish favorites and the reference to a Sicilian Vespers, John Chamberlain suggested that the Phelipses, father and son, might have been responsible: "for there be many presumptions that his hand was in it, his son being so busy and factious in the House, and Hoskyns one of his chief consorts and minions so far engaged, besides divers untoward speeches of his own." See John Chamberlain, *Letters* 1:540; and Linda Levy Peck, *Northampton: Patronage and Policy at the Court of James I* (London, 1982), 210, who cites

Chamberlain's suggestion as part of her argument that the conspiracy theory involving North-ampton—that Hoskyns' speech was planted in *order* to abort the session—was merely one of multiple rumors.

79. *Journal of the House of Commons* 1:494, 496.

80. When added to the misleading statement that Donne acquired his seat through "court influence" (87), when in fact he owed it to the father of one of the leading oppositionists, Carey's language quite unjustly suggests betrayal of friendship, another form of apostasy.

81. Donne, *Poetical Works*, 90, 22, 78.

82. Donne, *Poetical Works*, 145.

83. See also the ironic metaphor, in *Loves Growth*, that the relationship expands "as princes doe in times of action get / New taxes, and remit them not in peace" (*Poetical Works*, 31).

84. See *Proceedings in Parliament 1610* 2:241. This speech took place on July 2, 1610.

85. J. P. Sommerville, *Politics and Ideology*, 37, cited this passage as demonstrating that Donne supported the concept of free or unlimited monarchy. See also Donne's funeral elegy for Lord Harington, brother of Lucy, countess of Bedford, where, in reference to his early death in 1614, Donne commented:

> Yet I am farre from daring to dispute
> With that great soveraigntie, whose
>   absolute
> Prerogative hath thus dispens'd with thee,
> 'Gainst natures lawes.
>
>   (254)

The context here, of course, made the belief in divine absolutism appropriate.

86. See *Proceedings in Parliament 1610* 2:164, 190

87. Sir John Holles, *Historical Manuscripts Commission, Rutland* 9:139.

88. For one thing, it questions Kevin Sharpe's certainty ("Parliamentary History" 19) that in the summer of 1614 "the country gentlemen gave generously to a voluntary contribution which brought in at least as much as a subsidy," a statement intended to support Conrad Russell's position "that the Commons never successfully used, and seldom tried to use, the weapon of withholding supply in order to gain advantages." What one man stated, others may also have felt, imagining themselves also in the minority.

89. Donne, *Sermons*, ed. George Potter and Evelyn M. Simpson, 10 vols. (Berkeley and Los Angeles, 1953–62), 1:125.

90. *Habits of Thought*, 203.

Index

♦